Henry James, Elder Smith, William Makepeace Thackeray

The Paris Sketch Book

Henry James, Elder Smith, William Makepeace Thackeray

The Paris Sketch Book

ISBN/EAN: 9783337428730

Printed in Europe, USA, Canada, Australia, Japan

Cover: Foto ©Andreas Hilbeck / pixelio.de

More available books at **www.hansebooks.com**

PARIS SKETCH BOOK.

BY

W. M. THACKERAY.

[MR. TITMARSH.]

WITH NUMEROUS DESIGNS BY THE AUTHOR ON COPPER
AND WOOD.

LONDON:
SMITH, ELDER AND CO., 65, CORNHILL.
1866.

CONTENTS.

	PAGE
AN INVASION OF FRANCE	1
A CAUTION TO TRAVELLERS	19
THE FÊTES OF JULY	44
ON THE FRENCH SCHOOL OF PAINTING	56
THE PAINTER'S BARGAIN	85
CARTOUCHE	105
ON SOME FRENCH FASHIONABLE NOVELS	122
A GAMBLER'S DEATH	152
NAPOLEON AND HIS SYSTEM	167
THE STORY OF MARY ANCEL	187
BEATRICE MERGER	214
CARICATURES AND LITHOGRAPHY IN PARIS	225
LITTLE POINSINET	265
THE DEVIL'S WAGER	285
MADAME SAND AND THE NEW APOCALYPSE	299
THE CASE OF PEYTEL	335
FOUR IMITATIONS OF BERANGER	377
FRENCH DRAMAS AND MELODRAMAS	395
MEDITATIONS AT VERSAILLES	423

LIST OF ILLUSTRATIONS.

Paris Sketches	*Frontispiece.*	
Mr. Pogson's Temptation	*To face page*	23
A Puzzle for the Devil	,,	103
Cartouche	,,	121
How to Astonish the French	,,	126
Mary Ancel	,,	190
The Cheap Defence of Nations	,,	225
Poinsinet in Disguise	,,	271
The Chaplain Puzzled	,,	293
French Catholicism	,,	301
The Gallery at Deburau's Theatre Sketched from Nature	,,	413
Ludovicus Rex	,,	434

Dedicatory Letter

TO

M. ARETZ TAILOR, ETC.

27, RUE RICHELIEU, PARIS.

Sir,

It becomes every man in his station to acknowledge and praise virtue wheresoever he may find it, and to point it out for the admiration and example of his fellow-men.

Some months since, when you presented to the writer of these pages a small account for coats and pantaloons manufactured by you, and when you were met by a statement from your creditor, that an immediate settlement of your bill would be extremely inconvenient to him; your reply was, "Mon Dieu, Sir, let not that annoy you; if you want money, as a gentleman often does in a strange country, I have a thousand-franc note at my house which is quite at your service."

History or experience, Sir, makes us acquainted with so few actions that can be compared to yours,—an offer like this from a stranger and a tailor seems to me so astonishing,—that you must pardon me for thus making your virtue public, and acquainting the English nation with your merit and your name. Let me add, Sir, that you live on the first floor; that your clothes and fit are excellent, and your charges moderate and just; and, as a humble tribute of my admiration, permit me to lay these volumes at your feet.

Your obliged, faithful servant,

M. A. TITMARSH.

About half of the sketches in these volumes have already appeared in print, in various periodical works. A part of the text of one tale, and the plots of two others, have been borrowed from French originals; the other stories, which are, in the main, true, have been written upon facts and characters that came within the Author's observation during a residence in Paris.

As the remaining papers relate to public events which occurred during the same period, or to Parisian Art and Literature, he has ventured to give his publication the title which it bears.

LONDON, *July* 1, 1840.

THE PARIS SKETCH BOOK.

AN INVASION OF FRANCE.

"Cæsar venit in Galliam summâ diligentiâ."

ABOUT twelve o'clock, just as the bell of the packet is tolling a farewell to London Bridge, and warning off the blackguard-boys with the newspapers, who have been shoving *Times, Herald, Penny Paul-Pry, Penny Satirist, Flare-up,* and other abominations, into your face—just as the bell has tolled, and the Jews, strangers, people-taking-leave-of-their-families, and blackguard-boys aforesaid, are making a rush for the narrow plank which conducts from the paddle-box of the *Emerald* steamboat unto the quay —you perceive, staggering down Thames-street, those two hackney-coaches, for the arrival of which you have been praying, trembling, hoping, despairing, swearing—sw——, I beg your pardon, I believe the word is not used in polite company—and transpiring, for the last half-hour. Yes, at last, the two coaches draw near, and from thence an awful number of trunks, children, carpet-bags, nursery-maids, hat-boxes, band-boxes, bonnet-boxes, desks, cloaks, and an affectionate wife, are discharged on the quay.

"Elizabeth, take care of Miss Jane," screams that worthy woman, who has been for a fortnight employed in getting this tremendous body of troops and baggage into marching order. "Hicks! Hicks! for heaven's sake mind the babies!"—"George—Edward, sir, if you go near that porter with the trunk, he will tumble down and kill you, you naughty boy!—My love, *do* take the cloaks and umbrellas, and give a hand to Fanny and Lucy; and I wish you would speak to the hackney-coachmen, dear, they want fifteen shillings, and count the packages, love—twenty-seven packages,—and bring little Flo; where's little Flo?—Flo! Flo!"—(Flo comes sneaking in; she has been speaking a few parting words to a one-eyed terrier, that sneaks off similarly, landward.)

As when the hawk menaces the hen-roost, in like manner, when such a danger as a voyage menaces a mother, she becomes suddenly endowed with a ferocious presence of mind, and bristling up and screaming in the front of her brood, and in the face of circumstances, succeeds, by her courage, in putting her enemy to flight; in like manner you will always, I think, find your wife (if that lady be good for twopence) shrill, eager, and ill-humoured, before and during a great family move of this nature. Well, the swindling hackney-coachmen are paid, the mother leading on her regiment of little ones, and supported by her auxiliary nurse-maids, are safe in the cabin;—you have counted twenty-six of the twenty-seven parcels, and have them on board, and that horrid man on the paddle-box, who, for twenty minutes past, has been roaring out, NOW, SIR!—says, *now, sir*, no more.

I never yet knew how a steamer began to move, being always too busy among the trunks and children, for the first half hour, to mark any of the movements of the vessel. When these private arrangements are made, you find yourself opposite Greenwich (farewell, sweet, sweet whitebait!), and quiet begins to enter your soul. Your wife smiles for the first time these ten days; you pass by plantations of ship-masts, and forests of steam-chimneys; the sailors are singing on board the ships, the barges salute you with oaths, grins, and phrases facetious and familiar; the man on the paddle-box roars, "Ease her, stop her!" which mysterious words a shrill voice from below repeats, and pipes out, "Ease her, stop her!" in echo; the deck is crowded with groups of figures, and the sun shines over all.

The sun shines over all, and the steward comes up to say, "Lunch, ladies and gentlemen! Will any lady or gentleman please to take anythink?" About a dozen do: boiled beef and pickles, and great, red raw Cheshire cheese, tempt the epicure: little dumpy bottles of stout are produced, and fiz and bang about with a spirit one would never have looked for in individuals of their size and stature.

The decks have a strange look; the people on them, that is. Wives, elderly stout husbands, nurse-maids, and children predominate, of course, in English steam-boats. Such may be considered as the distinctive marks of the English gentleman at three or four and forty: two or three of such groups have pitched their camps on the deck. Then there are a number of young men, of whom three or four have allowed their moustaches to *begin* to grow since last Friday; for they are going "on the Continent," and they look, therefore, as if their upper lips were smeared with snuff.

A *danseuse* from the opera is on her way to Paris. Followed by her *bonne* and her little dog, she paces the deck, stepping out, in the real dancer fashion, and ogling all around. How happy the two young Englishmen are, who can speak French, and make up to her: and how all criticise her points and paces! Yonder is a group of young ladies, who are going to Paris to learn how to be governesses: those two splendidly dressed ladies are milliners from the Rue Richelieu, who have just brought over, and disposed of, their cargo of Summer fashions. Here sits the Rev. Mr. Snodgrass with his pupils, whom he is conducting to his establishment, near Boulogne, where, in addition to a classical and mathematical education (washing included), the young gentlemen have the benefit of learning French among *the French themselves.* Accordingly, the young gentlemen are locked up in a great rickety house, two miles from Boulogne, and never see a soul, except the French usher and the cook.

Some few French people are there already, preparing to be ill—(I never shall forget a dreadful sight I once had in the little dark, dirty, six-foot cabin of a Dover steamer.

Four gaunt Frenchmen, but for their pantaloons, in the costume of Adam in Paradise, solemnly anointing themselves with some charm against sea-sickness!)—a few Frenchmen are there, but these, for the most part, and with a proper philosophy, go to the fore-cabin of the ship, and you see them on the fore-deck (is that the name for that part of the vessel which is in the region of the bowsprit?) lowering in huge cloaks and caps; snuffy, wretched, pale, and wet; and not jabbering now, as their wont is on shore. I never could fancy the Mounseers formidable at sea.

There are, of course, many Jews on board. Who ever travelled by steam-boat, coach, diligence, eilwagen, vetturino, mule-back, or sledge, without meeting some of the wandering race?

By the time these remarks have been made the steward is on the deck again, and dinner is ready: and about two hours after dinner comes tea; and then there is brandy-and-water, which he eagerly presses as a preventive against what may happen; and about this time you pass the Foreland, the wind blowing pretty fresh; and the groups on deck disappear, and your wife, giving you an alarmed look, descends, and her little one, to the ladies' cabin, and you see the steward and his boys issuing from their den, under the paddle-box, with each a heap of round tin vases, like those which are called, I believe, in America, *expectoratoons*, only these are larger.

* * * * * *

The wind blows, the water looks greener and more beautiful than ever—ridge by ridge of long white rock passes away. "That's Ramsgit," says the man at the helm; and, presently, "that there's Deal—it's dreadful fallen off since the war;" and "that's Dover, round that there pint, only you can't see it;" and, in the meantime, the sun has plumped his hot face into the water, and the moon has shown hers as soon as ever his back is turned, and Mrs.—(the wife in general,) has brought up her children and self from the horrid cabin, in which, she says, it is impossible to breathe; and the poor little wretches are, by the officious stewardess and smart steward (expectoratoonifer), accommodated with a heap of blankets, pillows, and mattresses, in the midst of which they crawl, as best they may, and from the heaving heap of which, are, during the rest of the voyage, heard occasional faint cries, and sounds of puking woe!

Dear, dear Maria! Is this the woman who, anon, braved the jeers and brutal wrath of swindling hackney coachmen; who repelled the insolence of haggling porters, with a scorn that brought down their demands at least eighteenpence? Is this the woman at whose voice servants tremble; at the sound of whose steps the nursery, ay, and mayhap the parlour, is in order? Look at her now, prostrate, prostrate—no strength has she to speak, scarce power to push to her youngest one—her suffering, struggling Rosa,—to push to her the—the instrumentoon!

In the midst of all these throes and agonies, at which all the passengers, who have their own woes (you yourself—for how can you help *them*—you are on your back on a bench, and if you move all is up with you), are looking on indifferent—one man there is who has been watching you with the utmost care, and bestowing on your helpless family the tenderness that a father denies them. He is a foreigner, and you have been conversing with him, in the course of the morning, in French, which, he says, you speak remarkably well, like a native, in fact, and then in English (which, after all, you find, is more convenient). What can express your gratitude to this gentleman, for all his goodness towards your family and yourself—you talk to him, he has served under the Emperor, and is, for all that, sensible, modest, and well-informed. He speaks, indeed, of his countrymen almost with contempt, and readily admits the superiority of a Briton, on the seas and elsewhere. One loves to meet with such genuine liberality in a foreigner, and respects the man who can sacrifice vanity to truth. This distinguished foreigner has travelled much; he asks whither you are going?—where you stop? if you have a great quantity of luggage on board?—and laughs when he hears of the twenty-seven packages, and hopes you have some friend at the custom-house, who can spare you the monstrous trouble of unpacking that which has taken you weeks to put up. Nine, ten, eleven, the distinguished foreigner is ever at your side; you find him now, perhaps (with characteristic ingratitude), something of a bore, but, at least, he has been most tender to the children, and their mamma. At last a Boulogne light comes in sight (you see it over the bows of the vessel, when, having bobbed violently upwards, it sinks swiftly down), Boulogne harbour is in sight, and the foreigner says,—

The distinguished foreigner says, says he—" Sare, eef you af no 'otel, I sall recommend you, milor, to ze 'Otel

Betfort, in ze Quay, sare, close to the bathing machines and custom-ha-oose. Good bets and fine garten, sare; table d'hôte, sare, à cinq heures; breakfast, sare, in French or English style;—I am the commissionaire, sare, and vill see to your loggish."

* * Curse the fellow, for an impudent, swindling, sneaking, French humbug!—Your tone instantly changes, and you tell him to go about his business: but at twelve o'clock at night, when the voyage is over, and the custom-house business done, knowing not whither to go, with a wife and fourteen exhausted children, scarce able to stand, and longing for bed, you find yourself somehow, in the Hotel Bedford (and you can't be better), and smiling chambermaids carry off your children to snug beds; while smart waiters produce for your honour—a cold fowl, say, and a salad, and a bottle of Bordeaux and Seltzer water.

* * * * *

The morning comes—I don't know a pleasanter feeling than that of waking with the sun shining on objects quite new, and (although you have made the voyage a dozen times,) quite strange. Mrs. X. and you occupy a very light bed, which has a tall canopy of red *"percale;"* the windows are smartly draped with cheap gaudy calicoes and muslins, there are little mean strips of carpet about the tiled floor of the room, and yet all seems as gay and as comfortable as may be—the sun shines brighter than you have seen it for a year, the sky is a thousand times bluer, and what a cheery clatter of shrill quick French voices comes up from the court-yard under the windows! Bells are jangling; a family, mayhap, is going to Paris, en poste, and wondrous is the jabber of the courier, the postilion, the inn-waiters, and the lookers-on. The landlord calls out for "Quatre biftecks aux pommes, pour le trente-trois," —(O! my countrymen, I love your tastes and your ways!) —the chambermaid is laughing, and says, "Finissez donc, Monsieur Pierre!" (what can they be about?)—a fat Englishman has opened his window violently, and says, "*Dee dong, garsong, vooly voo me donny lo sho, ou vooly voo pah?*" He has been ringing for half an hour—the last energetic appeal succeeds, and shortly he is enabled to descend to the coffee-room, where, with three hot rolls, grilled ham, cold fowl, and four boiled eggs, he makes, what he calls, his first *French* breakfast.

It is a strange, mongrel, merry place, this town of Boulogne; the little French fishermen's children are beautiful, and the little French soldiers, four feet high, red-breeched, with huge *pompons* on their caps, and brown faces, and clear sharp eyes, look, for all their littleness, far more military and more intelligent than the heavy louts one has seen swaggering about the garrison towns in England. Yonder go a crowd of bare-legged fishermen; there is the town idiot, mocking a woman who is screaming "Flouve du Tage," at an inn-window, to a harp, and there are the little gamins mocking *him*. Lo! these seven young ladies, with red hair and green veils, they are from neighbouring Albion, and going to bathe. Here come three Englishmen, *habitués* evidently of the place,— dandy spécimens of our countrymen—one wears a marine dress, another has a shooting dress, a third has a blouse and a pair of guiltless spurs—all have as much hair on the face as nature or art can supply, and all wear their hats very much on one side. Believe me, there is on the face of this world no scamp like an English one, no blackguard like one of these half-gentlemen, so mean, so low, so vulgar,—so ludicrously ignorant and conceited, so desperately heartless and depraved.

But why, my dear sir, get into a passion ?—Take things coolly. As the poet has observed, " Those only is gentlemen who behave as sich;" with such, then, consort, be they cobblers or dukes. Don't give us, cries the patriotic reader, any abuse of our fellow-countrymen (anybody else can do that), but rather continue in that good-humoured, facetious, descriptive style, with which your letter has commenced.—Your remark, sir, is perfectly just, and does honour to your head and excellent heart.

There is little need to give a description of the good town of Boulogne ; which, haute and basse, with the new light-house and the new harbour, and the gas lamps, and the manufactures, and the convents, and the number of English and French residents, and the pillar erected in honour of the grand *Armée d'Angleterre*, so called because it *didn't* go to England, have all been excellently described by the facetious Coglan, the learned Dr. Millingen, and by innumerable guide-books besides. A fine thing it is to hear the stout old Frenchmen of Napoleon's time, argue how that audacious Corsican *would* have marched to London, after swallowing Nelson and all his gun-boats, but for *cette malheureuse guerre d'Espagne*, and *cette glorieuse campagne d'Autriche*, which the gold of Pitt caused to be raised at the Emperor's tail, in order to call him off from the helpless country in his front. Some Frenchmen go farther still, and vow that, in Spain, they were never beaten at all; indeed, if you read in the *Biographie des Hommes du Jour*, article "Soult," you will fancy that, with the exception of the disaster at Vittoria, the campaigns in Spain and Portugal were a series of triumphs. Only, by looking at a map, it is observable that Vimieiro is a mortal long way from Toulouse, where, at the end of certain years of victories, we somehow find the honest Marshal. And what then?—he went to Toulouse for the purpose of beating the English there, to be sure;—a known fact, on which comment would be superfluous. However, we shall never get to Paris at this rate; let us break off farther palaver, and away at once.   *   *

(During this pause, the ingenious reader is kindly requested to pay his bill at the Hotel at Boulogne, to mount the Diligence of Laffitte Caillard and Company, and to travel for twenty-five hours, amidst much jingling of harness-bells and screaming of postilions.)

*   *   *   *   *   *

The French milliner, who occupies one of the corners, begins to remove the greasy pieces of paper which have enveloped her locks during the journey. She withdraws the "Madras" of dubious hue which has bound her head for the last five-and-twenty hours, and replaces it by the black velvet bonnet, which, bobbing against your nose, has hung from the Diligence roof since your departure from Boulogne. The old lady in the opposite corner, who has been sucking bonbons, and smells dreadfully of anisette, arranges her little parcels in that immense basket of abominations which all old women carry in their laps. She rubs her mouth and eyes with her dusty cambric handkerchief, she ties up her nightcap into a little bundle, and replaces it by a more becoming head-piece, covered with withered artificial flowers, and crumpled tags of ribbon ; she looks wistfully at the company for an instant, and then places her handkerchief before her mouth :—her eyes roll strangely about for an instant, and you hear a faint clattering noise : the old lady has been getting ready her teeth, which had lain in her basket among the bonbons, pins, oranges, pomatum, bits of cake, lozenges, prayer-books, peppermint-water, copper-money, and false hair—stowed away there during the voyage. The Jewish gentleman, who has been so attentive to the milliner during the journey, and is a traveller and bag-man by profession, gathers together his various goods. The sallow-faced English lad, who has been drunk ever since we left Boulogne yesterday, and is coming to Paris to pursue the study of medicine, swears that he rejoices to leave the cursed Diligence, is sick of the infernal journey, and d—d glad that the d—d voyage is so nearly over. "*Enfin!*" says your neighbour, yawning, and inserting an elbow into the mouth of his right and left hand companion, "*nous voilà.*"

Nous Voilà!—We are at Paris! This must account for the removal of the milliner's curl papers, and the fixing of the old lady's teeth.—Since the last *relais*, the Diligence has been travelling with extraordinary speed. The postilion cracks his terrible whip, and screams shrilly. The conductor blows incessantly on his horn, the bells of the harness, the bumping and ringing of the wheels and chains, and the clatter of the great hoofs of the heavy snorting Norman stallions, have wondrously increased within this, the last ten minutes; and the Diligence, which has been proceeding hitherto at the rate of a league in an hour, now dashes gallantly forward, as if it would traverse at least six miles in the same space of time. Thus it is, when Sir Robert maketh a speech at Saint Stephen's—he useth his strength at the beginning, only, and the end. He gallopeth at the commencement; in the middle he lingers; at the close, again, he rouses the House, which has fallen asleep; he cracketh the whip of his satire; he shouts the shout of his patriotism; and, urging his eloquence to its roughest canter, awakens the sleepers, and inspires the weary, until men say, What a wondrous orator! What a capital coach! We will ride henceforth in it, and in no other!

But, behold us at Paris! The Diligence has reached a rude-looking gate, or *grille*, flanked by two lodges; the French Kings, of old, made their entry by this gate; some of the hottest battles of the late revolution were fought before it. At present, it is blocked by carts and peasants, and a busy crowd of men, in green, examining the packages before they enter, probing the straw with long needles. It is the Barrier of St. Denis, and the green men are the Customs' men of the city of Paris. If you are a countryman, who would introduce a cow into the Metropolis, the city demands twenty-four francs for such a privilege: if you have a hundredweight of tallow candles, you must, previously, disburse three francs: if a drove of hogs, nine francs per whole hog: but upon these subjects Mr. Bulwer, Mrs. Trollope, and other writers, have already enlightened the public. In the present instance, after a momentary pause, one of the men in green mounts by the side of the conductor, and the ponderous vehicle pursues its journey.

The street which we enter, that of the Faubourg St. Denis, presents a strange contrast to the dark uniformity of a London street, where everything, in the dingy and smoky atmosphere, looks as though it were painted in India-ink—black houses, black passengers, and black sky. Here, on the contrary, is a thousand times more life and colour. Before you, shining in the sun, is a long glistening line of *gutter*,—not a very pleasing object in a city, but in a picture invaluable. On each side are houses of all dimensions and hues; some, but of one story; some, as high as the tower of Babel. From these the haberdashers (and this is their favourite street) flaunt long strips of gaudy calicoes, which give a strange air of rude gaiety to the street. Milk-women, with a little crowd of gossips round each, are, at this early hour of morning, selling the chief material of the Parisian *café-au-lait*. Gay wine-shops, painted red, and smartly decorated with vines and gilded railings, are filled with workmen taking their morning's draught. That gloomy-looking prison on your right, is a prison for women; once it was a convent for Lazarists: a thousand unfortunate individuals of the softer sex now occupy that mansion: they bake, as we find in the guide-books, the bread of all the other prisons; they mend and wash the shirts and stockings of all the other prisoners; they make hooks and eyes and phosphorus boxes, and they attend chapel every

Sunday :—if occupation can help them, sure they have enough of it. Was it not a great stroke of the Legislature to superintend the morals and linen at once, and thus keep these poor creatures continually mending?—But we have passed the prison long ago, and are at the Port St. Denis itself.

There is only time to take a hasty glance as we pass; it commemorates some of the wonderful feats of arms of Ludovicus Magnus; and abounds in ponderous allegories —nymphs and river-gods, and pyramids crowned with fleurs-de-lis; Louis passing over the Rhine in triumph, and the Dutch Lion giving up the ghost, in the year of our Lord 1672. The Dutch Lion revived, and overcame the man some years afterwards; but of this fact, singularly enough, the inscriptions make no mention. Passing, then, *round* the gate, and not under it (after the general custom, in respect of triumphal arches), you cross the boulevard, which gives a glimpse of trees and sunshine, and gleaming white buildings; then, dashing down the Rue de Bourbon Villeneuve, a dirty street, which seems interminable, and the Rue St. Eustache, the conductor gives a last blast on his horn, and the great vehicle clatters into the court-yard, where its journey is destined to conclude.

If there was a noise before of screaming postilions and cracked horns, it was nothing to the Babel-like clatter which greets us now. We are in a great court, which Hajji Baba would call the father of Diligences—half-a-dozen other coaches arrive at the same minute; no light affairs, like your English vehicles, but ponderous machines, containing fifteen passengers inside, more in the cabriolet, and vast towers of luggage on the roof—others are loading: the yard is filled with passengers coming or departing;—bustling porters, and screaming *commissionaires*. These latter seize you as you descend from your place,—twenty cards are thrust into your hand, and as many voices, jabbering with inconceivable swiftness, shriek into your ear, "Dis way, sare; are you for ze Otel of Rhin? *Hôtel de l' Amirauté!*—Hôtel Bristol, sare!—*Monsieur, l' Hôtel de Lille? Sacr-rrré nom de Dieu, laissez passer ce petit, Monsieur!* Ow mosh loggish ave you, sare?"

And now, if you are a stranger in Paris, listen to the words of Titmarsh.—If you cannot speak a syllable of French, and love English comfort, clean rooms, breakfasts, and waiters; if you would have plentiful dinners, and are not particular (as how should you be?) concerning wine; if, in this foreign country, you *will* have your English companions, your porter, your friend, and your brandy-and-water—do not listen to any of these commissioner fellows, but, with your best English accent, shout out boldly, MEURICE! and straightway a man will step forward to conduct you to the Rue de Rivoli.

Here you will find apartments at any price; a very neat room, for instance, for three francs daily; an English breakfast of eternal boiled eggs, or grilled ham; a nondescript dinner, profuse but cold; and a society which will rejoice your heart. Here are young gentlemen from the universities; young merchants on a lark; large families of nine daughters, with fat father and mother; officers of dragoons, and lawyers' clerks. The last time we dined at Meurice's we hobbed and nobbed with no less a person than Mr. Moses, the celebrated bailiff of Chancery Lane; Lord Brougham was on his right, and a clergyman's lady, with a train of white-haired girls, sat on his left, wonderfully taken with the diamond rings of the fascinating stranger!

It is, as you will perceive, an admirable way to see Paris, especially if you spend your days reading the English papers at Galignani's, as many of our foreign tourists do.

But all this is promiscuous, and not to the purpose. If,—to continue on the subject of hotel choosing,—if you love quiet, heavy bills, and the best *table d'hôte* in the city, go, oh, stranger! to the Hôtel des Princes; it is close to the Boulevard, and convenient for *Frascati's*. The Hôtel Mirabeau possesses scarcely less attraction; but of this you will find, in Mr. Bulwer's Autobiography of Pelham, a faithful and complete account. Lawson's Hotel has likewise its merits, as also the Hôtel de Lille, which may be described as a "second chop" Meurice.

If you are a poor student come to study the humanities, or the pleasant art of amputation, cross the water forthwith, and proceed to the Hôtel Corneille, near the Odéon, or others of its species; there are many where you can live royally (until you economize by going into lodgings) on four francs a day; and where, if by any strange chance you are desirous for awhile to get rid of your countrymen, you will find that they scarcely ever penetrate.

But, above all, oh, my countrymen! shun boarding houses, especially if you have ladies in your train; or ponder well, and examine the characters of the keepers thereof, before you lead your innocent daughters, and their mamma, into places so dangerous. In the first place, you have bad dinners; and, secondly, bad company. If you play cards, you are very likely playing with a swindler; if you dance, you dance with a —— person with whom you had better have nothing to do.

Note (which ladies are requested not to read). In one of these establishments, daily advertised as most eligible for English, a friend of the writer lived. A lady, who had passed for some time as the wife of one of the inmates, suddenly changed her husband and name, her original husband remaining in the house, and saluting her by her new title.

A CAUTION TO TRAVELLERS.

A MILLION dangers and snares await the traveller, as soon as he issues out of that vast messagerie which we have just quitted: and as each man cannot do better than relate such events as have happened in the course of his own experience, and may keep the unwary from the path of danger, let us take this, the very earliest opportunity, of imparting to the public a little of the wisdom which we painfully have acquired.

And first, then, with regard to the city of Paris, it is to be remarked, that in that metropolis flourish a greater number of native and exotic swindlers than are to be found in any other European nursery. What young Englishman that visits it, but has not determined, in his heart, to have a little share of the gaieties that go on—just for once, just to see what they are like? How many, when the horrible gambling dens were open, did resist a sight of them?—nay, was not a young fellow rather flattered by a dinner invitation from the Salon, whither he went, fondly pretending that he should see "French society," in the persons of certain Dukes and Counts who used to frequent the place?

A CAUTION TO TRAVELLERS.

My friend Pogson is a young fellow, not much worse, although, perhaps, a little weaker and simpler than his neighbours; and coming to Paris with exactly the same notions that bring many others of the British youth to that capital, events befell him there, last winter, which are strictly true, and shall here be narrated, by way of warning to all.

Pog, it must be premised, is a city man, who travels in drugs for a couple of the best London houses, blows the flute, has an album, drives his own gig, and is considered, both on the road and in the metropolis, a remarkably nice, intelligent, thriving young man. Pogson's only fault is too great an attachment to the fair :—" the sex," as he says often, " will be his ruin : " the fact is, that Pog never travels without a " Don Juan " under his driving cushion, and is a pretty-looking young fellow enough.

Sam Pogson had occasion to visit Paris, last October; and it was in that city that his love of the sex had liked to have cost him dear. He worked his way down to Dover; placing, right and left, at the towns on his route, rhubarb, sodas, and other such delectable wares as his masters dealt in (" the sweetest sample of castor oil, smelt like a nosegay—went off like wildfire— hogshead and a half at Rochester, eight and twenty gallons at Canterbury : " and so on); and crossed to Calais; and thence voyaged to Paris, in the Coupé of the Diligence. He paid for two places, too, although a single man, and the reason shall now be made known.

Dining at the *table d'hôte* at Quillacq's—it is the best inn on the continent of Europe—our little traveller had the happiness to be placed next to a lady, who was, he saw at a glance, one of the extreme pink of the nobility. A large lady, in black satin, with eyes and hair as black as sloes, with gold chains, scent bottles, sable tippet, worked pocket-handkerchief, and four twinkling rings on each of her plump white fingers. Her cheeks were as pink as the finest Chinese rouge could make them. Pog knew the article: he travelled in it. Her lips were as red as the ruby lip salve: she used the very best, that was clear.

She was a fine-looking woman, certainly (holding down her eyes, and talking perpetually of "*mes trente-deux ans*"); and Pogson, the wicked young dog, who professed not to care for young misses, saying they smelt so of bread and butter, declared, at once, that the lady was one of *his* beauties; in fact, when he spoke to us about her, he said, "She's a slap-up thing, I tell you; a reg'lar good one; *one of my sort!*" And such was Pogson's credit in all commercial rooms, that one of *his* sort was considered to surpass all other sorts.

During dinner-time, Mr. Pogson was profoundly polite and attentive to the lady at his side, and kindly communicated to her, as is the way with the best bred English on their first arrival " on the Continent," all his impressions regarding the sights and persons he had seen. Such remarks having been made during half an hour's ramble about the ramparts and town, and in the course of a walk down to the custom-house, and a confidential communication with the *Commissionaire*, must be, doubtless, very valuable to Frenchmen in their own country; and the lady listened to Pogson's opinions: not only with benevolent attention, but actually, she said, with pleasure and delight. Mr. Pogson said that there was no such thing as good meat in France, and that's why they cooked their victuals in this queer way: he had seen many soldiers parading about the place, and expressed a true Englishman's abhorrence of an armed force; not that he feared such fellows as these—little whipper-snappers—our men would eat them. Hereupon the lady admitted that our guards were angels, but that Monsieur must not be too hard upon the French; " her father was a General of the Emperor."

Pogson felt a tremendous respect for himself, at the notion that he was dining with a General's daughter, and instantly ordered a bottle of Champagne to keep up his consequence.

" Mrs. Bironn, ma'am," said he, for he had heard the waiter call her by some such name, " if you *will* accept a glass of Champagne, ma'am, you'll do me, I'm sure, great *honour*: they say it's very good, and a precious sight cheaper than it is on our side of the way, too—not that I care for money. Mrs. Bironn, ma'am your health, ma'am."

The lady smiled very graciously, and drank the wine.

" Har you any relation, ma'am, if I may make so bold; har you any ways connected with the family of our immortal bard ?"

" Sir, I beg your pardon."

" Don't mention it, ma'am: but Bi*ronn* and *B*yron are hevidently the same names, only you pronounce in the French way; and I thought you might be related to his

Lordship : his horigin, ma'am, was of French extraction :" and here Pogson began to repeat,—

> "Have thy heyes like thy mother's, my fair child,
> Hada ! sole daughter of my ouse and art."

"O!" said the lady, laughing, "you speak of *Lor* Byron.

"Hauthor of Don Juan, Child Arold, and Cain, a Mystery," said Pogson:—"I do; and hearing the waiter calling you Madam la Bironn, took the liberty of hasking whether you were connected with his Lordship; that's hall:" and my friend here grew dreadfully red, and began twiddling his long ringlets in his fingers, and examining very eagerly the contents of his plate.

"O, no: Madame la Baronne means Mistress Baroness; my husband was Baron, and I am Baroness."

"What! ave I the honour—I beg your pardon, ma'am —is your Ladyship a Baroness, and I not know it? pray excuse me for calling you ma'am."

The Baroness smiled most graciously—with such a look as Juno cast upon unfortunate Jupiter when she wished to gain her wicked ends upon him—the Baroness smiled; and, stealing her hand into a black velvet bag, drew from it an ivory card-case, and from the ivory card-case extracted a glazed card, printed in gold; on it was engraved a coronet, and under the coronet the words

> BARONNE DE FLORVAL-DELVAL,
>
> NÉE DE MELVAL-NORVAL.
>
> *Rue Taitbout.*

The grand Pitt diamond—the Queen's own star of the garter—a sample of otto-of-roses at a guinea a drop, would not be handled more curiously, or more respectfully, than this porcelain card of the Baroness. Trembling he put it into his little Russia leather pocket-book: and when he ventured to look up, and saw the eyes of the Baroness de Floral-Delval, née de Melval-Norval, gazing upon him with friendly and serene glances, a thrill of pride tingled through Pogson's blood: he felt himself to be the very happiest fellow " on the Continent."

But Pogson did not, for some time, venture to resume that sprightly and elegant familiarity which generally forms the great charm of his conversation: he was too much frightened at the presence he was in, and contented himself by graceful and solemn bows, deep attention, and ejaculations of "Yes, my Lady," and "No, your Ladyship," for some minutes after the discovery had been made. Pogson piqued himself on his breeding: "I hate the aristocracy," he said, " but that's no reason why I shouldn't behave like a gentleman."

A surly, silent little gentleman, who had been the third at the ordinary, and would take no part either in the conversation or in Pogson's Champagne, now took up his hat, and, grunting, left the room, when the happy bagman had the delight of a *tête-à-tête*. The Baroness did not appear inclined to move: it was cold; a fire was comfortable, and she had ordered none in her apartment. Might Pogson give her one more glass of Champagne, or would her Ladyship prefer " something hot." Her Ladyship gravely said, she never took *anything* hot. " Some Champagne, then; a leetle drop?" She would! she would! Oh, gods! how Pogson's hand shook as he filled and offered her the glass!

What took place during the rest of the evening had better be described by Mr. Pogson himself, who has given us permission to publish his letter.

"Quillacq's Hotel (pronounced Killyax), Calais.

"DEAR TIT,

"I arrived at Cally, as they call it, this day, or, rather, yesterday; for it is past midnight, as I sit thinking of a wonderful adventure that has just befallen me. A woman, in course; that's always the case with *me*, you know: but, O, Tit! if you *could* but see her! Of the first family in France, the Florval-Melvals, beautiful as an angel, and no more caring for money than I do for split peas.

"I'll tell you how it occurred. Everybody in France, you know, dines at the ordinary—it's quite distangy to do so. There was only three of us to-day, however,—the Baroness, me, and a gent. who never spoke a word; and we didn't want him to, neither: do you mark that?

"You know my way with the women; Champagne's the thing; make 'em drink, make 'em talk;—make 'em talk, make 'em do anything. So I orders a bottle, as if for myself; and, 'Ma'am,' says I, 'will you take a glass of Sham—just one?' Take it she did—for you know it's quite distangy here: everybody dines at the *table de hôte*, and everybody accepts everybody's wine. Bob Irons, who travels in linen, on our circuit, told me that he had made some slap-up acquaintances among the genteelest people at Paris, nothing but by offering them Sham.

"Well, my Baroness takes one glass, two glasses, three glasses—the old fellow goes—we have a deal of chat (she took me for a military man, she said: is it not singular that so many people should?), and by ten o'clock we had grown so intimate, that I had from her her whole history, knew where she came from, and where she was going. Leave me alone with 'em: I can find out any woman's history in half an hour.

"And where do you think she *is* going? to Paris to be sure: she has her seat in what they call the coopy (though you're not near so cooped in it as in our coaches. I've been to the office and seen one of 'em). She has her place in the coopy, and the coopy holds *three;* so what does Sam Pogson do—he goes and takes the other two. Ain't I up to a thing or two? 'O no, not the least; but I shall have her to myself the whole of the way.

"We shall be in the French metropolis the day after this reaches you: please look out for a handsome lodging for me, and never mind the expense. And I say, if you could, in her hearing, when you came down to the coach, call me Captain Pogson, I wish you would—it sounds well travelling, you know; and when she asked me if I was not an officer, I couldn't say no. Adieu, then, my dear fellow, till Monday, and vive le joy, as they say. The Baroness says I speak French charmingly, she talks English as well as you or I.

"Your affectionate friend,
"S. Pogson."

This letter reached us duly, in our garrets, and we engaged such an apartment for Mr. Pogson, as beseemed a gentleman of his rank in the world and the army. At the appointed hour, too, we repaired to the Diligence office, and there beheld the arrival of the machine which contained him and his lovely Baroness.

Those who have much frequented the society of gentlemen of his profession (and what more delightful?) must be aware, that, when all the rest of mankind look hideous, dirty, peevish, wretched, after a forty hours' coach-journey, a bagman appears as gay and spruce as when he started; having within himself a thousand little conveniences for the voyage, which common travellers neglect. Pogson had a little portable toilet, of which he had not failed to take advantage, and with his long, curling, flaxen hair, flowing under a seal-skin cap, with a gold tassel, with a blue and gold satin handkerchief, a crimson velvet waistcoat, a light green cut-away coat, a pair of barred brick-dust coloured pantaloons, and a neat Macintosh, presented, altogether, as elegant and *distingué* an appearance as any one could desire. He had put on a clean collar at breakfast, and a pair of white kids as he entered the barrier, and looked, as he rushed into my arms, more like a man stepping out of a band-box, than one descending from a vehicle that has just performed one of the laziest, dullest, flattest, stalest, dirtiest journeys in Europe.

To my surprise, there were *two* ladies in the coach with my friend, and not *one*, as I had expected. One of these, a stout female, carrying sundry baskets, bags, umbrellas, and woman's wraps, was evidently a maid-servant:

the other, in black, was Pogson's fair one, evidently. I could see a gleam of curl-papers over a sallow face,—of a dusky night-cap flapping over the curl-papers,—but these were hidden by a lace veil and a huge velvet bonnet, of which the crowning birds of paradise were evidently in a moulting state. She was encased in many shawls and wrappers; she put, hesitatingly, a pretty little foot out of the carriage—Pogson was by her side in an instant, and, gallantly putting one of his white kids round her waist, aided this interesting creature to descend. I saw, by her walk, that she was five-and-forty, and that my little Pogson was a lost man.

After some brief parley between them—in which it was charming to hear how my friend Samuel *would* speak, what he called French, to a lady who could not understand one syllable of his jargon—the mutual hackney-coaches drew up; Madame la Baronne waved to the Captain a graceful French curtsey. "*Ad*you!" said Samuel, and waved his lily hand. "*Adyou-addimang.*"

A brisk little gentleman, who had made the journey in the same coach with Pogson, but had more modestly taken a seat in the Imperial, here passed us, and greeted me with a "How d'ye do?" He had shouldered his own little valise, and was trudging off, scattering a cloud of *commissionaires*, who would fain have spared him the trouble.

"Do you know that chap?" says Pogson; "surly fellow, ain't he?"

"The kindest man in existence," answered I; "all the world knows little Major British."

"He's a Major, is he?—why, that's the fellow that dined with us at Killyax's; it's lucky I did not call myself Captain before him, he mightn't have liked it, you know:" and then Sam fell into a reverie;—what was the subject of his thoughts soon appeared.

"Did you ever *see* such a foot and ankle?" said Sam, after sitting for some time, regardless of the novelty of the scene; his hands in his pockets, plunged in the deepest thought.

"*Isn't* she a slap-up woman, eh, now?" pursued he; and began enumerating her attractions, as a horse-jockey would the points of a favourite animal.

"You seem to have gone a pretty length already," said I, "by promising to visit her to-morrow."

"A good length?—I believe you. Leave *me* alone for that."

"But I thought you were only to be two in the *coupé*, you wicked rogue."

"Two in the *coopy*? Oh! ah! yes, you know—why, that is, I didn't know she had her maid with her (what an ass I was to think of a noblewoman travelling without one!) and couldn't, in course, refuse, when she asked me to let the maid in."

"Of course not."

"Couldn't, you know, as a man of *h*onour; but I made it up for all that," said Pogson, winking slily, and putting his hand to his little bunch of a nose, in a very knowing way.

"You did, and how?"

"Why, you dog, I sate next to her; sate in the middle

the whole way, and my back's half broke, I can tell you:" and thus, having depicted his happiness, we soon reached the inn where this back-broken young man was to lodge, during his stay in Paris.

The next day, at five, we met; Mr. Pogson had seen his Baroness, and described her lodgings, in his own expressive way, as "slap-up." She had received him quite like an old friend; treated him to *eau sucrée*, of which beverage he expressed himself a great admirer; and actually asked him to dine the next day. But there was a cloud over the ingenuous youth's brow, and I inquired still farther.

"Why," said he, with a sigh, "I thought she was a widow; and, hang it! who should come in but her husband, the Baron; a big fellow, sir, with a blue coat, a red ribbing, and *such* a pair of mustachios!"

"Well," said I, "he didn't turn you out, I suppose?"

"Oh, no! on the contrary, as kind as possible; his Lordship said that he respected the English army; asked me what corps I was in,—said he had fought in Spain against us,—and made me welcome."

"What could you want more?"

Mr. Pogson at this only whistled; and if some very profound observer of human nature had been there to read into this little bagman's heart, it would, perhaps, have been manifest, that the appearance of a whiskered soldier of a husband had counteracted some plans that the young scoundrel was concocting.

I live up a hundred and thirty-seven steps in the remote quarter of the Luxembourg, and it is not to be expected that such a fashionable fellow as Sam Pogson, with his pockets full of money, and a new city to see, should be always wandering to my dull quarters; so that, although he did not make his appearance for some time, he must not be accused of any lukewarmness of friendship on that score.

He was out, too, when I called at his hotel; but once, I had the good fortune to see him, with his hat curiously on one side, looking as pleased as Punch, and being driven, in an open cab, in the *Champs Elysées*. "That's *another* tip-top chap," said he, when we met, at length: "What do you think of an Earl's son, my boy? Honourable Tom Ringwood, son of the Earl of Cinqbars: what do you think of that, eh?"

I thought he was getting into very good society. Sam was a dashing fellow, and was always above his own line of life; he had met Mr. Ringwood at the Baron's, and they'd been to the play together; and the honourable gent, as Sam called him, had joked with him about being well to do *in a certain quarter;* and he had had a game of billiards with the Baron, at the *Estaminy,* "a very distangy place, where you smoke," said Sam; "quite select, and frequented by the tip-top nobility;" and they were as thick as peas in a shell; and they were to dine that day at Ringwood's, and sup, the next night, with the Baroness.

"I think the chaps down the road will stare," said Sam, "when they hear how I've been coming it." And stare, no doubt, they would; for it is certain that very few commercial gentlemen have had Mr. Pogson's advantages.

The next morning we had made an arrangement to go

out shopping together, and to purchase some articles of female gear, that Sam intended to bestow on his relations when he returned. Seven needle-books, for his sisters; a gilt buckle, for his mamma; a handsome French cashmere shawl and bonnet, for his aunt (the old lady keeps an inn in the Borough, and has plenty of money, and no heirs); and a tooth-pick case, for his father. Sam is a good fellow to all his relations, and as for his aunt, he adores her. Well, we were to go and make these purchases, and I arrived punctually at my time; but Sam was stretched on a sofa, very pale and dismal.

I saw how it had been.—"A little too much of Mr. Ringwood's claret, I suppose?"

He only gave a sickly stare.

"Where does the Honourable Tom live?" says I.

"*Honourable?*" says Sam, with a hollow horrid laugh; "I tell you, Dick, he's no more Honourable than you are."

"What, an impostor?"

"No, no; not that. He is a real Honourable, only—"

"Oh, ho! I smell a rat—a little jealous, eh?"

"Jealousy be hanged! I tell you he's a thief; and the Baron's a thief; and, hang me, if I think his wife is any better. Eight-and-thirty pounds he won of me before supper; and made me drunk, and sent me home:—is *that* honourable? How can *I* afford to lose forty pounds? It's took me two years to save it up:—if my old aunt gets wind of it, she'll cut me off with a shilling: hang me!"— and here Sam, in an agony, tore his fair hair.

While bewailing his lot in this lamentable strain, his bell was rung, which signal being answered by a surly

"Come in," a tall, very fashionable gentleman, with a fur coat, and a fierce tuft to his chin, entered the room. "Pogson, my buck, how goes it?" said he, familiarly, and gave a stare at me: I was making for my hat.

"Don't go," said Sam, rather eagerly; and I sat down again.

The Honourable Mr. Ringwood hummed and ha'd: and, at last, said he wished to speak to Mr. Pogson on business, in private, if possible.

"There's no secrets betwixt me and my friend," cried Sam.

Mr. Ringwood paused a little:—"An awkward business that of last night," at length exclaimed he.

"I believe it *was* an awkward business," said Sam, drily.

"I really am very sorry for your losses."

"Thank you: and so am I, *I* can tell you," said Sam.

"You must mind, my good fellow, and not drink; for, when you drink, you *will* play high: by Gad, you led *us* in, and not we you."

"I dare say," answered Sam, with something of peevishness; "losses is losses: there's no use talking about 'em when they're over and paid."

"And paid?" here wonderingly spoke Mr. Ringwood: "why, my dear fel—what the deuce—has Florval been with you?"

"D— Florval!" growled Tom, "I've never set eyes on his face since last night; and never wish to see him again."

"Come, come, enough of this talk; how do you intend to settle the bills which you gave him last night?"

"Bills! what do you mean?"

"I mean, sir, these bills," said the Honourable Tom, producing two out of his pocket-book, and looking as stern as a lion. "I promise to pay, on demand, to the Baron de Florval, the sum of four hundred pounds. October 20, 1838." "Ten days after date I promise to pay the Baron de et cætera, et cætera, one hundred and ninety-eight pounds. Samuel Pogson." "You didn't say what regiment you were in."

"WHAT!" shouted poor Sam, as from a dream, starting up and looking preternaturally pale and hideous.

"D— it, sir, you don't affect ignorance: you don't pretend not to remember that you signed these bills, for money lost in my rooms: money *lent to* you, by Madame de Melval, at your own request, and lost to her husband? You don't suppose, sir, that I shall be such an infernal idiot as to believe you, or such a coward as to put up with a mean subterfuge of this sort. Will you, or will you not pay the money, sir?"

"I will not," said Sam, stoutly, "it's a d—d swin—"

Here Mr. Ringwood sprung up, clenching his riding-whip, and looking so fierce that Sam and I bounded back to the other end of the room. "Utter that word again, and, by Heaven, I'll murder you!" shouted Mr. Ringwood, and looked as if he would, too: "once more, will you, or will you not, pay this money?"

"I can't," said Sam, faintly.

"I'll call again, Captain Pogson," said Mr. Ringwood, "I'll call again in one hour; and, unless you come to some arrangement, you must meet my friend, the Baron de Melval, or I'll post you for a swindler and a coward."

With this he went out: the door thundered to after him, and when the clink of his steps departing had subsided, I was enabled to look round at Pog. The poor little man had his elbows on the marble table, his head between his hands, and looked, as one has seen gentlemen look over a steam-vessel off Ramsgate, the wind blowing remarkably fresh : at last he fairly burst out crying.

"If Mrs. Pogson heard of this," said I, "what would become of the Three Tuns? (for I wished to give him a lesson :) if your Ma, who took you every Sunday to meeting, should know that her boy was paying attention to married women;—if Drench, Glauber and Co., your employers, were to know that their confidential agent was a gambler, and unfit to be trusted with their money, how long do you think your connexion would last with them, and who would afterwards employ you?"

To this poor Pog had not a word of answer; but sate on his sofa, whimpering so bitterly that the sternest of moralists would have relented towards him, and would have been touched by the little wretch's tears. Everything, too, must be pleaded in excuse for this unfortunate bagman: who, if he wished to pass for a Captain, had only done so because he had an intense respect and longing for rank: if he had made love to the Baroness, had only done so because he was given to understand, by Lord Byron's *Don Juan*, that making love was a very correct, natty thing; and if he had gambled, had only been induced to do so by the bright eyes and example of the Baron and the Baroness. O ye Barons and Baronesses of England! if ye knew what a number of small commoners are daily occupied in studying your lives, and imitating your aristocratic ways, how careful would ye be of your morals, manners, and conversation!

My soul was filled, then, with a gentle yearning pity for Pogson, and revolved many plans for his rescue: none of these seeming to be practicable, at last we hit on the very wisest of all; and determined to apply for counsel to no less a person than Major British.

A blessing it is to be acquainted with my worthy friend, little Major British; and heaven, sure, it was that put the Major into my head, when I heard of this awkward scrape of poor Pog's. The Major is on half-pay, and occupies a modest apartment, *au quatrième*, in the very hotel which Pogson had patronised, at my suggestion: indeed, I had chosen it from Major British's own peculiar recommendation.

There is no better guide to follow than such a character as the honest Major, of whom there are many likenesses now scattered over the continent of Europe; men who love to live well, and are forced to live cheaply, and who find the English, abroad, a thousand times easier, merrier, and more hospitable than the same persons at home. I, for my part, never landed on Calais pier, without feeling that a load of sorrows was left on the other side of the water; and have always fancied that black care stepped on board the steamer, along with the custom-house officers, at Gravesend, and accompanied one to yonder black louring towers of London—so busy, so dismal, and so vast.

British would have cut any foreigner's throat, who ventured to say so much, but entertained, no doubt, private sentiments of this nature; for he passed eight months of the year, regularly, abroad, with head-quarters at Paris (the garrets before alluded to), and only went to England for the month's shooting, on the grounds of his old Colonel, now an old Lord, of whose acquaintance the Major was passably inclined to boast.

He loved and respected, like a good stanch Tory as he is, every one of the English nobility; gave himself certain little airs of a man of fashion, that were by no means disagreeable; and was, indeed, kindly regarded by such English aristocracy as he met, in his little annual tours among the German courts, in Italy or in Paris, where he never missed an ambassador's night: he retailed to us, who didn't go, but were delighted to know all that had taken place, accurate accounts of the dishes, the dresses, and the scandal which had there fallen under his observation.

He is, moreover, one of the most useful persons in society that can possibly be; for besides being incorrigibly duelsome on his own account, he is, for others, the most acute and peaceable counsellor in the world, and has carried more friends through scrapes, and prevented more deaths than any member of the Humane Society. British never bought a single step in the army, as is well known. In '14 he killed a celebrated French fire-eater, who had slain a young friend of his; and living, as he does, a great deal with young men of pleasure, and good, old, sober, family people, he is loved by them both, and has as welcome a place made for him at a roaring bachelor's supper at the *Café Anglais*, as at a staid Dowager's dinner-table in the *Faubourg St. Honoré*. Such pleasant old boys are very profitable acquaintances, let me tell you; and lucky is the young man who has one or two such friends in his list.

Hurrying on Pogson in his dress, I conducted him, panting, up to the Major's *quatrième*, where we were cheerfully bidden to come in. The little gentleman was in his travelling jacket, and occupied in painting, elegantly, one of those natty pairs of boots in which he daily promenaded the *Boulevards*. A couple of pairs of tough buff gloves had been undergoing some pipe-claying operation under his hands: no man stepped out so speck and span, with a hat so nicely brushed, with a stiff cravat tied so neatly, under a fat, little red face, with a blue frock coat so scrupulously fitted to a punchy little person, as Major British, about whom we have written these two pages. He stared rather hardly at my companion, but gave me a kind shake of the hand, and we proceeded at once to business. "Major British," said I, "we want your advice in regard to an unpleasant affair, which has just occurred to my friend Pogson."

"Pogson, take a chair."

"You must know, sir, that Mr. Pogson, coming from Calais, the other day, encountered, in the diligence, a very handsome woman."

British winked at Pogson, who, wretched as he was, could not help feeling pleased.

"Mr. Pogson was not more pleased with this lovely creature than was she with him; for, it appears, she gave him her card, invited him to her house, where he has been constantly, and has been received with much kindness."

"I see," says British.

"Her husband, the Baron——"

"*Now* it's coming," said the Major, with a grin: "her husband is jealous, I suppose, and there is a talk of the *Bois de Boulogne:* my dear sir, you can't refuse—can't refuse."

"It's not that," said Pogson, wagging his head passionately.

"Her husband, the Baron, seemed quite as much taken with Pogson as his lady was, and has introduced him to some very *distingué* friends of his own set. Last night one of the Baron's friends gave a party in honour of my friend Pogson, who lost forty-eight pounds at cards *before* he was made drunk, and heaven knows how much after.

"Not a shilling, by sacred heaven!—not a shilling!" yelled out Pogson. "After the supper I 'ad such an 'eadach', I couldn't do anything but fall asleep on the sofa."

"You 'ad such an 'eadach', sir," says British, sternly, who piques himself on his grammar and pronunciation, and scorns a cockney.

"Such a *h*-eadach, sir," replied Pogson, with much meekness.

"The unfortunate man is brought home at two o'clock, as tipsy as possible, dragged upstairs, senseless, to bed, and, on waking, receives a visit from his entertainer of the night before—a Lord's son, Major, a tip-top fellow,—who brings a couple of bills that my friend Pogson is said to have signed."

"Well, my dear fellow, the thing's quite simple,—he must pay them."

"I can't pay them."

"He can't pay them," said we both in a breath:

"Pogson is a commercial traveller, with thirty shillings a week, and how the deuce is he to pay five hundred pounds?"

"A bagman, sir! and what right has a bagman to gamble? Gentlemen gamble, sir; tradesmen, sir, have no business with the amusements of the gentry. What business had you with Barons and Lords' sons, sir?—serve you right, sir."

"Sir," says Pogson, with some dignity, "merit, and not birth, is the criterion of a man: I despise an hereditary aristocracy, and admire only Nature's gentlemen. For my part, I think that a British merch——"

"Hold your tongue, sir," bounced out the Major, "and don't lecture me; don't come to me, sir, with your slang about Nature's gentlemen—Nature's Tomfools, sir! Did Nature open a cash account for you at a banker's, sir? Did Nature give you an education, sir? What do you mean by competing with people to whom Nature has given all these things? Stick to your bags, Mr. Pogson, and your bagmen, and leave Barons and their like to their own ways."

"Yes, but, Major," here cried that faithful friend, who has always stood by Pogson; "they won't leave him alone."

"The honourable gent says I must fight if I don't pay," whimpered Sam.

"What! fight *you?* Do you mean that the honourable gent, as you call him, will go out with a bagman?"

"He doesn't know I'm a—I'm a commercial man," blushingly said Sam: "he fancies I'm a military gent."

The Major's gravity was quite upset at this absurd notion; and he laughed outrageously. "Why, the fact is, sir," said I, "that my friend Pogson, knowing the value of the title of Captain, and being complimented by the Baroness on his warlike appearance, said, boldly, he was in the army. He only assumed the rank in order to dazzle her weak imagination, never fancying that there was a husband, and a circle of friends, with whom he was afterwards to make an acquaintance; and then, you know, it was too late to withdraw."

"A pretty pickle you have put yourself in, Mr. Pogson, by making love to other men's wives, and calling yourself names," said the Major, who was restored to good humour. "And pray, who is the *h*onourable gent.?"

"The Earl of Cinqbars' son," says Pogson, "the Honourable Tom Ringwood."

"I thought it was some such character: and the Baron is the Baron de Florval Melval?"

"The very same."

"And his wife a black-haired woman, with a pretty foot and ankle; calls herself Athenais; and is always talking about her *trente deux ans?* Why, sir, that woman was an actress, on the Boulevard, when we were here in '15. She's no more his wife than I am. Melval's name is Chicot. The woman is always travelling between London and Paris: I saw she was hooking you at Calais; she has hooked ten men, in the course of the last two years, in this very way. She lent you money, didn't she?" "Yes." "And she leans on your shoulder, and whispers, 'Play half for me,' and somebody wins it, and the poor thing is as sorry as you are, and her husband storms and rages, and insists on double stakes; and she leans over your shoulder again, and tells every card in your hand to your adversary; and that's the way it's done, Mr. Pogson."

"I've been 'ad, I see I 'ave," said Pogson, very humbly.

"Well, sir," said the Major, "in consideration, not of you, sir—for, give me leave to tell you, Mr. Pogson, that you are a pitiful little scoundrel—in consideration for my Lord Cinqbars, sir, with whom, I am proud to say, I am intimate (the Major dearly loved a Lord, and was, by his own showing, acquainted with half the peerage), I will aid you in this affair. Your cursed vanity, sir, and want of principle, has set you, in the first place, intriguing with other men's wives; and if you had been shot for your pains, a bullet would have only served you right, sir. You must go about as an impostor, sir, in society; and you pay richly for your swindling, sir, by being swindled yourself: but, as I think your punishment has been already pretty severe, I shall do my best, out of regard for my friend, Lord Cinqbars, to prevent the matter going any farther; and I recommend you to leave Paris without delay. Now let me wish you a good morning."—Wherewith British made a majestic bow, and began giving the last touch to his varnished boots.

We departed: poor Sam perfectly silent and chapfallen; and I meditating on the wisdom of the half-pay philosopher, and wondering what means he would employ to rescue Pogson from his fate.

What these means were I know not; but Mr. Ringwood did *not* make his appearance at six; and, at eight, a letter arrived for "Mr. Pogson, commercial traveller," &c. &c. It was blank inside, but contained his two bills. Mr. Ringwood left town, almost immediately, for Vienna; nor did the Major explain the circumstances which caused his departure; but he muttered something about "knew some of his old tricks," "threatened police, and made him disgorge directly."

Mr. Ringwood is, as yet, young at his trade; and I have often thought it was very green of him to give up the bills to the Major, who, certainly, would never have pressed the matter before the police, out of respect for his friend, Lord Cinqbars.

THE FÊTES OF JULY.

IN A LETTER TO THE EDITOR OF THE "BUNGAY BEACON."

Paris, July 30*th*, 1839.

WE have arrived here just in time for the fêtes of July. —You have read, no doubt, of that glorious revolution which took place here nine years ago, and which is now commemorated annually, in a pretty facetious manner, by gun-firing, student-processions, pole-climbing-for-silver-spoons, gold-watches, and legs-of-mutton, monarchical orations, and what not, and sanctioned, moreover, by Chamber-of-Deputies, with a grant of a couple of hundred thousand francs to defray the expenses of all the crackers, gun-firings, and legs-of-mutton aforesaid. There is a new fountain in the Place Louis Quinze, otherwise called the Place Louis Seize, or else the Place de la Révolution, or else the Place de la Concorde (who can say why ?)—which I am told, is to run bad wine during certain hours to-morrow, and there *would* have been a review of the National Guards and the Line—only, since the Fieschi business, reviews are no joke, and so this latter part of the festivity has been discontinued.

Do you not laugh—O Pharos of Bungay—at the continuance of a humbug such as this?—at the humbugging anniversary of a humbug? The King of the Barricades is, next to the Emperor Nicholas, the most absolute Sovereign in Europe; yet there is not in the whole of this fair kingdom of France, a single man who cares sixpence about him, or his dynasty: except, mayhap, a few hangers-on at the Château, who eat his dinners, and put their hands in his purse. The feeling of loyalty is as dead as old Charles the Tenth; the Chambers have been laughed at, the country has been laughed at, all the successive ministries have been laughed at (and you know who is the wag that has amused himself with them all); and, behold, here come three days at the end of July, and cannons think it necessary to fire off, squibs and crackers to blaze and fiz, fountains to run wine, Kings to make speeches, and subjects to crawl up greasy mâts-de-cocagne in token of gratitude, and *réjouissance-publique!*—My dear sir, in their aptitude to swallow, to utter, to enact humbugs, these French people, from Majesty downwards, beat all the other nations of this earth. In looking at these men, their manners, dresses, opinions, politics, actions, history, it is impossible to preserve a grave countenance; instead of having Carlyle to write a History of the French Revolution, I often think it should be handed over to Dickens or Theodore Hook: and, oh! where is the Rabelais to be the faithful historian of the last phase of the Revolution—the last glorious nine years of which we are now commemorating the last glorious three days?

I had made a vow not to say a syllable on the subject, although I have seen, with my neighbours, all the gingerbread stalls down the Champs-Elysées, and some of the "catafalques" erected to the memory of the heroes of July, where the students and others, not connected personally with the victims, and not having in the least profited by their deaths, come and weep; but the grief shown on the first day is quite as absurd and fictitious as the joy exhibited on the last. The subject is one which admits of much wholesome reflection, and food for mirth; and, besides, is so richly treated by the French themselves, that it would be a sin and a shame to pass it over. Allow me to have the honour of translating, for your edification, an account of the first day's proceedings—it is mighty amusing, to my thinking.

CELEBRATION OF THE DAYS OF JULY.

"To-day (Saturday), funeral ceremonies, in honour of the victims of July, were held in the various edifices consecrated to public worship.

"These edifices, with the exception of some churches (especially that of the Petits-Pères), were uniformly hung with black on the outside; the hangings bore only this inscription: 27, 28, 29 July, 1830—surrounded by a wreath of oak-leaves.

"In the interior of the Catholic churches, it had only been thought proper to dress *little catafalques*, as for burials of the third and fourth class. Very few clergy attended; but a considerable number of the National Guard.

"The Synagogue of the Israelites was entirely hung with black; and a great concourse of people attended. The service was performed with the greatest pomp.

"In the Protestant temples there was likewise a very full attendance: *apologetical discourses* on the Revolution of July were pronounced by the pastors.

"The absence of M. de Quélen (Archbishop of Paris), and of many members of the superior clergy, was remarked at Notre Dame.

"The civil authorities attended service in their several districts.

"The poles ornamented with tri-coloured flags, which formerly were placed on Notre Dame, were, it was remarked, suppressed. The flags on the Pont Neuf were, during the ceremony, only half-mast high, and covered with crape."

Et cætera, et cætera, et cætera.

"The tombs of the Louvre were covered with black hangings, and adorned with tri-coloured flags. In front and in the middle was erected an expiatory monument of a pyramidical shape, and surmounted by a funeral vase.

"*These tombs were guarded by the* MUNICIPAL GUARD, THE TROOPS OF THE LINE, THE SERJENS DE VILLE (*town patrol*), AND A BRIGADE OF AGENTS OF POLICE IN PLAIN CLOTHES, under the orders of peace-officer Vassal.

"Between eleven and twelve o'clock, some young men, to the number of 400 or 500, assembled on the Place de la Bourse, one of them bearing a tri-coloured banner with an inscription, 'TO THE MANES OF JULY:' ranging themselves in order, they marched five abreast to the Marché-des-Innocens. On their arrival, the Municipal Guards of the Halle-aux-Draps, where the post had been doubled, issued out without arms, and the town-sergeants placed themselves before the market to prevent the entry of the procession. The young men passed in perfect order, and without saying a word—only lifting their hats as they defiled before the tombs. When they arrived at the Louvre, they found the gates shut, and the garden evacuated. The troops were under arms, and formed in battalion.

"After the passage of the procession, the Garden was again open to the public."

And the evening and the morning were the first day.

There's nothing serious in mortality: is there, from the beginning of this account to the end thereof, aught but sheer, open, monstrous, undisguised humbug? I said, before, that you should have a history of these people by Dickens or Theodore Hook, but there is little need of professed wags;—do not the men write their own tale with an admirable Sancho-like gravity and naïveté, which one could not desire improved? How good is that touch of sly indignation about the *little catafalques!* how rich the contrast presented by the economy of the Catholics to the splendid disregard of expense exhibited by the devout Jews! and how touching the "*apologetical discourses* on the Revolution," delivered by the Protestant pastors! Fancy the profound affliction of the Gardes-Municipaux, the Sergens de Ville, the police agents in plain clothes, and the troops, with fixed bayonets, sobbing round the "expiatory-monuments-of-a-pyramidical shape, surmounted by funeral-vases," and compelled, by sad duty, to fire into the public who might wish to indulge in the same woe! O "manes of July!" (the phrase is pretty and grammatical), why did you with sharp bullets break those Louvre windows? Why did you bayonet red-coated Swiss behind that fair white façade, and, braving cannon, musket, sabre, perspective guillotine, burst yonder bronze gates, rush through that peaceful picture-gallery, and hurl royalty, loyalty, and a thousand years of Kings, head over heels, out of yonder Tuileries' windows?

It is, you will allow, a little difficult to say :—there is, however, *one* benefit that the country has gained (as for liberty of press, or person, diminished taxation, a juster representation, who ever thinks of them?)—*one* benefit they have gained, or nearly—*abolition de la peine-de-mort pour délit politique*—no more wicked guillotining for revolutions—a Frenchman must have his revolution—it is his nature to knock down omnibuses in the street, and across them to fire at troops of the line—it is a sin to balk it. Did not the King send off Revolutionary Prince Napoleon in a coach-and-four? Did not the jury, before the face of God and Justice, proclaim Revolutionary Colonel Vaudrey not guilty?—One may hope, soon, that if a man shows decent courage and energy in half-a-dozen *émeutes*, he will get promotion and a premium.

I do not (although, perhaps, partial to the subject,) want to talk more nonsense than the occasion warrants, and will pray you to cast your eyes over the following anecdote, that is now going the round of the papers, and respects the commutation of the punishment of that wretched, fool-hardy Barbés, who, on his trial, seemed to invite the penalty which has just been remitted to him. You recollect the braggart's speech : " When the Indian falls into the power of the enemy, he knows the fate that awaits him, and submits his head to the knife:—*I am the Indian!*"

"Well——"

"M. Hugo was at the Opera on the night the sentence of the Court of Peers, condemning Barbés to death, was published. The great poet composed thefollowing verses:—

> 'Par votre ange envolée, ainsi qu'une colombe,
> Par le royal enfant, doux et frêle roseau,
> Grace encore une fois! Grace au nom de la tombe!
> Grace au nom du berceau!'*

"M. Victor Hugo wrote the lines out instantly on a sheet of paper, which he folded, and simply despatched them to the King of the French by the penny-post.

"That truly is a noble voice, which can at all hours thus speak to the throne. Poetry, in old days, was called the language of the Gods—it is better named now—it is the language of the Kings.

"But the clemency of the King had anticipated the letter of the Poet. His Majesty had signed the commutation of Barbés, while the Poet was still writing.

"Louis Philippe replied to the author of Ruy Blas most graciously, that he had already subscribed to a wish so noble, and that the verses had only confirmed his previous disposition to mercy."

Now in countries where fools most abound, did one ever read of more monstrous, palpable folly? In any

---

* Translated for the benefit of country gentlemen:—

> "By your angel flown away just like a dove,
> By the royal infant, that frail and tender reed,
> Pardon yet once more! Pardon in the name of the tomb!
> Pardon in the name of the cradle!"

country, save this, would a poet who chose to write four crack-brained verses, comparing an angel to a dove, and a little boy to a reed, and calling upon the chief-magistrate, in the name of the angel, or dove (the Princess Mary), in her tomb, and the little infant in his cradle, to spare a criminal, have received a "gracious answer" to his nonsense? Would he have ever despatched the nonsense? and would any Journalist have been silly enough to talk of "the noble voice that could thus speak to the throne," and the noble throne that could return such a noble answer to the noble voice? You get nothing done here gravely and decently. Tawdry stage tricks are played, and braggadocio claptraps uttered, on every occasion, however sacred or solemn; in the face of death, as by Barbés with his hideous Indian metaphor; in the teeth of reason, as by M. Victor Hugo with his twopenny-post poetry; and of justice, as by the King's absurd reply to this absurd demand! Suppose the Count of Paris to be twenty times a reed, and the Princess Mary a host of angels, is that any reason why the law should not have its course? Justice is the God of our lower world, our great omnipresent guardian: as such it moves, or should move on, majestic, awful, irresistible, having no passions—like a God: but, in the very midst of the path across which it is to pass, lo! M. Victor Hugo trips forward, smirking, and says, O divine Justice! I will trouble you to listen to the following trifling effusion of mine:—

"*Par votre ange envolée, ainsi qu'une,*" &c.

Awful Justice stops, and, bowing gravely, listens to M. Hugo's verses, and, with true French politeness, says,

"Mon cher Monsieur, these verses are charming, *ravissans, délicieux*, and, coming from such a *célébrité littéraire* as yourself, shall meet with every possible attention—in fact, had I required anything to confirm my own previous opinions, this charming poem would have done so. Bon jour, mon cher Monsieur Hugo, au revoir!"—and they part:—Justice taking off his hat and bowing, and the Author of "Ruy Blas" quite convinced that he has been treating with him, *d'égal en égal*. I can hardly bring my mind to fancy that anything is serious in France—it seems to be all rant, tinsel, and stage-play. Sham liberty, sham monarchy, sham glory, sham justice,—*où diable donc la verité va-t-elle se nicher?*

* * * * *

The last rocket of the fête of July has just mounted, exploded, made a portentous bang, and emitted a gorgeous show of blue-lights, and then (like many reputations) disappeared totally: the hundredth gun on the invalid-terrace has uttered its last roar—and a great comfort it is for eyes and ears that the festival is over. We shall be able to go about our every-day business again, and not be hustled by the gendarmes or the crowd.

The sight which I have just come away from is as brilliant, happy, and beautiful as can be conceived; and if you want to see French people to the greatest advantage, you should go to a festival like this, where their manners, and innocent gaiety, show a very pleasing contrast to the coarse and vulgar hilarity which the same class would exhibit in our own country—at Epsom Race-course, for instance, or Greenwich Fair. The greatest noise that I heard was that of a company of jolly villagers from a place in the neighbourhood of Paris, who, as soon as the fireworks were over, formed themselves into a line, three or four abreast, and so marched singing home. As for the fireworks, squibs and crackers are very hard to describe, and very little was to be seen of them : to me, the prettiest sight was the vast, orderly, happy crowd, the number of children, and the extraordinary care and kindness of the parents towards these little creatures. It does one good to see honest, heavy *épiciers*, fathers of families, playing with them in the Tuileries, or, as to-night, bearing them stoutly on their shoulders, through many long hours, in order that the little ones, too, may have their share of the fun. John Bull, I fear, is more selfish : he does not take Mrs. Bull to the public-house ; but leaves her, for the most part, to take care of the children at home.

The fête, then, is over ; the pompous black pyramid at the Louvre is only a skeleton now ; all the flags have been miraculously whisked away during the night, and the fine chandeliers which glittered down the Champs Elysées for full half a mile, have been consigned to their dens and darkness. Will they ever be reproduced for other celebrations of the glorious 29th of July ?—I think not ; the Government which vowed that there should be no more persecutions of the press, was, on that very 29th, seizing a legitimist paper, for some real or fancied offence against it : it had seized, and was seizing daily, numbers of persons merely suspected of being disaffected (and you may fancy how liberty is understood, when some of these prisoners, the other day, on coming to trial, were found guilty and sentenced to *one* day's imprisonment, after *thirty-six days detention on suspicion*). I think the Government which follows such a system, cannot be very anxious about any farther revolutionary fêtes, and that the Chamber may reasonably refuse to vote more money for them. Why should men be so mighty proud of having, on a certain day, cut a certain number of their fellow-countrymen's throats? The guards and the line employed, this time nine years, did no more than those who cannonaded the starving Lyonnese, or bayoneted the luckless inhabitants of the Rue Transnounain;—they did but fulfil the soldier's honourable duty:—his superiors bid him kill and he killeth:—perhaps, had he gone to his work with a little more heart, the result would have been different, and then —would the conquering party have been justified in annually rejoicing over the conquered? Would we have thought Charles X. justified in causing fireworks to be blazed, and concerts to be sung, and speeches to be spouted, in commemoration of his victory over his slaughtered countrymen?—I wish, for my part, they would allow the people to go about their business as on the other 362 days of the year, and leave the Champs Elysées free for the omnibuses to run, and the Tuileries in quiet, so that the nursemaids might come as usual, and the newspapers be read for a halfpenny a piece.

Shall I trouble you with an account of the speculations of these latter, and the state of the parties which they represent? The complication is not a little curious, and may form, perhaps, a subject of graver disquisition. The July fêtes occupy, as you may imagine, a considerable part of their columns just now, and it is amusing to follow them, one by one; to read Tweedledum's praise, and Tweedledee's indignation—to read, in the Débats, how the King was received with shouts and loyal vivats—in the Nation, how not a tongue was wagged in his praise, but, on the instant of his departure, how the people called for the Marseillaise and applauded *that*.—But best say no more about the fête. The legitimists were always indignant at it. The high Philippist party sneers at, and despises it; the republicans hate it: it seems a joke against *them*. Why continue it?—If there be anything sacred in the name and idea of loyalty, why renew this fête? It only shows how a rightful monarch was hurled from his throne, and a dexterous usurper stole his precious diadem. If there be anything noble in the memory of a day, when citizens, unused to war, rose against practised veterans, and, armed with the strength of their cause, overthrew them, why speak of it now? or renew the bitter recollections of the bootless struggle and victory? O Lafayette! O hero of two worlds! O accomplished Cromwell Grandison! you have to answer for more than any mortal man who has played a part in history: two republics and one monarchy does the world owe to you; and especially grateful should your country be to you. Did you not, in '90, make clear the path for honest Robespierre, and, in '30, prepare the way for—

* * * * *

[The Editor of the "Bungay Beacon" would insert no more of this letter, which is, therefore, for ever lost to the public.]

ON THE FRENCH SCHOOL OF PAINTING:

WITH APPROPRIATE ANECDOTES, ILLUSTRATIONS, AND PHILOSOPHICAL DISQUISITIONS.

IN A LETTER TO MR. MACGILP, OF LONDON.

The three collections of pictures at the Louvre, the Luxembourg, and the Ecole des Beaux Arts, contain a number of specimens of French art, since its commencement almost, and give the stranger a pretty fair opportunity to study and appreciate the school. The French list of painters contains some very good names—no very great ones, except Poussin (unless the admirers of Claude choose to rank him among great painters),—and I think the school was never in so flourishing a condition as it is at the present day. They say there are three thousand artists in this town alone: of these a handsome minority paint not merely tolerably, but well understand their business; draw the figure accurately; sketch with cleverness; and paint portraits, churches, or restaurateurs' shops, in a decent manner.

To account for a superiority over England—which, I

think, as regards art, is incontestable—it must be remembered that the painter's trade, in France, is a very good one; better appreciated, better understood, and, generally, far better paid than with us. There are a dozen excellent schools in which a lad may enter here, and, under the eye of a practised master, learn the apprenticeship of his art at an expense of about ten pounds a year. In England there is no school except the Academy, unless the student can afford to pay a very large sum, and place himself under the tuition of some particular artist. Here, a young man, for his ten pounds, has all sorts of accessory instruction, models, &c.; and has further, and for nothing, numberless incitements to study his profession which are not to be found in England:—the streets are filled with pictureshops, the people themselves are pictures walking about; the churches, theatres, eating-houses, concert-rooms are covered with pictures: Nature itself is inclined more kindly to him, for the sky is a thousand times more bright and beautiful, and the sun shines for the greater part of the year. Add to this, incitements more selfish, but quite as powerful: a French artist is paid very handsomely; for five hundred a year is much where all are poor; and has a rank in society rather above his merits than below them, being caressed by hosts and hostesses in places where titles are laughed at and a baron is thought of no more account than a banker's clerk.

The life of the young artist here is the easiest, merriest, dirtiest existence possible. He comes to Paris, probably at sixteen, from his province; his parents settle forty pounds a year on him, and pay his master; he establishes himself in the Pays Latin, or in the new quarter of Notre Dame de Lorette (which is quite peopled with painters); he arrives at his atelier at a tolerably early hour, and labours among a score of companions as merry and poor as himself. Each gentleman has his favourite tobacco-pipe; and the pictures are painted in the midst of a cloud of smoke, and a din of puns and choice French slang, and a roar of choruses, of which no one can form an idea who has not been present at such an assembly.

You see here every variety of *coiffure* that has ever been known. Some young men of genius have ringlets hanging over their shoulders—you may smell the tobacco with which they are scented across the street; some have straight locks, black, oily, and redundant; some have *toupets* in the famous Louis-Philippe fashion; some are cropped close; some have adopted the present mode— which he who would follow must, in order to do so, part his hair in the middle, grease it with grease, and gum it with gum, and iron it flat down over his ears; when arrived at the ears, you take the tongs and make a couple of ranges of curls close round the whole head,—such curls as you may see under a gilt three-cornered hat, and in her Britannic Majesty's coachman's state wig.

This is the last fashion. As for the beards, there is no end to them; all my friends, the artists, have beards who can raise them; and Nature, though she has rather stinted the bodies and limbs of the French nation, has been very liberal to them of hair, as you may see by the following specimen. Fancy these heads and beards under all sorts of caps—Chinese caps, mandarin caps, Greek skull-caps,

English jockey caps, Russian or Kuzzilbash caps, middle-age caps (such as are called, in heraldry, caps of maintenance), Spanish nets, and striped worsted nightcaps. Fancy all the jackets you have ever seen, and you have before you, as well as the pen can describe, the costumes of these indescribable Frenchmen.

In this company and costume the French student of art passes his days and acquires knowledge; how he passes his evenings, at what theatres, at what *guinguettes*, in company with what seducing little milliner, there is no need to say; but I knew one who pawned his coat to go to a carnival ball, and walked abroad very cheerfully in his *blouse*, for six weeks, until he could redeem the absent garment.

These young men (together with the students of sciences) comport themselves towards the sober citizen pretty much as the German *bursch* towards the *philister*, or as the military man, during the empire, did to the *pékin* :—from the height of their poverty they look down upon him with the greatest imaginable scorn—a scorn, I think, by which the citizen seems dazzled, for his respect for the arts is intense. The case is very different in England, where a grocer's daughter would think she made a misalliance by marrying a painter, and where a literary man (in spite of all we can say against it) ranks below that class of gentry composed of the apothecary, the attorney, the wine-merchant, whose positions, in country towns at least, are so equivocal. As for instance, my friend, the Rev. James Asterisk, who has an undeniable pedigree, a paternal estate, and a living to boot, once dined in Warwickshire, in company with several squires and parsons of that enlightened county. Asterisk, as usual, made himself extraordinarily agreeable at dinner, and delighted all present with his learning and wit. " Who is that monstrous pleasant fellow ? " said one of the squires. " Don't you know ? " replied another. " It's Asterisk, the author of so-and-so, and a famous contributor to such-and-such a magazine. " Good heavens ! " said the squire, quite horrified ; " a literary man ! I thought he had been a gentleman ! "

Another instance. M. Guizot, when he was minister here, had the grand hotel of the ministry, and gave entertainments to all the great *de par le monde*, as Brantôme says, and entertained them in a proper ministerial magnificence. The splendid and beautiful Duchess of Dash was at one of his ministerial parties ; and went, a fortnight afterwards, as in duty bound, to pay her respects to M.

Guizot. But it happened, in this fortnight, that M. Guizot was minister no longer; having given up his portfolio, and his grand hotel, to retire into private life, and to occupy his humble apartments in the house which he possesses, and of which he lets the greater portion. A friend of mine was present at one of the ex-minister's *soirées*, where the Duchess of Dash made her appearance. He says, the Duchess, at her entrance, seemed quite astounded, and examined the premises with a most curious wonder. Two or three shabby little rooms, with ordinary furniture, and a minister *en retraite*, who lives by letting lodgings! In our country was ever such a thing heard of? No, thank Heaven! and a Briton ought to be proud of the difference.

But to our muttons. This country is surely the paradise of painters and penny-a-liners; and when one reads of M. Horace Vernet at Rome, exceeding ambassadors at Rome, by his magnificence, and leading such a life as Rubens or Titian did of old; when one sees M. Thiers's grand villa in the Rue St. George (a dozen years ago he was not even a penny-a-liner: no such luck); when one contemplates, in imagination, M. Gudin, the marine painter, too lame to walk through the picture gallery of the Louvre, accommodated, therefore, with a wheel-chair, a privilege of princes only, and accompanied—nay, for what I know, actually trundled — down the gallery by majesty itself—who does not long to make one of the great nation, exchange his native tongue for the melodious jabber of France; or, at least, adopt it for his native country, like Marshal Saxe, Napoleon, and Anacharsis Clootz? Noble people! they made Tom Paine a deputy; and as for Tom Macaulay, they would make a *dynasty* of him.

Well, this being the case, no wonder there are so many painters in France; and here, at least, we are back to them. At the Ecole Royale des Beaux Arts, you see two or three hundred specimens of their performances; all the prize-men, since 1750, I think, being bound to leave their prize sketch or picture. Can anything good come out of the Royal Academy? is a question which has been considerably mooted in England (in the neighbourhood of Suffolk Street, especially). The hundreds of French samples are, I think, not very satisfactory. The subjects are almost all what are called classical: Orestes pursued by every variety of Furies; numbers of little wolf-sucking Romuluses; Hectors and Andromaches in a complication of parting embraces, and so forth; for it was the absurd maxim of our forefathers, that because these subjects had been the fashion twenty centuries ago, they must remain so in *sæcula sæculorum;* because to these lofty heights giants had scaled, behold the race of pigmies must get upon stilts and jump at them likewise! and on the canvas, and in the theatre, the French frogs (excuse the pleasantry) were instructed to swell out and roar as much as possible like bulls.

What was the consequence, my dear friend? In trying to make themselves into bulls, the frogs make themselves into jackasses, as might be expected. For a hundred and ten years the classical humbug oppressed the nation; and you may see, in this gallery of the Beaux Arts, seventy years' specimens of the dulness which it engendered.

Now, as Nature made every man with a nose and eyes of his own, she gave him a character of his own too; and yet we, O foolish race! must try our very best to ape some one or two of our neighbours, whose ideas fit us no more than their breeches! It is the study of nature, surely, that profits us, and not of these imitations of her. A man, as a man, from a dustman up to Æschylus, is God's work, and good to read, as all works of Nature are: but the silly animal is never content; is ever trying to fit itself into another shape; wants to deny its own identity, and has not the courage to utter its own thoughts. Because Lord Byron was wicked, and quarrelled with the world; and found himself growing fat, and quarrelled with his victuals, and thus, naturally, grew ill-humoured, did not half Europe grow ill-humoured too? Did not every poet feel his young affections withered, and despair and darkness cast upon his soul? Because certain mighty men of old could make heroical statues and plays, must we not be told that there is no other beauty but classical beauty?—must not every little whipster of a French poet chalk you out plays, *Henriades,* and such-like, and vow that here was the real thing, the undeniable Kalon?

The undeniable fiddlestick! For a hundred years, my dear sir, the world was humbugged by the so-called classical artists, as they now are by what is called the Christian art (of which anon); and it is curious to look at the pictorial traditions as here handed down. The consequence of them is, that scarce one of the classical pictures exhibited is worth much more than two and sixpence. Borrowed from statuary, in the first place, the colour of the paintings seems, as much as possible, to participate in it; they are, mostly, of a misty, stony, green, dismal hue, as if they had been painted in a world where no colour was. In every picture there are, of course, white mantles, white urns, white columns, white statues — those *obligé* accomplishments of the sublime. There are the endless straight noses, long eyes, round chins, short upper lips, just as they are ruled down for you in the drawing-books, as if the latter were the revelations of beauty, issued by supreme authority, from which there was no appeal? Why is the classical reign to endure? Why is yonder simpering Venus de Medicis to be our standard of beauty, or the Greek tragedies to bound our notions of the sublime? There was no reason why Agamemnon should set the fashions, and remain ἄναξ ἀνδρῶν to eternity: and there is a classical quotation, which you may have occasionally heard, beginning *Vixere fortes*, &c., which, as it avers that there were a great number of stout fellows before Agamemnon, may not unreasonably induce us to conclude that similar heroes were to succeed him. Shakspeare made a better man when his imagination moulded the mighty figure of Macbeth. And if you will measure Satan by Prometheus, the blind old Puritan's work by that of the fiery Grecian poet, does not Milton's angel surpass Æschylus's — surpass him by " many a rood ? "

In the same school of the Beaux Arts, where are to be found such a number of pale imitations of the antique, Monsieur Thiers (and he ought to be thanked for it) has caused to be placed a full-sized copy of " The Last Judgment" of Michel Angelo, and a number of casts from statues by the same splendid hand. There *is* the sublime, if you please—a new sublime—an original sublime—quite as sublime as the Greek sublime. See yonder, in the midst of his angels, the Judge of the world descending in glory; and near him, beautiful and gentle, and yet indescribably august and pure, the Virgin by his side. There is the " Moses," the grandest figure that ever was carved in stone. It has about it something frightfully majestic, if one may so speak. In examining this, and the astonishing picture of " The Judgment," or even a single figure of it, the spectator's sense amounts almost to pain. I would not like to be left in a room alone with the " Moses." How did the artist live amongst them, and create them? How did he suffer the painful labour of invention? One fancies that he would have been scorched up, like Semele, by sights too tremendous for his vision to bear. One cannot imagine him, with our small physical endowments and weaknesses, a man like ourselves.

As for the Ecole Royale des Beaux Arts, then, and all the good its students have done, as students, it is stark naught. When the men did anything, it was after they had left the academy, and began thinking for themselves. There is only one picture among the many hundreds that has, to my idea, much merit (a charming composition of Homer singing, signed Jourdy); and the only good that the academy has done by its pupils was to send them to Rome, where they might learn better things. At home, the intolerable, stupid classicalities, taught by men who, belonging to the least erudite country in Europe, were themselves, from their profession, the least learned among their countrymen, only weighed the pupils down, and cramped their hands, their eyes, and their imaginations; drove them away from natural beauty, which, thank God, is fresh and attainable by us all, to-day, and yesterday, and to-morrow; and sent them rambling after artificial grace, without the proper means of judging or attaining it.

A word for the building of the Palais des Beaux Arts. It is beautiful, and as well finished and convenient as beautiful. With its light and elegant fabric, its pretty fountain, its archway of the *Renaissance*, and fragments of sculpture, you can hardly see, on a fine day, a place more *riant* and pleasing.

Passing from thence up the picturesque Rue de Seine, let us walk to the Luxembourg, where *bonnes*, students, grisettes, and old gentlemen with pigtails, love to wander in the melancholy, quaint, old gardens; where the peers have a new and comfortable court of justice, to judge all the *émeutes* which are to take place; and where, as everybody knows, is the picture gallery of modern French artists, whom government thinks worthy of patronage.

A very great proportion of these, as we see by the catalogue, are by the students whose works we have just been to visit at the Beaux Arts, and who, having performed their pilgrimage to Rome, have taken rank among the professors of the art. I don't know a more pleasing exhibition; for there are not a dozen really bad pictures in the collection, some very good, and the rest showing great skill and smartness of execution.

In the same way, however, that it has been supposed that no man could be a great poet unless he wrote a very big poem, the tradition is kept up among the painters, and we have here a vast number of large canvases, with figures of the proper heroical length and nakedness. The anti-classicists did not arise in France until about 1827; and, in consequence, up to that period, we have here the old classical faith in full vigour. There is Brutus, having chopped his son's head off, with all the agony of a father, and then, calling for number two; there is Æneas carrying off old Anchises; there are Paris and Venus, as naked as two Hottentots, and many more such choice subjects from Lemprière.

But the chief specimens of the sublime are in the way of murders, with which the catalogue swarms. Here are a few extracts from it:—

7. Beaume, Chevalier de la Légion d'Honneur. "The Grand Dauphiness Dying."

18. Blondel, Chevalier de la, &c. "Zenobia found Dead."

36. Debay, Chevalier. "The Death of Lucretia."

38. Dejuinne. "The Death of Hector."

34. Court, Chevalier de la, &c. "The Death of Cæsar."

39, 40, 41. Delacroix, Chevalier. "Dante and Virgil in the Infernal Lake," "The Massacre of Scio," and "Medea going to Murder her Children."

43. Delaroche, Chevalier. "Joas taken from among the Dead."

44. "The Death of Queen Elizabeth."

45. "Edward V. and his Brother" (preparing for death).

50. "Hecuba going to be Sacrificed." Drolling, Chevalier.

51. Dubois. "Young Clovis found Dead."

56. Henry, Chevalier. "The Massacre of St. Bartholomew."

75. Guerin, Chevalier. "Cain, after the Death of Abel."

83. Jacquand. "Death of Adelaide de Comminges."

88. "The Death of Eudamidas.

93. "The Death of Hymetto."

103. "The Death of Philip of Austria."—And so on.

You see what woful subjects they take, and how profusely they are decorated with knighthood. They are like the Black Brunswickers these painters, and ought to be called *Chevaliers de la Mort*. I don't know why the merriest people in the world should please themselves with such grim representations and varieties of murder, or why murder itself should be considered so eminently sublime and poetical. It is good at the end of a tragedy; but, then, it is good because it is the end, and because, by the events foregone, the mind is prepared for it. But these men will have nothing but fifth acts; and seem to skip, as unworthy, all the circumstances leading to them. This, however, is part of the scheme—the bloated, unnatural, stilted, spouting, sham sublime, that our teachers have believed and tried to pass off as real, and which your humble servant and other antihumbuggists should heartily, according to the strength that is in them, endeavour to pull down. What, for instance, could Monsieur Lafond care about the death of Eudamidas? What was Hecuba to Chevalier Drolling, or Chevalier Drolling, to Hecuba? I would lay a wager that neither of them ever conjugated τύπτω, and that their school learning carried them not as far as the letter, but only to the game of taw. How were they to be inspired by such subjects? From having seen Talma and Mademoiselle Georges flaunting in sham Greek costumes, and having read up the articles Eudamidas, Hecuba, in the *Mythological Dictionary*. What a classicism, inspired by rouge, gas-lamps, and a few lines in Lemprière, and copied, half from ancient statues, and half from a naked guardsman at one shilling and sixpence the hour!

Delacroix is a man of a very different genius, and his " Medea " is a genuine creation of a noble fancy. For most of the others, Mrs. Brownrigg, and her two female 'prentices, would have done as well as the desperate Colchian, with her τέκνα φίλτατα. M. Delacroix has produced a number of rude, barbarous pictures; but there is the stamp of genius on all of them,—the great poetical *intention*, which is worth all your execution. Delaroche is another man of high merit; with not such a great *heart*, perhaps, as the other, but a fine and careful draughtsman, and an excellent arranger of his subject. " The Death of Elizabeth " is a raw, young performance, seemingly— not, at least, to my taste. The " Enfans d'Edouard " is renowned over Europe, and has appeared in a hundred different ways in print. It is properly pathetic and gloomy, and merits fully its high reputation. This painter rejoices in such subjects—in what Lord Portsmouth used to call " black jobs." He has killed Charles I., and Lady

Jane Grey, and the Dukes of Guise, and I don't know whom besides. He is, at present, occupied with a vast work at the Beaux Arts, where the writer of this had the honour of seeing him,—a little, keen-looking man, some five feet in height. He wore, on this important occasion, a bandanna round his head, and was in the act of smoking a cigar.

Horace Vernet, whose beautiful daughter Delaroche married, is the king of French battle-painters—an amazingly rapid and dexterous draughtsman, who has Napoleon and all the campaigns by heart, and has painted the Grenadier Français under all sorts of attitudes. His pictures on such subjects are spirited, natural, and excellent; and he is so clever a man, that all he does is good to a certain degree. His "Judith" is somewhat violent, perhaps. His "Rebecca" most pleasing; and not the less so for a little pretty affectation of attitude and needless singularity of costume. "Raphael and Michael Angelo" is as clever a picture as can be—clever is just the word—the groups and drawing excellent, the colouring pleasantly bright and gaudy; and the French students study it incessantly: there are a dozen who copy it for one who copies Delacroix. His little scraps of wood-cuts, in the now publishing *Life of Napoleon*, are perfect gems in their way, and the noble price paid for them not a penny more than he merits.

The picture, by Court, of "The Death of Cæsar," is remarkable for effect and excellent workmanship; and the head of Brutus (who looks like Armand Carrel) is full of energy. There are some beautiful heads of women, and some very good colour in the picture. Jacquand's "Death of Adelaide de Comminge" is neither more nor less than beautiful. Adelaide had, it appears, a lover, who betook himself to a convent of Trappists. She followed him thither, disguised as a man, took the vows, and was not discovered by him till on her death-bed. The painter has told this story in a most pleasing and affecting manner: the picture is full of *onction* and melancholy grace. The objects, too, are capitally represented; and the tone and colour very good. Decaisne's "Guardian Angel" is not so good in colour, but is equally beautiful in expression and grace. A little child and a nurse are asleep: an angel watches the infant. You see women look very wistfully at this sweet picture; and what triumph would a painter have more?

We must not quit the Luxembourg without noticing the dashing sea-pieces of Gudin, and one or two landscapes by Giroux (the plain of Grasivaudan), and "The Prometheus" of Aligny. This is an imitation, perhaps; as is a noble picture of "Jesus Christ and the Children," by Flandrin: but the artists are imitating better models, at any rate; and one begins to perceive that the odious classical dynasty is no more. Poussin's magnificent "Polyphemus" (I only know a print of that marvellous composition) has, perhaps, suggested the first-named picture; and the latter has been inspired by a good enthusiastic study of the Roman schools.

Of this revolution, Monsieur Ingres has been one of the chief instruments. He was, before Horace Vernet, president of the French Academy at Rome, and is famous as a chief of a school. When he broke up his atelier here, to set out for his presidency, many of his pupils attended him faithfully some way on his journey; and some, with scarcely a penny in their pouches, walked through France, and across the Alps, in a pious pilgrimage to Rome, being determined not to forsake their old master. Such an action was worthy of them, and of the high rank which their profession holds in France, where the honours to be acquired by art are only inferior to those which are gained in war. One reads of such peregrinations in old days, when the scholars of some great Italian painter followed him from Venice to Rome, or from Florence to Ferrara. In regard of Ingres' individual merit, as a painter, the writer of this is not a fair judge, having seen but three pictures by him; one being a *plafond* in the Louvre, which his disciples much admire.

Ingres stands between the Imperio-Davido-classical school of French art, and the namby-pamby mystical German school, which is for carrying us back to Cranach and Dürer, and which is making progress here.

For everything here finds imitation: the French have the genius of imitation and caricature. This absurd humbug, called the Christian or Catholic art, is sure to tickle our neighbours, and will be a favourite with them, when better known. My dear MacGilp, I do believe this to be a greater humbug than the humbug of David and Girodet, inasmuch as the latter was founded on Nature at least; whereas the former is made up of silly affectations, and improvements upon Nature. Here, for instance, is Chevalier Ziegler's picture of " St. Luke painting the

Virgin." St. Luke has a monk's dress on, embroidered, however, smartly round the sleeves. The Virgin sits in an immense yellow-ochre halo, with her son in her arms. She looks preternaturally solemn; as does St. Luke, who is eyeing his paint-brush with an intense ominous mystical look. They call this Catholic art. There is nothing, my dear friend, more easy in life. First, take your colours, and rub them down clean,—bright carmine, bright yellow, bright sienna, bright ultramarine, bright green. Make the costumes of your figures as much as possible like the costumes of the early part of the fifteenth century. Paint them in with the above colours; and if on a gold ground, the more "Catholic" your art is. Dress your apostles like priests before the altar; and remember to have a good commodity of crosiers, censers, and other such gimcracks, as you may see in the Catholic chapels, in Sutton Street, and elsewhere. Deal in Virgins, and dress them like a burgomaster's wife by Cranach or Van Eyck. Give them all long twisted tails to their gowns, and proper angular draperies. Place all their heads on one side, with the eyes shut, and the proper solemn simper. At the back of the head, draw, and gild with gold-leaf, a halo, or glory, of the exact shape of a cart-wheel: and you have the thing done. It is Catholic art *tout craché*, as Louis Philippe says. We have it still in England, handed down to us for four centuries, in the pictures on the cards, as the redoubtable king and queen of clubs. Look at them: you will see that the costumes and attitudes are precisely similar to those which figure in the catholicities of the school of Overbeck and Cornelius.

Before you take your cane at the door, look for one instant at the statue-room. Yonder is Jouffley's " Jeune Fille confiant son premier secret à Vénus." Charming, charming! It is from the exhibition of this year only; and, I think, the best sculpture in the gallery—pretty, fanciful, *naïve;* admirable in workmanship and imitation of Nature. I have seldom seen flesh better represented in marble. Examine, also, Jaley's "Pudeur," Jacquot's "Nymph," and Rude's "Boy with the Tortoise." These are not very exalted subjects, or what are called exalted, and do not go beyond simple, smiling, beauty and nature. But what then? Are we gods, Miltons, Michel Angelos, that can leave earth when we please, and soar to heights immeasurable? No, my dear MacGilp; but the fools of academicians would fain make us so. Are you not, and half the painters in London, panting for an opportunity to show your genius in a great "historical picture?" O blind race! Have you wings? Not a feather: and yet you must be ever puffing, sweating up to the tops of rugged hills; and, arrived there, clapping and shaking your ragged elbows, and making as if you would fly! Come down, silly Dædalus; come down to the lowly places in which Nature ordered you to walk. The sweet flowers are springing there; the fat muttons are waiting there; the pleasant sun shines there; be content and humble, and take your share of the good cheer.

While we have been indulging in this discussion, the omnibus has gaily conducted us across the water; and "Le garde qui veille à la porte du Louvre ne défend pas" our entry.

What a paradise this gallery is for French students, or

foreigners who sojourn in the capital! It is hardly necessary to say that the brethren of the brush are not usually supplied by Fortune with any extraordinary wealth, or means of enjoying the luxuries with which Paris, more than any other city, abounds. But here they have a luxury which surpasses all others, and spend their days in a palace which all the money of all the Rothschilds could not buy. They sleep, perhaps, in a garret, and dine in a cellar; but no grandee in Europe has such a drawing-room. Kings' houses have, at best, but damask hangings, and gilt cornices. What are these, to a wall covered with canvas by Paul Veronese, or a hundred yards of Rubens? Artists from England, who have a national gallery that resembles a moderate-sized gin-shop, who may not copy pictures, except under particular restrictions, and on rare and particular days, may revel here to their hearts' content. Here is a room half a mile long, with as many windows as Aladdin's palace, open from sunrise till evening, and free to all manners and all varieties of study: the only puzzle to the student, is to select the one he shall begin upon, and keep his eyes away from the rest.

Fontaine's grand staircase, with its arches, and painted ceilings, and shining Doric columns, leads directly to the gallery; but it is thought too fine for working days, and is only opened for the public entrance on Sabbath. A little back stair (leading from a court, in which stand numerous bas-reliefs, and a solemn sphinx, of polished granite), is the common entry for students and others, who, during the week, enter the gallery.

Hither have lately been transported a number of the

works of French artists, which formerly covered the walls of the Luxembourg (death only entitles the French painter to a place in the Louvre); and let us confine ourselves to the Frenchmen only, for the space of this letter.

I have seen, in a fine private collection at St. Germain, one or two admirable single figures of David, full of life, truth, and gaiety. The colour is not good, but all the rest excellent; and one of these so much-lauded pictures is the portrait of a washerwoman. "Pope Pius," at the Louvre, is as bad in colour, and as remarkable for its vigour and look of life. The man had a genius for painting portraits and common life, but must attempt the heroic;—failed signally; and, what is worse, carried a whole nation blundering after him. Had you told a Frenchman so, twenty years ago, he would have thrown the *démenti* in your teeth; or, at least, laughed at you in scornful incredulity. They say of us that we don't know when we are beaten: they go a step further, and swear their defeats are victories. David was a part of the glory of the empire; and one might as well have said there that "Romulus" was a bad picture, as that Toulouse was a lost battle. Old-fashioned people, who believe in the Emperor, believe in the Théâtre Français, and believe that Ducis improved upon Shakspeare, have the above opinion. Still, it is curious to remark, in this place, how art and literature become party matters, and political sects have their favourite painters and authors.

Nevertheless, Jacques Louis David is dead. He died about a year after his bodily demise in 1825. The romanticism killed him. Walter Scott, from his Castle of Abbotsford, sent out a troop of gallant young Scotch adventurers,

ON THE FRENCH SCHOOL OF PAINTING.

merry outlaws, valiant knights, and savage Highlanders, who, with trunk hosen and buff jerkins, fierce two-handed swords, and harness on their back, did challenge, combat, and overcome the heroes and demigods of Greece and Rome. *Notre Dame à la rescousse!* Sir Brian de Bois Guilbert has borne Hector of Troy clear out of his saddle. Andromache may weep: but her spouse is beyond the reach of physic. See! Robin Hood twangs his bow, and the heathen gods fly, howling. *Montjoie Saint Dénis!* down goes Ajax under the mace of Dunois; and yonder are Leonidas and Romulus begging their lives of Rob Roy Macgregor. Classicism is dead. Sir John Froissart has taken Dr. Lemprière by the nose, and reigns sovereign.

Of the great pictures of David, the defunct, we need not, then, say much. Romulus is a mighty fine young fellow, no doubt; and if he has come out to battle stark naked (except a very handsome helmet), it is because the costume became him, and shows off his figure to advantage. But was there ever anything so absurd as this passion for the nude, which was followed by all the painters of the Davidian epoch? And how are we to suppose yonder straddle to be the true characteristic of the heroic and the sublime? Romulus stretches his legs as far as ever nature will allow; the Horatii, in receiving their swords, think proper to stretch their legs too, and to thrust forward their arms, thus,—

Romulus.   The Horatii.

Romulus's is the exact action of a telegraph; and the Horatii are all in the position of the lunge. Is this the sublime? Mr. Angelo, of Bond Street, might admire the attitude; his namesake, Michael, I don't think would.

The little picture of "Paris and Helen," one of the master's earliest, I believe, is likewise one of his best: the details are exquisitely painted. Helen looks needlessly sheepish, and Paris has a most odious ogle; but the limbs of the male figure are beautifully designed, and have not the green tone which you see in the later pictures of the master. What is the meaning of this green? Was it the fashion, or the varnish? Girodet's pictures are green; Gros's emperor's and grenadiers have universally the jaundice. Gerard's "Psyche" has a most decided green sickness; and I am at a loss, I confess, to account for the enthusiasm which this performance inspired on its first appearance before the public.

In the same room with it, is Girodet's ghastly "Deluge," and Gericault's dismal "Medusa." Gericault died, they say, for want of fame. He was a man who possessed a considerable fortune of his own; but pined because no one in his day would purchase his pictures, and so acknowledge his talent. At present, a scrawl from his pencil brings an enormous price. All his works have a grand *cachet*: he never did anything mean. When he painted the "Raft of the Medusa," it is said he lived for a long time among the corpses which he painted, and that his studio was a second Morgue. If you have not seen the picture, you are familiar, probably, with Reynolds's admirable engraving of it. A huge black sea; a raft beating upon it; a horrid company of men dead, half dead, writhing and frantic with hideous hunger or hideous hope; and, far away, black, against a stormy sunset, a sail. The story is powerfully told, and has a legitimate tragic interest, so to speak,—deeper, because more natural, than Girodet's green "Deluge," for instance; or his livid "Orestes," or red-hot "Clytemnestra."

Seen from a distance the latter's "Deluge" has a certain awe-inspiring air with it. A slimy green man stands on a green rock, and clutches hold of a tree. On the green man's shoulders is his old father, in a green old age; to him hangs his wife, with a babe on her breast, and dangling at her hair, another child. In the water floats a corpse (a beautiful head); and a green sea and atmosphere envelops all this dismal group. The old father is represented with a bag of money in his hand; and the tree, which the man catches, is cracking, and just on the point of giving way. These two points were considered very fine by the critics: they are two such ghastly epigrams as continually disfigure French Tragedy. For this reason I have never been able to read Racine with pleasure, — the dialogue is so crammed with these lugubrious good things — melancholy antitheses — sparkling undertakers' wit; but this is heresy, and had better be spoken discreetly.

The gallery contains a vast number of Poussin's pictures; they put me in mind of the colour of objects in dreams,—a strange, hazy, lurid hue. How noble are some of his landscapes! What a depth of solemn shadow is in yonder wood, near which, by the side of a black water, halts Diogenes. The air is thunder-laden, and breathes heavily. You hear ominous whispers in the vast forest gloom.

Near it is a landscape, by Carel Dujardin, I believe, conceived in quite a different mood, but exquisitely poetical too. A horseman is riding up a hill, and giving money to a blowsy beggar-wench. *O matutini rores auræque salubres !* in what a wonderful way has the artist managed to create you out of a few bladders of paint and pots of varnish. You can see the matutinal dews twinkling in the grass, and feel the fresh, salubrious airs ("the breath of Nature blowing free," as the corn-law man sings) blowing free over the heath; silvery vapours are rising up from the blue lowlands. You can tell the hour of the morning and the time of the year : you can do anything but describe it in words. As with regard to the Poussin above-mentioned, one can never pass it without bearing away a certain pleasing, dreamy feeling of awe and musing; the other landscape inspires the spectator infallibly with the most delightful briskness and cheerfulness of spirit. Herein lies the vast privilege of the landscape-painter : he does not address you with one fixed particular subject or expression, but with a thousand never contemplated by himself, and which only arise out of occasion. You may always be looking at a natural landscape as at a fine pictorial imitation of one; it seems eternally producing new thoughts in your bosom, as it does fresh beauties from its own. I cannot fancy more delightful, cheerful, silent companions for a man than half a dozen landscapes hung round his study. Portraits, on the contrary, and large pieces of figures, have a painful, fixed, staring look, which must jar upon the mind in many of its moods. Fancy living in a room with David's sans-culotte Leonidas staring perpetually in your face!

There is a little Watteau here, and a rare piece of fantastical brightness and gaiety it is. What a delightful affectation about yonder ladies flirting their fans, and trailing about in their long brocades! What splendid dandies are those, ever-smirking, turning out their toes, with broad blue ribbons to tie up their crooks and their pigtails, and wonderful gorgeous crimson satin breeches! Yonder, in the midst of a golden atmosphere, rises a bevy of little round Cupids, bubbling up in clusters as out of a champagne bottle, and melting away in air. There is, to be sure, a hidden analogy between liquors and pictures: the eye is deliciously tickled by these frisky Watteaus, and yields itself up to a light, smiling, gentlemanlike intoxication. Thus, were we inclined to pursue further this mighty subject, yonder landscape of Claude,—calm, fresh, delicate, yet full of flavour,—should be likened to a bottle of Château-Margaux. And what is the Poussin before spoken of but Romanée-Gelée?—heavy, sluggish,—the luscious odour almost sickens you; a sultry sort of drink; your limbs sink under it; you feel as if you had been drinking hot blood.

An ordinary man would be whirled away in a fever, or would hobble off this mortal stage, in a premature gout-fit, if he too early or too often indulged in such tremendous drink. I think in my heart I am fonder of pretty third-rate pictures than of your great thundering first-rates. Confess how many times you have read Béranger, and how many Milton? If you go to the Star-and-Garter, don't you grow sick of that vast, luscious landscape, and long for the sight of a couple of cows, or a donkey, and a few yards of common? Donkeys, my dear MacGilp, since we have come to this subject, say not so; Richmond Hill for them. Milton they never grow tired of; and are as familiar with Raphael as Bottom with exquisite Titania. Let us thank Heaven, my dear sir, for according to us the power to taste and appreciate the pleasures of mediocrity. I have never heard that we were great geniuses. Earthy are we, and of the earth; glimpses of the sublime are but rare to us; leave we them to great geniuses, and to the donkeys; and if it nothing profit us, *aërias tentâsse domos* along with them, let us thankfully remain below, being merry and humble.

I have now only to mention the charming "Cruche Cassée" of Greuze, which all the young ladies delight to copy; and of which the colour (a thought too blue, perhaps) is marvellously graceful and delicate. There are three more pictures by the artist, containing exquisite female heads and colour; but they have charms for French critics which are difficult to be discovered by English eyes; and the pictures seem weak to me. A very fine picture by Bon Bollongue, "Saint Benedict resuscitating a Child," deserves particular attention, and is superb in vigour and richness of colour. You must look, too, at the large, noble, melancholy landscapes of Philippe de Champagne; and the two magnificent Italian pictures of

Léopold Robert; they are, perhaps, the very finest pictures that the French school has produced,—as deep as Poussin, of a better colour, and of a wonderful minuteness and veracity in the representation of objects.

Every one of Lesueur's church-pictures are worth examining and admiring; they are full of "unction," and pious mystical grace. "Saint Scholastica" is divine; and the taking down from the cross as noble a composition as ever was seen; I care not by whom the other may be. There is more beauty, and less affectation, about this picture than you will find in the performances of many Italian masters, with high-sounding names (out with it, and say RAPHAEL at once). I hate those simpering Madonnas. I declare that the Jardinière is a puking, smirking miss, with nothing heavenly about her. I vow that the "Saint Elizabeth" is a bad picture,—a bad composition, badly drawn, badly coloured, in a bad imitation of Titian,—a piece of vile affectation. I say, that when Raphael painted this picture, two years before his death, the spirit of painting had gone from out of him; he was no longer inspired; *it was time that he should die!!*

There,—the murder is out! My paper is filled to the brim, and there is no time to speak of Lesueur's "Crucifixion," which is odiously coloured, to be sure; but earnest, tender, simple, holy. But such things are most difficult to translate into words;—one lays down the pen, and thinks and thinks. The figures appear, and take their places one by one: ranging themselves according to order, in light or in gloom, the colours are reflected duly in the little camera obscura of the brain, and the whole picture lies there complete; but can you describe it? No, not if pens were fitch-brushes, and words were bladders of paint. With which, for the present, adieu.

Your faithful
M. A. T.

To Mr. Robert MacGilp,
    Newman Street, London.

THE PAINTER'S BARGAIN.

Simon Gambouge was the son of Solomon Gambouge; and as all the world knows, both father and son were astonishingly clever fellows at their profession. Solomon painted landscapes, which nobody bought; and Simon took a higher line, and painted portraits to admiration, only nobody came to sit to him.

As he was not gaining five pounds a year by his profession, and had arrived at the age of twenty, at least, Simon determined to better himself by taking a wife,—a plan which a number of other wise men adopt, in similar years and circumstances. So Simon prevailed upon a butcher's daughter (to whom he owed considerably for cutlets) to quit the meat-shop and follow him. Griskinissa—such was the fair creature's name—was as lovely a bit of mutton, her father said, as ever a man would wish to stick a knife into. She had sat to the painter for all sorts of characters; and the curious who possess any of Gambouge's pictures will see her as Venus, Minerva, Madonna, and in numberless other characters: Portrait of a lady—Griskinissa; Sleeping Nymph—Griskinissa, without a rag of clothes, lying in a forest; Maternal Solicitude—Griskinissa again, with young Master Gambouge, who was by this time the offspring of their affections.

The lady brought the painter a handsome little fortune of a couple of hundred pounds; and as long as this sum lasted no woman could be more lovely or loving. But want began speedily to attack their little household; bakers' bills were unpaid; rent was due, and the reckless landlord gave no quarter; and, to crown the whole, her father, unnatural butcher! suddenly stopped the supplies of mutton-chops; and swore that his daughter, and the dauber, her husband, should have no more of his wares. At first they embraced tenderly, and, kissing and crying over their little infant, vowed to Heaven that they would do without; but in the course of the evening Griskinissa grew peckish, and poor Simon pawned his best coat.

When this habit of pawning is discovered, it appears to the poor a kind of Eldorado. Gambouge and his wife were so delighted, that they, in the course of a month, made away with her gold chain, her great warming-pan, his best crimson plush inexpressibles, two wigs, a washhand-basin and ewer, fire-irons, window-curtains, crockery, and armchairs. Griskinissa said, smiling, that she had found a second father in *her uncle*,—a base pun, which showed that her mind was corrupted, and that she was no longer the tender, simple Griskinissa of other days.

I am sorry to say that she had taken to drinking; she swallowed the warming-pan in the course of three days, and fuddled herself one whole evening with the crimson plush breeches.

THE PAINTER'S BARGAIN.

Drinking is the devil—the father, that is to say, of all vices. Griskinissa's face and her mind grew ugly together; her good humour changed to bilious, bitter discontent; her pretty, fond epithets, to foul abuse and swearing; her tender blue eyes grew watery and blear, and the peach colour on her cheeks fled from its old habitation, and crowded up into her nose, where, with a number of pimples, it stuck fast. Add to this a dirty, draggle-tailed chintz; long, matted hair, wandering into her eyes, and over her lean shoulders, which were once so snowy, and you have the picture of drunkenness and Mrs. Simon Gambouge.

Poor Simon, who had been a gay, lively fellow enough in the days of his better fortune, was completely cast down by his present ill luck, and cowed by the ferocity of his wife. From morning till night the neighbours could hear this woman's tongue, and understand her doings; bellows went skimming across the room, chairs were flumped down on the floor, and poor Gambouge's oil and varnish-pots went clattering through the windows, or down the stairs. The baby roared all day; and Simon sat pale and idle in a corner, taking a small sup at the brandy-bottle, when Mrs. Gambouge was out of the way.

One day, as he sat disconsolately at his easel, furbishing up a picture of his wife, in the character of Peace, which he had commenced a year before, he was more than ordinarily desperate, and cursed and swore in the most pathetic manner. "Oh, miserable fate of genius!" cried he, "was I, a man of such commanding talents, born for this? to be bullied by a fiend of a wife; to have my master-pieces neglected by the world, or sold only for a few pieces?

Cursed be the love which has misled me; cursed be the art which is unworthy of me! Let me dig or steal, let me sell myself as a soldier, or sell myself to the devil, I should not be more wretched than I am now!"

"Quite the contrary," cried a small, cheery voice.

"What!" exclaimed Gambouge, trembling and surprised. "Who's there?—where are you?—who are you?"

"You were just speaking of me," said the voice.

Gambouge held, in his left hand, his palette; in his right, a bladder of crimson lake, which he was about to squeeze out upon the mahogany. "Where are you?" cried he again.

"S-q-u-e-e-z-e!" exclaimed the little voice.

Gambouge picked out the nail from the bladder, and gave a squeeze; when, as sure as I am living, a little imp spurted out from the hole upon the palette, and began laughing in the most singular and oily manner.

When first born he was little bigger than a tadpole; then he grew to be as big as a mouse; then he arrived at the size of a cat; and then he jumped off the palette, and, turning head over heels, asked the poor painter what he wanted with him.

* * * * *

The strange little animal twisted head over heels, and fixed himself at last upon the top of Gambouge's easel,— smearing out, with his heels, all the white and vermilion which had just been laid on the allegoric portrait of Mrs. Gambouge.

"What!" exclaimed Simon, "is it the——"

"Exactly so; talk of me, you know, and I am always at hand: besides, I am not half so black as I am painted, as you will see when you know me a little better."

"Upon my word," said the painter, "it is a very singular surprise which you have given me. To tell truth, I did not even believe in your existence."

The little imp put on a theatrical air, and, with one of Mr. Macready's best looks, said,—

> There are more things in heaven and earth, Gambogio,
> Than are dreamed of in your philosophy.

Gambouge, being a Frenchman, did not understand the

quotation, but felt somehow strangely and singularly interested in the conversation of his new friend.

Diabolus continued: "You are a man of merit, and want money; you will starve on your merit; you can only get money from me. Come, my friend, how much is it? I ask the easiest interest in the world; old Mordecai, the usurer, has made you pay twice as heavily before now: nothing but the signature of a bond, which is a mere ceremony, and the transfer of an article which, in itself, is a supposition — a valueless, windy, uncertain property of yours, called, by some poet of your own, I think, an *animula, vagula, blandula;* bah! there is no use beating about the bush — I mean *a soul.* Come, let me have it; you know you will sell it some other way, and not get such good pay for your bargain!"—and, having made this speech, the Devil pulled out from his fob a sheet as big as a double *Times*, only there was a different *stamp* in the corner.

It is useless and tedious to describe law documents: lawyers only love to read them; and they have as good in Chitty as any that are to be found in the devil's own; so nobly have the apprentices emulated the skill of the master. Suffice it to say, that poor Gambouge read over the paper, and signed it. He was to have all he wished for seven years, and at the end of that time was to become the property of the ——; 𝔓𝔯𝔬𝔳𝔦𝔡𝔢𝔡 that, during the course of the seven years, every single wish which he might form should be gratified by the other of the contracting parties; otherwise the deed became null and non-avenue, and Gambouge should be left " to go to the —— his own way."

"You will never see me again," said Diabolus, in shaking hands with poor Simon, on whose fingers he left such a mark as is to be seen at this day—"never, at least unless you want me; for everything you ask will be performed in the most quiet and every-day manner: believe me, it is best and most gentlemanlike, and avoids anything like scandal. But if you set me about anything which is extraordinary, and out of the course of nature, as it were, come I must, you know; and of this you are the best judge." So saying, Diabolus disappeared; but whether up the chimney, through the keyhole, or by any other aperture or contrivance, nobody knows. Simon Gambouge was left in a fever of delight, as, Heaven forgive me! I believe many a worthy man would be, if he were allowed an opportunity to make a similar bargain.

"Heigho!" said Simon. "I wonder whether this be a reality or a dream. I am sober, I know; for who will give me credit for the means to be drunk? and as for sleeping, I'm too hungry for that. I wish I could see a capon and a bottle of white wine."

"Monsieur Simon!" cried a voice on the landing-place.

"*C'est ici*," quoth Gambouge, hastening to open the door. He did so; and, lo! there was a *restaurateur's* boy at the door, supporting a tray, a tin-covered dish, and plates on the same; and, by its side, a tall amber-coloured flask of Sauterne.

"I am the new boy, sir," exclaimed this youth, on entering; "but I believe this is the right door, and you asked for these things."

Simon grinned, and said, "Certainly, I did *ask for* these things." But such was the effect which his interview with the demon had had on his innocent mind, that he took them, although he knew that they were for old Simon, the Jew dandy, who was mad after an opera girl, and lived on the floor beneath.

"Go, my boy," he said; "it is good: call in a couple of hours, and remove the plates and glasses."

The little waiter trotted down-stairs, and Simon sate greedily down to discuss the capon and the white wine. He bolted the legs, he devoured the wings, he cut every morsel of flesh from the breast;—seasoning his repast with pleasant draughts of wine, and caring nothing for the inevitable bill, which was to follow all.

"Ye gods!" said he, as he scraped away at the backbone, "what a dinner! what wine!—and how gaily served up too!" There were silver forks and spoons, and the remnants of the fowl were upon a silver dish. "Why, the money for this dish and these spoons," cried Simon, "would keep me and Mrs. G. for a month! I WISH"— and here Simon whistled, and turned round to see that nobody was peeping—"I wish the plate were mine."

O the horrid progress of the devil! "Here they are," thought Simon to himself; "why should not I *take them?*" And take them he did. "Detection," said he, "is not so bad as starvation; and I would as soon live at the galleys as live with Madame Gambouge."

So Gambouge shovelled dish and spoons into the flap of his surtout, and ran down-stairs as if the devil were behind him—as, indeed, he was.

He immediately made for the house of his old friend the pawnbroker — that establishment which is called in France the Mont de Piété. "I am obliged to come to you again, my old friend," said Simon, "with some family plate, of which I beseech you to take care."

The pawnbroker smiled as he examined the goods. "I can give you nothing upon them," said he.

"What!" cried Simon; "not even the worth of the silver?"

"No; I could buy them at that price at the Café Morisot, Rue de la Verrerie, where, I suppose, you got them a little cheaper." And, so saying, he showed to the guilt-stricken Gambouge how the name of that coffee-house was inscribed upon every one of the articles which he had wished to pawn.

The effects of conscience are dreadful indeed. Oh! how fearful is retribution, how deep is despair, how bitter is remorse for crime—*when crime is found out!*—otherwise, conscience takes matters much more easily. Gambouge cursed his fate, and swore henceforth to be virtuous.

"But, hark ye, my friend," continued the honest broker, "there is no reason why, because I cannot lend upon these things, I should not buy them: they will do to melt, if for no other purpose. Will you have half the money?—speak, or I peach."

Simon's resolves about virtue were dissipated instantaneously. "Give me half," he said, "and let me go.— What scoundrels are these pawnbrokers!" ejaculated he, as he passed out of the accursed shop, "seeking every wicked pretext to rob the poor man of his hard-won gain."

When he had marched forwards for a street or two, Gambouge counted the money which he had received, and found that he was in possession of no less than a hundred francs. It was night, as he reckoned out his equivocal gains, and he counted them at the light of a lamp. He looked up at the lamp, in doubt as to the course he should next pursue: upon it was inscribed the simple number, 152. "A gambling-house," thought Gambouge. "I wish I had half the money that is now on the table, upstairs."

He mounted, as many a rogue has done before him, and found half a hundred persons busy at a table of *rouge et noir*. Gambouge's five napoleons looked insignificant by the side of the heaps which were around him; but the effects of the wine, of the theft, and of the detection by the pawnbroker, were upon him, and he threw down his capital stoutly upon the 0 0.

It is a dangerous spot that 0 0, or double zero; but to Simon it was more lucky than to the rest of the world. The ball went spinning round—in "its predestined circle rolled," as Shelley has it, after Goethe—and plumped down at last in the double zero. One hundred and thirty-five gold napoleons (louis they were then) were counted out to the delighted painter. "Oh, Diabolus!" cried he, "now it is that I begin to believe in thee! Don't talk about merit," he cried; "talk about fortune. Tell me not about heroes for the future—tell me of *zeroes*." And down went twenty napoleons more upon the 0.

The devil was certainly in the ball: round it twirled, and dropped into zero as naturally as a duck pops its head into a pond. Our friend received five hundred pounds for his stake; and the croupiers and lookers-on began to stare at him.

There were twelve thousand pounds on the table. Suffice it to say, that Simon won half, and retired from the Palais Royal with a thick bundle of bank-notes crammed into his dirty three-cornered hat. He had been but half-an-hour in the place, and he had won the revenues of a prince for half-a-year!

Gambouge, as soon as he felt that he was a capitalist, and that he had a stake in the country, discovered that he was an altered man. He repented of his foul deed, and his base purloining of the *restaurateur's* plate. "Oh, honesty!" he cried, "how unworthy is an action like this of a man who has a property like mine!" So he went back to the pawnbroker with the gloomiest face imaginable. "My friend," said he, "I have sinned against all that I hold most sacred: I have forgotten my family and my religion. Here is thy money. In the name of Heaven, restore me the plate which I have wrongfully sold thee!"

But the pawnbroker grinned, and said, "Nay, Mr. Gambouge, I will sell that plate for a thousand francs to you, or I never will sell it at all."

"Well," cried Gambouge, "thou art an inexorable ruffian, Troisboules; but I will give thee all I am worth." And here he produced a billet of five hundred francs. "Look," said he, "this money is all I own; it is the payment of two years' lodging. To raise it, I have toiled for many months; and, failing, I have been a criminal. Oh, Heaven! I *stole* that plate, that I might pay my debt, and keep my dear wife from wandering houseless. But I cannot bear this load of ignominy.—I cannot suffer the thought of this crime. I will go to the person to whom I did wrong. I will starve, I will confess; but I will, I *will* do right!"

The broker was alarmed. "Give me thy note," he cried; "here is the plate."

"Give me an acquittal first," cried Simon, almost broken-hearted; "sign me a paper, and the money is yours." So Troisboules wrote according to Gambouge's dictation: "Received, for thirteen ounces of plate, twenty pounds."

"Monster of iniquity!" cried the painter, "fiend of wickedness! thou art caught in thine own snares. Hast thou not sold me five pounds' worth of plate for twenty? Have I it not in my pocket? Art thou not a convicted dealer in stolen goods? Yield, scoundrel, yield thy money, or I will bring thee to justice!"

The frightened pawnbroker bullied and battled for awhile; but he gave up his money at last, and the dispute ended. Thus it will be seen that Diabolus had rather a hard bargain in the wily Gambouge. He had taken a victim prisoner, but he had assuredly caught a Tartar. Simon now returned home, and, to do him justice, paid the bill for his dinner, and restored the plate.

* * * * *

And now I may add (and the reader should ponder upon this, as a profound picture of human life), that Gambouge, since he had grown rich, grew likewise abundantly moral. He was a most exemplary father. He fed the poor, and was loved by them. He scorned a base action. And I have no doubt that Mr. Thurtell, or the late lamented Mr. Greenacre, in similar circumstances, would have acted like the worthy Simon Gambouge.

There was but one blot upon his character—he hated Mrs. Gam. worse than ever. As he grew more benevolent, she grew more virulent: when he went to plays, she went to bible societies, and *vice versâ:* in fact, she led him such a life as Xantippe led Socrates, or as a dog leads a cat in the same kitchen. With all his fortune—for, as may be supposed, Simon prospered in all worldly things—he was the most miserable dog in the whole city of Paris. Only in the point of drinking did he and Mrs. Simon agree; and for many years, and during a considerable number of hours in each day, he thus dissipated, partially, his domestic chagrin. Oh, philosophy! we may talk of thee: but, except at the bottom of the wine-cup, where thou liest like truth in a well, where shall we find thee?

He lived so long, and in his worldly matters prospered so much, there was so little sign of devilment in the accomplishment of his wishes, and the increase of his prosperity, that Simon, at the end of six years, began to doubt whether he had made any such bargain at all, as that which we have described at the commencement of this history. He had grown, as we said, very pious and moral. He went regularly to mass, and had a confessor into the bargain. He resolved, therefore, to consult that reverend gentleman, and to lay before him the whole matter.

"I am inclined to think, holy sir," said Gambouge, after he had concluded his history, and shown how, in some miraculous way, all his desires were accomplished, "that, after all, this demon was no other than the creation of my own brain, heated by the effects of that bottle of wine, the cause of my crime and my prosperity."

The confessor agreed with him, and they walked out of church comfortably together; and entered afterwards a *café*, where they sate down to refresh themselves after the fatigues of their devotion.

A respectable old gentleman, with a number of orders at his button-hole, presently entered the room, and sauntered up to the marble table, before which reposed Simon and his clerical friend. "Excuse me, gentlemen," he said, as he took a place opposite them, and began reading the papers of the day.

"Bah!" said he, at last; "sont-ils grands ces journaux Anglais? Look, sir," he said, handing over an immense sheet of the *Times* to Mr. Gambouge, "was ever anything so monstrous?"

Gambouge smiled politely, and examined the proffered page. "It is enormous," he said; "but I do not read English."

"Nay," said the man with the orders, "look closer at it, Signor Gambouge; it is astonishing how easy the language is."

Wondering, Simon took the sheet of paper. He turned pale as he looked at it, and began to curse the ices and the waiter. "Come, M. l'Abbé," he said; "the heat and glare of this place are intolerable."

* * * * *

The stranger rose with them. "Au plaisir de vous

revoir, mon cher monsieur," said he; " I do not mind speaking before the abbé here, who will be my very good friend one of these days; but I thought it necessary to refresh your memory, concerning our little business transaction six years since; and could not exactly talk of it *at church*, as you may fancy."

Simon Gambouge had seen, in the double-sheeted *Times*, the paper signed by himself, which the little devil had pulled out of his fob.

* * * * *

There was no doubt on the subject; and Simon, who had but a year to live, grew more pious, and more careful than ever. He had consultations with all the doctors of the Sarbonne and all the lawyers of the Palais. But his magnificence grew as wearisome to him as his poverty had been before; and not one of the doctors whom he consulted could give him a pennyworth of consolation.

Then he grew outrageous in his demands upon the devil, and put him to all sorts of absurd and ridiculous tasks; but they were all punctually performed, until Simon could invent no new ones, and the devil sate all day with his hands in his pockets doing nothing.

One day, Simon's confessor came bounding into the room, with the greatest glee. " My friend," said he, " I have it! Eureka!—I have found it. Send the pope a hundred thousand crowns, build a new Jesuit college at Rome, give a hundred gold candlesticks to St. Peter's; and tell his holiness you will double all, if he will give you absolution!"

Gambouge caught at the notion, and hurried off a

courier to Rome, *ventre à terre.* His holiness agreed to the request of the petition, and sent him an absolution, written out with his own fist, and all in due form.

"Now," said he, "foul fiend, I defy you! arise, Diabolus! your contract is not worth a jot: the pope has absolved me, and I am safe on the road to salvation." In a fervour of gratitude he clasped the hand of his confessor, and embraced him: tears of joy ran down the cheeks of these good men.

They heard an inordinate roar of laughter, and there was Diabolus sitting opposite to them, holding his sides, and lashing his tail about, as if he would have gone mad with glee.

"Why," said he, "what nonsense is this! do you suppose I care about *that?*" and he tossed the pope's missive into a corner. "M. l'Abbé knows," he said, bowing and grinning, "that though the pope's paper may pass current *here,* it is not worth twopence in our country. What do I care about the pope's absolution? You might just as well be absolved by your under butler."

"Egad," said the abbé, "the rogue is right—I quite forgot the fact, which he points out clearly enough."

"No, no, Gambouge," continued Diabolus, with horrid familiarity, "go thy ways, old fellow, that *cock won't fight;*" and he retired up the chimney, chuckling at his wit and his triumph. Gambouge heard his tail scuttling all the way up, as if he had been a sweeper by profession.

Simon was left in that condition of grief in which, according to the newspapers, cities and nations are found when a murder is committed, or a lord ill of the gout

—a situation, we say, more easy to imagine than to describe.

To add to his woes, Mrs. Gambouge, who was now first made acquainted with his compact, and its probable consequences, raised such a storm about his ears, as made him wish almost that his seven years were expired. She screamed, she scolded, she swore, she wept, she went into such fits of hysterics, that poor Gambouge, who had completely knocked under to her, was worn out of his life. He was allowed no rest, night or day: he moped about his fine house, solitary and wretched, and cursed his stars that he ever had married the butcher's daughter.

It wanted six months of the time.

A sudden and desperate resolution seemed all at once to have taken possession of Simon Gambouge. He called his family and his friends together—he gave one of the greatest feasts that ever was known in the city of Paris—he gaily presided at one end of his table, while Mrs. Gam., splendidly arrayed, gave herself airs at the other extremity.

After dinner, using the customary formula, he called upon Diabolus to appear. The old ladies screamed, and hoped he would not appear naked; the young ones tittered, and longed to see the monster: everybody was pale with expectation and affright.

A very quiet, gentlemanly man, neatly dressed in black, made his appearance, to the surprise of all present, and bowed all round to the company. "I will not show my *credentials*," he said, blushing, and pointing to his hoofs, which were cleverly hidden by his pumps and shoe-buckles, "unless the ladies absolutely wish it; but I am the person you want, Mr. Gambouge; pray tell me what is your will."

"You know," said that gentleman, in a stately and determined voice, "that you are bound to me, according to our agreement, for six months to come."

"I am," replied the new comer.

"You are to do all that I ask, whatsoever it may be, or you forfeit the bond which I gave you?"

"It is true."

"You declare this before the present company?"

"Upon my honour, as a gentleman," said Diabolus, bowing, and laying his hand upon his waistcoat.

A whisper of applause ran round the room: all were charmed with the bland manners of the fascinating stranger.

"My love," continued Gambouge, mildly addressing his lady, "will you be so polite as to step this way? You know I must go soon, and I am anxious, before this noble company, to make a provision for one who, in sickness as in health, in poverty as in riches, has been my truest and fondest companion."

Gambouge mopped his eyes with his handkerchief—all the company did likewise. Diabolus sobbed audibly, and Mrs. Gambouge sidled up to her husband's side, and took him tenderly by the hand. "Simon!" said she, "is it true? and do you really love your Griskinissa?"

Simon continued solemnly: "Come hither, Diabolus; you are bound to obey me in all things for the six months during which our contract has to run; take, then, Gris-

kinissa Gambouge, live alone with her for half a year, never leave her from morning till night, obey all her caprices, follow all her whims, and listen to all the abuse which falls from her infernal tongue. Do this, and I ask no more of you; I will deliver myself up at the appointed time."

Not Lord G——, when flogged by Lord B—— in the House,—not Mr. Cartlitch, of Astley's Amphitheatre, in his most pathetic passages, could look more crest-fallen, and howl more hideously, than Diabolus did now. "Take another year, Gambouge," screamed he; "two more—ten more—a century; roast me on Lawrence's gridiron, boil me in holy water, but don't ask that: don't, don't bid me live with Mrs. Gambouge!"

Simon smiled sternly. "I have said it," he cried; "do this, or our contract is at an end."

The devil, at this, grinned so horribly that every drop of beer in the house turned sour: he gnashed his teeth so frightfully that every person in the company well nigh fainted with the cholic. He slapped down the great parchment upon the floor, trampled upon it madly, and lashed it with his hoofs and his tail: at last, spreading out a mighty pair of wings as wide as from here to Regent Street, he slapped Gambouge with his tail over one eye, and vanished, abruptly, through the keyhole.

* * * * *

Gambouge screamed with pain and started up. "You drunken, lazy scoundrel!" cried a shrill and well-known voice, "you have been asleep these two hours:" and here he received another terrific box on the ear.

It was too true, he had fallen asleep at his work; and the beautiful vision had been dispelled by the thumps of the tipsy Griskinissa. Nothing remained to corroborate his story, except the bladder of lake, and this was spirted all over his waistcoat and breeches.

"I wish," said the poor fellow, rubbing his tingling cheeks, "that dreams were true;" and he went to work again at his portrait.

* * * * *

My last accounts of Gambouge are, that he has left the arts, and is footman in a small family. Mrs. Gam. takes in washing; and it is said that her continual dealings with soap-suds and hot water have been the only things in life which have kept her from spontaneous combustion.

CARTOUCHE.

I HAVE been much interested with an account of the exploits of Monsieur Louis Dominic Cartouche, and as Newgate and the highways are so much the fashion with us in England, we may be allowed to look abroad for histories of a similar tendency. It is pleasant to find that virtue is cosmopolite, and may exist among wooden-shoed Papists as well as honest Church-of-England men.

Louis Dominic was born in a quarter of Paris called the Courtille, says the historian whose work lies before me;—born in the Courtille, and in the year 1693. Another biographer asserts that he was born two years later, and in the Marais;—of respectable parents, of course. Think of the talent that our two countries produced about this time: Marlborough, Villars, Mandrin, Turpin, Boileau, Dryden, Swift, Addison, Molière, Racine, Jack Sheppard, and Louis Cartouche,—all famous within the same twenty years, and fighting, writing, robbing, à l'envi!

Well, Marlborough was no chicken when he began to shew his genius; Swift was but a dull, idle, college lad; but if we read the histories of some other great men mentioned in the above list—I mean the thieves, especially—we shall find that they all commenced very early: they shewed a passion for their art, as little Raphael did, or little Mozart; and the history of Cartouche's knaveries begins almost with his breeches.

Dominic's parents sent him to school at the college of Clermont (now Louis le Grand); and although it has never been discovered that the Jesuits, who directed that seminary, advanced him much in classical or theological knowledge, Cartouche, in revenge, shewed, by repeated instances, his own natural bent and genius, which no difficulties were strong enough to overcome. His first great action on record, although not successful in the end, and tinctured with the innocence of youth, is yet highly creditable to him. He made a general swoop of a hundred and twenty nightcaps belonging to his companions, and disposed of them to his satisfaction; but as it was discovered that of all the youths in the college of Clermont, he only was the possessor of a cap to sleep in, suspicion (which, alas! was confirmed) immediately fell upon him: and by this little piece of youthful *naïveté*, a scheme, prettily conceived and smartly performed, was rendered naught.

Cartouche had a wonderful love for good eating, and put all the apple-women and cooks, who came to supply the students, under contribution. Not always, however, desirous of robbing these, he used to deal with them, occasionally, on honest principles of barter; that is, whenever he could get hold of his schoolfellows' knives, books, rulers, or playthings, which he used fairly to exchange for tarts and gingerbread.

It seemed as if the presiding genius of evil was determined to patronize this young man; for before he had been long at college, and soon after he had, with the greatest difficulty, escaped from the nightcap scrape, an opportunity occurred by which he was enabled to gratify both his propensities at once, and not only to steal, but to steal sweetmeats. It happened that the principal of the college received some pots of Narbonne honey, which came under the eyes of Cartouche, and in which that young gentleman, as soon as ever he saw them, determined to put his fingers. The president of the college put aside his honey-pots in an apartment within his own; to which, except by the one door which led into the room which his reverence usually occupied, there was no outlet. There was no chimney in the room; and the windows looked into the court, where there was a porter at night, and where crowds passed by day. What was Cartouche to do?—have the honey he must.

Over this chamber, which contained what his soul longed after, and over the president's rooms, there ran a set of unoccupied garrets, into which the dexterous Cartouche penetrated. These were divided from the rooms below, according to the fashion of those days, by a set of large beams, which reached across the whole building, and across which rude planks were laid, which formed the ceiling of the lower story and the floor of the upper. Some of these planks did young Cartouche remove; and having descended by means of a rope, tied a couple of others to the neck of the honey-pots, climbed back again, and drew up his prey in safety. He then cunningly fixed the planks again in their old places, and retired to gorge himself upon his booty. And, now, see the punishment of avarice! Everybody knows that the brethren of the order of Jesus are bound by a vow to have no more than a certain small sum of money in their possession. The principal of the college of Clermont had amassed a larger sum, in defiance of this rule: and where do you think the old gentleman had hidden it? In the honey-pots! As Cartouche dug his spoon into one of them, he brought out, besides a quantity of golden honey, a couple of golden louis, which, with ninety-eight more of their fellows, were comfortably hidden in the pots. Little Dominic, who, before, had cut rather a poor figure among his fellow-students, now appeared in as fine clothes as any of them could boast of; and when asked by his parents, on going home, how he came by them, said that a young nobleman of his school-fellows had taken a violent fancy to him, and made him a present of a couple of his suits. Cartouche the elder, good man, went to thank the young nobleman; but none such could be found, and young Cartouche disdained to give any explanation of his manner of gaining the money.

Here, again, we have to regret and remark the inadvertence of youth. Cartouche lost a hundred louis—for what? For a pot of honey not worth a couple of shillings. Had he fished out the pieces, and replaced the pots and the honey, he might have been safe, and a respectable citizen all his life after. The principal would not have dared to confess the loss of his money, and did not, openly; but he vowed vengeance against the stealer of his sweetmeat, and a rigid search was made. Cartouche, as usual, was fixed upon; and in the tick of his bed, lo! there were found a couple of empty honey-pots! From this scrape there is no knowing how he would have escaped, had not the president himself been a little anxious to hush the matter up; and accordingly, young Cartouche was made to disgorge the residue of his ill-gotten gold pieces, old Cartouche made up the deficiency, and his son was allowed to remain unpunished —until the next time.

This, you may fancy, was not very long in coming; and though history has not made us acquainted with the exact crime which Louis Dominic next committed, it must have been a serious one; for Cartouche, who had borne philosophically all the whippings and punishments which were administered to him at college, did not dare to face that one which his indignant father had in pickle for him. As he was coming home from school, on the first day after his crime, when he received permission to go abroad, one of his brothers, who was on the look-out for him, met him, at a short distance from home, and told him what was in preparation; which so frightened this young thief, that he declined returning home altogether, and set out upon the wide world to shift for himself as he could.

Undoubted as his genius was, he had not arrived at the full exercise of it, and his gains were by no means equal to his appetite. In whatever professions he tried,—whether he joined the gipsies, which he did,—whether he picked pockets on the Pont Neuf, which occupation history attributes to him,—poor Cartouche was always hungry. Hungry and ragged, he wandered from one place and profession to another, and regretted the honey-pots at Clermont, and the comfortable soup and *bouilli* at home.

Cartouche had an uncle, a kind man, who was a merchant, and had dealings at Rouen. One day, walking on the quays of that city, this gentleman saw a very miserable, dirty, starving lad, who had just made a pounce upon some bones and turnip-peelings, that had been flung out on the quay, and was eating them as greedily as if they had been turkeys and truffles. The worthy man examined the lad a little closer. O heavens! it was their runaway prodigal—it was little Louis Dominic! The merchant was touched by his case; and forgetting the nightcaps, the honey-pots, and the rags and dirt of little Louis, took him to his arms, and kissed and hugged him with the tenderest affection. Louis kissed and hugged too, and blubbered a great deal: he was very repentant, as a man often is when he is hungry; and he went home with his uncle, and his peace was made; and his mother got him new clothes, and filled his belly, and for a while Louis was as good a son as might be.

But why attempt to balk the progress of genius? Louis's was not to be kept down. He was sixteen years of age by this time—a smart, lively young fellow, and, what is more, desperately enamoured of a lovely washerwoman. To be successful in your love, as Louis knew, you must have something more than mere flames and sentiment;—a washer, or any other woman, cannot live upon sighs only; but must have new gowns and caps, and a necklace every now and then, and a few handkerchiefs and silk stockings, and a treat into the country or to the play. Now, how are all these things to be had without money? Cartouche saw at once that it was impossible; and as his father would give him none, he was obliged to look for it elsewhere. He took to his old courses, and lifted a purse here, and a watch there; and found, moreover, an accommodating gentleman, who took the wares off his hands.

This gentleman introduced him into a very select and agreeable society, in which Cartouche's merit began speedily to be recognized, and in which he learned how pleasant it is in life to have friends to assist one, and how much may be done by a proper division of labour. M. Cartouche, in fact, formed part of a regular company or gang of gentlemen, who were associated together for the purpose of making war on the public and the law.

Cartouche had a lovely young sister, who was to be married to a rich young gentleman from the provinces. As is the fashion in France, the parents had arranged the match among themselves; and the young people had never met until just before the time appointed for the marriage, when the bridegroom came up to Paris with his title-deeds, and settlements, and money. Now, there can hardly be found in history a finer instance of devotion than Cartouche now exhibited. He went to his captain, explained the matter to him, and actually, for the good of his country, as it were (the thieves might be called his country), sacrificed his sister's husband's property. Informations were taken, the house of the bridegroom was reconnoitred, and, one night, Cartouche, in company with some chosen friends, made his first visit to the house of his brother-in-law. All the people were gone to bed; and, doubtless, for fear of disturbing the porter, Cartouche and his companions spared him the trouble of opening the door, by ascending quietly at the window. They arrived at the room where the bridegroom kept his great chest, and set industriously to work, filing and picking the locks which defended the treasure.

The bridegroom slept in the next room; but however tenderly Cartouche and his workmen handled their tools, from fear of disturbing his slumbers, their benevolent design was disappointed, for awaken him they did; and quietly slipping out of bed, he came to a place where he had a complete view of all that was going on. He did not cry out, or frighten himself sillily; but, on the contrary, contented himself with watching the countenances of the robbers, so that he might recognize them on another occasion; and, though an avaricious man, he did not feel the slightest anxiety about his money-chest; for the fact is, he had removed all the cash and papers the day before.

As soon, however, as they had broken all the locks, and found the nothing which lay at the bottom of the chest, he shouted with such a loud voice, "Here, Thomas!—John! —officer!—keep the gate, fire at the rascals!" that they, incontinently taking fright, skipped nimbly out of window, and left the house free.

Cartouche, after this, did not care to meet his brother-in-law, but eschewed all those occasions on which the latter was to be present at his father's house. The evening before the marriage came; and then his father insisted upon his appearance among the other relatives of the bride's and bridegroom's families, who were all to assemble and make merry. Cartouche was obliged to yield; and brought with him one or two of his companions, who had been, by the way, present in the affair of the empty money-boxes; and though he never fancied that there was any danger in meeting his brother-in-law, for he had no idea that he had been seen in the night of the attack, with a natural modesty, which did him really credit, he kept out of the young bridegroom's sight as much as he could, and showed no desire to be presented to him. At supper, however, as he was sneaking modestly down to a side-table, his father shouted after him, "Ho, Dominic, come hither, and sit opposite your brother-in-law:" which Dominic did, his friends following. The bridegroom pledged him very gracefully in a bumper; and was in the act of making him a pretty speech, on the honour of an alliance with such a family, and on the pleasures of brother-in-lawship in general, when, looking in his face—ye gods! he saw the very man who had been filing at his money-chest a few nights ago! By his side, too, sat a couple more of the gang. The poor fellow turned deadly pale and sick, and, setting his glass down, ran quickly out of the room, for he thought he was in company of a whole gang of robbers. And when he got home, he wrote a letter to the elder Cartouche, humbly declining any connexion with his family.

Cartouche the elder, of course, angrily asked the reason of such an abrupt dissolution of the engagement; and then, much to his horror, heard of his eldest son's doings. "You would not have me marry into such a family?" said the ex-bridegroom. And old Cartouche, an honest old citizen, confessed, with a heavy heart, that he would not. What was he to do with the lad? He did not like to ask for a *lettre de cachet*, and shut him up in the Bastile. He determined to give him a year's discipline at the monastery of St. Lazare.

But how to catch the young gentleman? Old Cartouche knew that, were he to tell his son of the scheme, the latter would never obey, and, therefore, he determined to be very cunning. He told Dominic that he was about to make a heavy bargain with the fathers, and should require a witness; so they stepped into a carriage together, and drove unsuspectingly to the Rue St. Denis. But, when they arrived near the convent, Cartouche saw several ominous figures gathering round the coach, and felt that his doom was sealed. However, he made as if he knew nothing of the conspiracy; and the carriage drew up, and his father descended, and, bidding him wait for a minute in the coach, promised to return to him. Cartouche looked out; on the other side of the way half-a-dozen men were posted, evidently with the intention of arresting him.

Cartouche now performed a great and celebrated stroke of genius, which, if he had not been professionally employed in the morning, he never could have executed. He had in his pocket a piece of linen, which he had laid hold of at the door of some shop, and from which he quickly tore three suitable stripes. One he tied round his head, after the fashion of a nightcap; a second round his waist, like an apron; and with the third he covered his hat, a round one, with a large brim. His coat and his periwig he left behind him in the carriage; and when he stepped out from it (which he did without asking the coachman to let down the steps), he bore exactly the appearance of a cook's boy carrying a dish; and with this he slipped through the exempts quite unsuspected, and bade adieu to the Lazarists and his honest father, who came out speedily to seek him, and was not a little annoyed to find only his coat and wig.

With that coat and wig, Cartouche left home, father, friends, conscience, remorse, society, behind him. He discovered (like a great number of other philosophers and poets, when they have committed rascally actions,) that the world was all going wrong, and he quarrelled with it outright. One of the first stories told of the illustrious Cartouche, when he became professionally and openly a robber, redounds highly to his credit, and shows that he knew how to take advantage of the occasion, and how much he had improved in the course of a very few years' experience. His courage and ingenuity were vastly admired by his friends; so much so, that, one day, the captain of the band thought fit to compliment him, and vowed that when he (the captain) died, Cartouche should infallibly be called to the command-in-chief. This conversation, so flattering to Cartouche, was carried on between the two gentlemen, as they were walking, one night, on the quays by the side of the Seine. Cartouche, when the captain made the last remark, blushingly protested against it, and pleaded his extreme youth as a reason why his comrades could never put entire trust in him. "Psha, man!" said the captain, "thy youth is in thy favour; thou wilt live only the longer to lead thy troops to victory. As for strength, bravery, and cunning, wert thou as old as Methuselah, thou couldst not be better provided than thou art now, at eighteen."

What was the reply of Monsieur Cartouche? He answered, not by words, but by actions. Drawing his knife from his girdle, he instantly dug it into the captain's left side, as near his heart as possible; and then, seizing that imprudent commander, precipitated him violently into the waters of the Seine, to keep company with the gudgeons and river-gods. When he returned to the band, and recounted how the captain had basely attempted to assassinate him, and how he, on the contrary, had, by exertion of superior skill, overcome the captain, not one of the society believed a word of his history; but they elected him captain forthwith. I think his excellency Don Rafael Maroto, the pacificator of Spain, is an amiable character, for whom history has not been written in vain.

Being arrived at this exalted position, there is no end of the feats which Cartouche performed; and his band reached to such a pitch of glory, that if there had been a hundred thousand, instead of a hundred of them, who knows but that a new and popular dynasty might not have been founded, and "Louis Dominic, premier Empereur des Français," might have performed innumerable glorious actions, and fixed himself in the hearts of his people, just as other monarchs have done, a hundred years after Cartouche's death.

A story similar to the above, and equally moral, is that of Cartouche, who, in company with two other gentlemen, robbed the *coche*, or packet-boat, from Melun, where they took a good quantity of booty,—making the passengers lie down on the decks, and rifling them at leisure. "This money will be but very little among three," whispered

Cartouche to his neighbour, as the three conquerors were making merry over their gains; "if you were but to pull the trigger of your pistol in the neighbourhood of your comrade's ear, perhaps it might go off, and then there would be but two of us to share." Strangely enough, as Cartouche said, the pistol *did* go off, and No. 3 perished. "Give him another ball," said Cartouche; and another was fired into him. But no sooner had Cartouche's comrade discharged both his pistols, than Cartouche himself, seized with a furious indignation, drew his: "Learn, monster," cried he, "not to be so greedy of gold, and perish, the victim of thy disloyalty and avarice!" So Cartouche slew the second robber; and there is no man in Europe who can say that the latter did not merit well his punishment.

I could fill volumes, and not mere sheets of paper, with tales of the triumphs of Cartouche and his band; how he robbed the Countess of O——, going to Dijon, in her coach, and how the Countess fell in love with him, and was faithful to him ever after; how, when the lieutenant of police offered a reward of a hundred pistoles to any man who would bring Cartouche before him, a noble Marquess, in a coach and six, drove up to the hotel of the police; and the noble Marquess, desiring to see Monsieur de la Reynie, on matters of the highest moment, alone, the latter introduced him into his private cabinet; and how, when there, the Marquess drew from his pocket a long, curiously shaped dagger: "Look at this, Monsieur de la Reynie," said he; "this dagger is poisoned!"

"Is it possible?" said M. de la Reynie.

"A prick of it would do for any man," said the Marquess.

"You don't say so!" said M. de la Reynie.

"I do, though; and, what is more," says the Marquess, in a terrible voice, "if you do not instantly lay yourself flat on the ground, with your face towards it, and your hands crossed over your back, or if you make the slightest noise or cry, I will stick this poisoned dagger between your ribs, as sure as my name is Cartouche?"

At the sound of this dreadful name, M. de la Reynie sunk incontinently down on his stomach, and submitted to be carefully gagged and corded; after which Monsieur Cartouche laid his hands upon all the money which was kept in the lieutenant's cabinet. Alas! and alas! many a stout bailiff, and many an honest fellow of a spy, went, for that day, without his pay and his victuals.

There is a story that Cartouche once took the diligence to Lille, and found in it a certain Abbé Potter, who was full of indignation against this monster of a Cartouche, and said that when he went back to Paris, which he proposed to do in about a fortnight, he should give the lieutenant of police some information, which would infallibly lead to the scoundrel's capture. But poor Potter was disappointed in his designs; for, before he could fulfil them, he was made the victim of Cartouche's cruelty.

A letter came to the lieutenant of police, to state that Cartouche had travelled to Lille, in company with the Abbé de Potter, of that town; that on the reverend gentleman's return towards Paris, Cartouche had waylaid him, murdered him, taken his papers, and would come to Paris himself, bearing the name and clothes of the unfortunate abbé, by the Lille coach, on such a day. The Lille coach arrived, was surrounded by police agents; the monster Cartouche was there, sure enough, in the abbé's guise. He was seized, bound, flung into prison, brought out to be examined, and, on examination, found to be no other than the Abbé Potter himself! It is pleasant to read thus of the relaxations of great men, and find them condescending to joke like the meanest of us.

Another diligence adventure is recounted of the famous Cartouche. It happened that he met, in the coach, a young and lovely lady, clad in widow's weeds, and bound to Paris, with a couple of servants. The poor thing was the widow of a rich old gentleman of Marseilles, and was going to the capital to arrange with her lawyers, and to settle her husband's will. The Count de Grinche (for so her fellow-passenger was called) was quite as candid as the pretty widow had been, and stated that he was a Captain in the regiment of Nivernois; that he was going to Paris to buy a colonelcy, which his relatives, the Duke de Bouillon, the Prince de Montmorency, the Commandeur de la Trémoille, with all their interest at court, could not fail to procure for him. To be short, in the course of the four days' journey, the Count Louis Dominic de Grinche played his cards so well, that the poor little widow half forgot her late husband; and her eyes glistened with tears as the Count kissed her hand at parting,—at parting, he hoped, only for a few hours.

Day and night the insinuating Count followed her; and when, at the end of a fortnight, and in the midst of a tête-à-tête, he plunged, one morning, suddenly on his knees, and said, "Leonora, do you love me?" the poor thing heaved the gentlest, tenderest, sweetest sigh in the world; and, sinking her blushing head on his shoulder, whispered, "Oh, Dominic, je t'aime! Ah!" said she, "how noble is it of my Dominic to take me with the little I have, and he so rich a nobleman!" The fact is, the old Baron's titles and estates had passed away to his nephews; his dowager was only left with three hundred thousand livres, in *rentes sur l'état*,—a handsome sum, but nothing to compare to the rent-roll of Count Dominic, Count de la Grinche, Seigneur de la Haute Pigre, Baron de la Bigorne; he had estates and wealth which might authorize him to aspire to the hand of a duchess, at least.

The unfortunate widow never for a moment suspected the cruel trick that was about to be played on her; and, at the request of her affianced husband, sold out her money, and realized it in gold, to be made over to him on the day when the contract was to be signed. The day arrived; and, according to the custom in France, the relations of both parties attended. The widow's relatives, though respectable, were not of the first nobility, being chiefly persons of the *finance* or the *robe:* there was the president of the court of Arras, and his lady; a farmer-general; a judge of a court of Paris; and other such grave and respectable people. As for Monsieur le Comte de la Grinche, he was not bound for names; and, having the whole peerage to choose from, brought a host of Montmorencies, Crequis, De la Tours, and Guises at his back. His *homme d'affaires* brought his papers in a sack, and displayed the plans of his estates, and the titles of his

glorious ancestry. The widow's lawyers had her money in sacks; and between the gold on the one side, and the parchments on the other, lay the contract which was to make the widow's three hundred thousand francs the property of the Count de Grinche. The Count de la Grinche was just about to sign; when the Marshal de Villars, stepping up to him, said, "Captain, do you know who the president of the court of Arras, yonder, is? It is old Manasseh, the fence, of Brussels. I pawned a gold watch to him, which I stole from Cadogan, when I was with Malbrook's army in Flanders."

Here the Duc de la Roche Guyon came forward, very much alarmed. "Run me through the body!" said his Grace, "but the comptroller-general's lady, there, is no other than that old hag of a Margoton who keeps the ——." Here the Duc de la Roche Guyon's voice fell.

Cartouche smiled graciously, and walked up to the table. He took up one of the widow's fifteen thousand gold pieces;—it was as pretty a bit of copper as you could wish to see. "My dear," said he, politely, "there is some mistake here, and this business had better stop."

"Count!" gasped the poor widow.

"Count be hanged!" answered the bridegroom, sternly; "my name is CARTOUCHE!"

ON SOME FRENCH FASHIONABLE NOVELS:

WITH A PLEA FOR ROMANCES IN GENERAL.

THERE is an old story of a Spanish court painter, who, being pressed for money, and having received a piece of damask, which he was to wear in a state procession, pawned the damask, and appeared, at the show, dressed out in some very fine sheets of paper, which he had painted so as exactly to resemble silk. Nay, his coat looked so much richer than the doublets of all the rest, that the Emperor Charles, in whose honour the procession was given, remarked the painter, and so his deceit was found out.

I have often thought that, in respect of sham and real histories, a similar fact may be noticed; the sham story appearing a great deal more agreeable, life-like, and natural than the true one: and all who, from laziness as well as principle, are inclined to follow the easy and comfortable study of novels, may console themselves with the notion that they are studying matters quite as important as history, and that their favourite duodecimos are as instructive as the biggest quartos in the world.

If, then, ladies, the big-wigs begin to sneer at the course of our studies, calling our darling romances foolish, trivial, noxious to the mind, enervators of intellect, fathers of idleness, and what not, let us at once take a high ground, and say,—Go you to your own employments, and to such dull studies as you fancy; go and bob for triangles, from the Pons Asinorum; go enjoy your dull black draughts of metaphysics; go fumble over history books, and dissert upon Herodotus and Livy; *our* histories are, perhaps, as true as yours; our drink is the brisk sparkling champagne drink, from the presses of Colburn, Bentley, and Co.; our walks are over such sunshiny pleasure-grounds as Scott and Shakspeare have laid out for us; and if our dwellings are castles in the air, we find them excessively splendid and commodious;—be not you envious because you have no wings to fly thither. Let the big-wigs despise us; such contempt of their neighbours is the custom of all barbarous tribes;—witness, the learned Chinese : Tippoo Sultaun declared that there were not in all Europe ten thousand men: the Sklavonic hordes, it is said, so entitled themselves from a word in their jargon, which signifies "to speak;" the ruffians imagining that they had a monopoly of this agreeable faculty, and that all other nations were dumb.

Not so : others may be *deaf;* but the novelist has a loud, eloquent, instructive language, though his enemies may despise or deny it ever so much. What is more, one could, perhaps, meet the stoutest historian on his own ground, and argue with him; showing that sham histories were much truer than real histories; which are, in fact, mere contemptible catalogues of names and places, that can have no moral effect upon the reader.

As thus:—

Julius Cæsar beat Pompey, at Pharsalia.
The Duke of Marlborough beat Marshal Tallard, at Blenheim.
The Constable of Bourbon beat Francis the First, at Pavia.

And what have we here?—so many names, simply. Suppose Pharsalia had been, at that mysterious period when names were given, called Pavia; and that Julius Cæsar's family name had been John Churchill;—the fact would have stood, in history, thus:—

"Pompey ran away from the Duke of Marlborough at Pavia."

And why not?—we should have been just as wise. Or it might be stated, that—

"The tenth legion charged the French infantry at Blenheim; and Cæsar, writing home to his mamma, said, '*Madame, tout est perdu fors l'honneur.*'"

What a contemptible science this is, then, about which quartos are written, and sixty-volumed Biographies Universelles, and Lardner's Cabinet Cyclopædias, and the like! the facts are nothing in it, the names everything; and a gentleman might as well improve his mind by learning Walker's Gazetteer, or getting by heart a fifty-years-old edition of the Court Guide.

Having thus disposed of the historians, let us come to the point in question—the novelists.

———

On the title-page of these volumes the reader has, doubtless, remarked, that among the pieces introduced, some are announced as "copies" and "compositions." Many of the histories have, accordingly, been neatly stolen from the collections of French authors (and mutilated, according to the old saying, so that their owners should not know them); and, for compositions, we intend to favour the public with some studies of French modern works, that have not as yet, we believe, attracted the notice of the English public.

Of such works there appear many hundreds yearly, as may be seen by the French catalogues; but the writer has not so much to do with works political, philosophical, historical, metaphysical, scientifical, theological, as with those for which he has been putting forward a plea—novels, namely; on which he has expended a great deal of time and study. And passing from novels in general to French novels, let us confess, with much humiliation, that we borrow from these stories a great deal more knowledge of French society than from our own personal observation we ever can hope to gain: for, let a gentleman who has dwelt two, four, or ten years in Paris (and has not gone thither for the purpose of making a book, when three weeks are sufficient)—let an English gentleman say, at the end of any given period, how much he knows of French society; how many French houses he has entered, and how many French friends he has made?—He has enjoyed, at the end of the year, say—

    At the English Amassador's, so many soirées.
    At houses to which he has brought letters, so many tea-parties.
    At Cafés, so many dinners.
    At French private houses, say three dinners, and very lucky too.

He has, we say, seen an immense number of wax

candles, cups of tea, glasses of orgeat, and French people, in best clothes, enjoying the same; but intimacy there is none; we see but the outsides of the people. Year by year we live in France, and grow grey, and see no more. We play écarté, with Monsieur de Trèfle, every night; but what know we of the heart of the man—of the inward ways, thoughts, and customs of Trèfle? If we have good legs, and love the amusement, we dance with Countess Flicflac, Tuesdays and Thursdays, ever since the Peace; and how far are we advanced in acquaintance with her since we first twirled her round a room? We know her velvet gown, and her diamonds (about three-fourths of them are sham, by the way); we know her smiles, and her simpers, and her rouge—but no more: she may turn into a kitchen wench at twelve on Thursday night, for aught we know; her *voiture*, a pumpkin; and her *gens*, so many rats: but the real, rougeless, *intime* Flicflac, we know not. This privilege is granted to no Englishman: we may understand the French language as well as Monsieur de Levizac, but never can penetrate into Flicflac's confidence: our ways are not her ways; our manners of thinking, not hers: when we say a good thing, in the course of the night, we are wondrous lucky and pleased; Flicflac will trill you off fifty in ten minutes, and wonder at the *bêtise* of the Briton, who has never a word to say. We are married, and have fourteen children, and would just as soon make love to the Pope of Rome as to any one but our own wife. If you do not make love to Flicflac, from the day after her marriage to the day she reaches sixty, she thinks you a fool. We won't play at

écarté with Trèfle on Sunday nights; and are seen walking, about one o'clock (accompanied by fourteen red-haired children, with fourteen gleaming prayer-books), away from the church. "*Grand Dieu!*" cries Trèfle, "is that man mad? He won't play at cards on a Sunday; he goes to church on a Sunday: he has fourteen children!"

Was ever Frenchman known to do likewise? Pass we on to our argument, which is, that, with our English notions, and moral and physical constitution, it is quite impossible that we should become intimate with our brisk neighbours; and when such authors as Lady Morgan and Mrs. Trollope, having frequented a certain number of tea-parties in the French capital, begin to prattle about French manners and men,—with all respect for the talents of those ladies, we do believe their information not to be worth a sixpence; they speak to us, not of men, but of tea-parties. Tea-parties are the same all the world over; with the exception that, with the French, there are more lights and prettier dresses; and with us, a mighty deal more tea in the pot.

There is, however, a cheap and delightful way of travelling, that a man may perform in his easy chair, without expense of passports or postboys. On the wings of a novel, from the next circulating library, he sends his imagination a gadding, and gains acquaintance with people and manners, whom he could not hope otherwise to know. Twopence a volume bears us whithersoever we will;—back to Ivanhoe and Cœur de Lion, or to Waverley and the Young Pretender, along with Walter Scott; up to the heights of fashion with the charming enchanters of the silver-fork school; or, better still, to the snug inn parlour, or the jovial tap-room, with Mr. Pickwick and his faithful Sancho Weller. I am sure that a man who, a hundred years hence, should sit down to write the history of our time, would do wrong to put that great contemporary history of Pickwick aside, as a frivolous work. It contains true character under false names; and, like Roderick Random, an inferior work, and Tom Jones (one that is immeasurably superior), gives us a better idea of the state and ways of the people, than one could gather from any more pompous or authentic histories.

We have, therefore, introduced into these volumes one or two short reviews of French fiction-writers, of particular classes, whose Paris sketches may give the reader some notion of manners in that capital. If not original, at least the drawings are accurate; for, as a Frenchman might have lived a thousand years in England, and never could have written Pickwick, an Englishman cannot hope to give a good description of the inward thoughts and ways of his neighbours.

To a person inclined to study these, in that light and amusing fashion in which the novelist treats them, let us recommend the works of a new writer, Monsieur de Bernard, who has painted actual manners, without those monstrous and terrible exaggerations in which late French writers have indulged; and who, if he occasionally wounds the English sense of propriety (as what French man or woman alive will not?) does so more by slighting than by outraging it, as, with their laboured descriptions of all sorts of imaginable wickedness, some of his brethren of the press have done. M. de Bernard's characters are men and women of genteel society—rascals enough, but living in no state of convulsive crimes; and we follow him in his lively, malicious account of their manners, without risk of lighting upon any such horrors as Balzac or Dumas have provided for us.

Let us give an instance:—it is from the amusing novel called "Les Ailes d'Icare," and contains what is to us quite a new picture of a French fashionable rogue. The fashions will change in a few years, and the rogue, of course, with them. Let us catch this delightful fellow ere he flies. It is impossible to sketch the character in a more sparkling, gentlemanlike way, than M. de Bernard's; but such light things are very difficult of translation, and the sparkle sadly evaporates during the process of *decanting.*

A FRENCH FASHIONABLE LETTER.

"My dear Victor, it is six in the morning: I have just come from the English Ambassador's ball, and as my plans for the day do not admit of my sleeping, I write you a line; for, at this moment, saturated as I am with the enchantments of a fairy night, all other pleasures would be too wearisome to keep me awake, except that of conversing with you. Indeed, were I not to write to you now, when should I find the possibility of doing so? Time flies here with such a frightful rapidity, my pleasures and my affairs whirl onwards together in such a torrentuous galopade, that I am compelled to seize occasion by the forelock; for each moment has its imperious employ. Do not then accuse me of negligence: if my correspondence has not always that regularity which I would fain give it, attribute the fault solely to the whirlwind in which I live, and which carries me hither and thither at its will.

"However, you are not the only person with whom I am behindhand: I assure you, on the contrary, that you are one of a very numerous and fashionable company, to whom, towards the discharge of my debts, I propose to consecrate four hours to-day. I give you the preference to all the world, even to the lovely Duchess of San Severino, a delicious Italian, whom for my special happiness, I met last summer at the Waters of Aix. I have also a most important negotiation to conclude with one of our Princes of Finance: but, *n'importe*, I commence with thee: friendship before love or money—friendship before everything. My despatches concluded, I am engaged to ride with the Marquis de Grigneure, the Comte de Castijars, and Lord Cobham, in order that we may recover, for a breakfast at the Rocher de Cancale that Grigneure has lost, the appetite which we all of us so cruelly abused last night at the Ambassador's gala. On my honour, my dear fellow, everybody was of a *caprice prestigieux* and a *comfortable mirobolant*. Fancy, for a banquet-hall, a royal orangery hung with white damask; the boxes of the shrubs transformed into so many sideboards; lights gleaming through the foliage; and, for guests, the loveliest women and most brilliant cavaliers of Paris. Orleans and Nemours were there, dancing and eating like simple mortals. In a word, Albion did the thing very handsomely, and I accord it my esteem.

"Here I pause, to call for my valet de chambre, and call for tea; for my head is heavy, and I've no time for a headache. In serving me, this rascal of a Frederic has broken a cup, true Japan, upon my honour—the rogue does nothing else. Yesterday, for instance, did he not thump me prodigiously, by letting fall a goblet, after Cellini, of which the carving alone cost me three hundred francs? I must positively put the wretch out of doors, to ensure the safety of my furniture; and, in consequence of this, Eneas, an audacious young negro, in whom wisdom hath not waited for years—Eneas, my groom, I say, will probably be elevated to the post of valet de chambre. But where was I? I think I was speaking to you of an oyster breakfast, to which, on our return from the Park (du Bois), a company of pleasant rakes are invited. After quitting Borel's, we propose to adjourn to the Barrière du Combat, where Lord Cobham proposes to try some bull-dogs, which he has brought over from England, one of these, O'Connell (Lord Cobham is a Tory), has a face in which I place much confidence : I have a bet of ten louis with Castijars on the strength of it. After the fight, we shall make our accustomed appearance at the Café de Paris (the only place, by the way, where a man who respects himself may be seen), —and then away with frocks and spurs, and on with our dress-coats for the rest of the evening. In the first place, I shall go doze for a couple of hours at the Opera, where my presence is indispensable; for Coralie, a charming creature, passes this evening from the rank of the *rats* to that of the *tigers*, in a *pas-de-trois*, and our box patronizes her. After the Opera, I must show my face at two or three *salons* in the Faubourg St. Honoré; and having thus performed my duties to the world of fashion, I return to the exercise of my rights as a member of the Carnival. At two o'clock all the world meets at the Theatre Ventadour: lions and tigers—the whole of our menagerie, will be present. Evoé! off we go! roaring and bounding Bacchanal and Saturnal; 'tis agreed that we shall be everything that is low. To conclude, we sup with Castijars, the most 'furiously dishevelled' orgy that ever was known."

* * * * *

The rest of the letter is on matters of finance, equally curious and instructive. But pause we for the present, to consider the fashionable part: and, caricature as it is, we have an accurate picture of the actual French dandy. Bets, breakfasts, riding, dinners at the Café de Paris, and delirious Carnival balls; the animal goes through all such frantic pleasures at the season that precedes Lent. He has a wondrous respect for English "gentlemen-sportsmen;" he imitates their clubs—their love of horse-flesh, he calls his palefrenier a groom, wears blue bird's-eye neckcloths, sports his pink out hunting, rides steeple-chases, and has his Jockey-club. The "tigers and lions" alluded to in the report, have been borrowed from our own country, and a great compliment is it to Monsieur de Bernard, the writer of the above amusing sketch, that he has such a knowledge of English names and things, as to give a Tory Lord the decent title of Lord Cobham, and to call his dog O'Connell. Paul de Kock calls an English nobleman, in one of his last novels, *Lord Boulingrog*, and appears vastly delighted at the verisimilitude of the title.

For the "*rugissements et bondissements, bacchanale et saturnale galop infernal, ronde du sabbat tout le tremblement,*" these words give a most clear, untranslateable idea of the Carnival ball. A sight more hideous can hardly strike a man's eye. I was present at one where the four thousand guests whirled screaming, reeling, roaring, out of the ball-room in the Rue St. Honoré, and tore down to the column in the Place Vendôme, round which they went shrieking their own music, twenty miles an hour, and so tore madly back again. Let a man go alone to such a place of amusement, and the sight for him is perfectly terrible: the horrid frantic gaiety of the place puts him in mind more of the merriment of demons than of men: bang, bang, drums, trumpets, chairs, pistol-shots, pour out of the orchestra, which seems as mad as the dancers; whiz! a whirlwind of paint and patches, all the costumes under the sun, all the ranks in the empire, all the he and she scoundrels of the capital, writhed and twisted together, rush by you; if a man falls, woe be to him: two thousand screaming menads go trampling over his carcass: they have neither power nor will to stop.

A set of Malays, drunk with bhang, and running amuck, a company of howling dervishes, may possibly, at our own day, go through similar frantic vagaries; but I doubt if any civilized European people, but the French, would permit and enjoy such scenes. Yet our neighbours see little shame in them; and it is very true that men of all classes, high and low, here congregate and give themselves up to the disgusting worship of the genius of the place.—From the dandy of the Boulevart and the Café Anglais, let us turn to the dandy of Flicoteau's and the Pays Latin—the Paris student, whose exploits among the grisettes are so celebrated, and whose fierce republicanism keeps gendarmes for ever on the alert. The following is M. de Bernard's description of him:—

"I became acquainted with Dambergeac when we were students at the Ecole de Droit; we lived in the same hotel, on the Place du Panthéon. No doubt, madam, you have occasionally met little children dedicated to the Virgin, and, to this end, clothed in white raiment from head to foot: my friend, Dambergeac, had received a different consecration. His father, a great patriot of the Revolution, had determined that his son should bear into the world a sign of indelible republicanism; so, to the great displeasure of his godmother and the parish curate, Dambergeac was christened by the Pagan name of Harmodius. It was a kind of moral tricolor-cockade, which the child was to bear through the vicissitudes of all the revolutions to come. Under such influences, my friend's character began to develop itself, and, fired by the example of his father, and by the warm atmosphere of his native place, Marseilles, he grew up to have an independent spirit, and a grand liberality of politics, which were at their height when first I made his acquaintance.

"He was then a young man of eighteen, with a tall, slim figure, a broad chest, and a flaming black eye, out of all which personal charms he knew how to draw the most advantage; and though his costume was such as Staub might probably have criticized, he had, nevertheless, a style peculiar to himself—to himself and the students, among whom he was the leader of the fashion. A tight black coat, buttoned up to the chin, across the chest, set off that part of his person; a low-crowned hat, with a voluminous rim, cast solemn shadows over a countenance bronzed by a southern sun: he wore, at one time, enormous flowing black locks, which he sacrificed pitilessly, however, and adopted a Brutus, as being more revolutionary: finally, he carried an enormous club, that was his code and digest: in like manner, De Retz used to carry a stiletto in his pocket, by way of a breviary.

"Although of different ways of thinking in politics, certain sympathies of character and conduct united Dambergeac and myself, and we speedily became close friends. I don't think, in the whole course of his three years' residence, Dambergeac ever went through a single course of lectures. For the examinations, he trusted to luck, and to his own facility, which was prodigious: as for honours, he never aimed at them, but was content to do exactly as little as was necessary for him to gain his degree. In like manner he sedulously avoided those horrible circulating libraries, where daily are seen to congregate the 'reading men' of our schools. But, in revenge, there was not a milliner's shop, or a *lingère's*, in all our quartier Latin, which he did not industriously frequent, and of which he was not the oracle. Nay, it was said that his victories were not confined to the left bank of the Seine: reports did occasionally come to us of fabulous adventures by him accomplished in the far regions of the Rue de la Paix and the Boulevard Poissonnière. Such recitals were, for us less favoured mortals, like tales of Bacchus conquering in the East; they excited our ambition, but not our jealousy; for the superiority of Harmodious was acknowledged by us all, and we never thought of a rivalry with him. No man ever cantered a hack through the Champs Elysées with such elegant assurance; no man ever made such a massacre of dolls at the shooting gallery; or won you a rubber at billiards with more easy grace; or thundered out a couplet out of Béranger with such a roaring melodious bass. He was the monarch of the Prado in winter; in summer, of the Chaumière and Mont Parnasse. Not a frequenter of those fashionable places of entertainment showed a more amiable *laisser-aller* in the dance—that peculiar dance at which gendarmes think proper to blush, and which squeamish society has banished from her salons. In a word, Harmodious was the prince of *mauvais sujets*, a youth with all the accomplishments of Göttingen and Jena, and all the eminent graces of his own country.

"Besides dissipation and gallantry, our friend had one other vast and absorbing occupation—politics, namely; in which he was as turbulent and enthusiastic as in pleasure. La Patrie was his idol, his heaven, his nightmare: by day he spouted, by night he dreamed, of his country. I have spoken to you of his coiffure à la Sylla; need I mention his pipe, his meerschaum pipe, of which General Foy's head was the bowl; his handkerchief with the Charte printed thereon; and his celebrated tricolor braces, which kept the rallying-sign of his country ever close to his heart? Besides these outward and visible signs of sedition, he had inward and secret plans of revolution : he belonged to clubs, frequented associations, read the *Constitutionnel* (liberals, in those days, swore by the *Constitutionnel*), harangued peers and deputies who had deserved well of their country; and if death happened to fall on such, and the *Constitutionnel* declared their merit, Harmodious was the very first to attend their obsequies, or to set his shoulder to their coffins.

"Such were his tastes and passions: his antipathies were not less lively. He detested three things: a jesuit, a gendarme, and a *claqueur* at a theatre. At this period, missionaries were rife about Paris, and endeavoured to re-illume the zeal of the faithful by public preachings in the churches. ' *Infâmes jesuites!* ' would Harmodius exclaim, who, in the excess of his toleration, tolerated nothing; and, at the head of a band of philosophers like himself, would attend with scrupulous exactitude the meetings of the reverend gentlemen. But, instead of a contrite heart, Harmodius only brought the abomination of desolation into their sanctuary. A perpetual fire of fulminating balls would bang from under the feet of the faithful; odours of impure asafœtida would mingle with the fumes of the incense; and wicked drinking choruses would rise up along with the holy canticles, in hideous dissonance, reminding one of the old orgies under the reign of the Abbot of Unreason.

"His hatred of the gendarmes was equally ferocious: and as for the claqueurs, woe be to them when Harmodius was in the pit! They knew him, and trembled before him, like the earth before Alexander; and his famous war-cry, '*La Carte au chapeau!*' was so much dreaded, that the '*entrepreneurs de succès dramatiques*' demanded twice as much to '*do*' the Odéon Theatre (which we students and Harmodius frequented), as to applaud at any other place of amusement: and, indeed, their double pay was hardly gained; Harmodius taking care that they should earn the most of it under the benches."

This passage, with which we have taken some liberties, will give the reader a more lively idea of the reckless, jovial, turbulent Paris student, than any with which a foreigner could furnish him: the grisette is his heroine; and dear old Béranger, the cynic-epicurean, has celebrated him and her in the most delightful verses in the world. Of these we may have occasion to say a word or two anon. Meanwhile let us follow Monsieur de Bernard in his amusing descriptions of his countrymen somewhat farther; and, having seen how Dambergeac was a ferocious republican, being a bachelor, let us see how age, sense, and a little government pay—the great agent of conversions in France —nay, in England—has reduced him to be a pompous, quiet, loyal supporter of the juste milieu: his former portrait was that of the student, the present will stand for an admirable lively likeness of

THE SOUS-PREFET.

"Saying that I would wait for Dambergeac in his own study, I was introduced into that apartment, and saw around me the usual furniture of a man in his station.

There was, in the middle of the room, a large bureau, surrounded by orthodox arm-chairs; and there were many shelves, with boxes duly ticketed; there were a number of maps, and, among them, a great one of the department over which Dambergeac ruled; and, facing the windows, on a wooden pedestal, stood a plaster-cast of the "*Roi des Français.*" Recollecting my friend's former republicanism, I smiled at this piece of furniture; but, before I had time to carry my observations any farther, a heavy rolling sound of carriage-wheels, that caused the windows to rattle and seemed to shake the whole edifice of the sub-prefecture, called my attention to the court without. Its iron gates were flung open, and in rolled, with a great deal of din, a chariot escorted by a brace of gendarmes, sword in hand. A tall gentleman, with a cocked-hat and feathers, wearing a blue and silver uniform coat, descended from the vehicle; and having, with much grave condescension, saluted his escort, mounted the stair. A moment afterwards the door of the study was opened, and I embraced my friend.

"After the first warmth and salutations, we began to examine each other with an equal curiosity, for eight years had elapsed since we had last met.

"You are grown very thin and pale," said Harmodius, after a moment.

"In revenge, I find you fat and rosy: if I am a walking satire on celibacy,—you, at least, are a living panegyric on marriage."

"In fact, a great change, and such an one as many people would call a change for the better, had taken place in my friend: he had grown fat, and announced a decided disposition to become, what French people call, a *bel homme:* that is, a very fat one. His complexion, bronzed before, was now clear white and red: there were no more political allusions in his hair, which was, on the contrary, neatly frizzed, and brushed over the forehead, shell-shape. This head-dress, joined to a thin pair of whiskers, cut crescent-wise from the ear to the nose, gave my friend a regular bourgeois physiognomy, wax-doll-like: he looked a great deal too well; and, added to this, the solemnity of his prefectural costume, gave his whole appearance a pompous, well-fed look, that by no means pleased.

"I surprise you," said I, "in the midst of your splendour: do you know that this costume and yonder attendants have a look excessively awful and splendid? You entered your palace just now with the air of a pasha."

"You see me in uniform in honour of Monseigneur the Bishop, who has just made his diocesan visit, and whom I have just conducted to the limit of the *arrondissement.*"

"What!" said I, "you have gendarmes for guards, and dance attendance on bishops? There are no more janissaries and jesuits, I suppose?" The sub-prefect smiled.

"I assure you that my gendarmes are very worthy fellows; and that among the gentlemen who compose our clergy there are some of the very best rank and talent: besides, my wife is niece to one of the vicars-general."

"What have you done with that great Tasso beard that poor Armandine used to love so?"

"My wife does not like a beard; and you know that what is permitted to a student is not very becoming to a magistrate."

I began to laugh. "Harmodius and a magistrate!—how shall I ever couple the two words together? But tell me, in your correspondences, your audiences, your sittings with village mayors and petty councils, how do you manage to remain awake?"

"In the commencement," said Harmodius, gravely, "it *was* very difficult; and, in order to keep my eyes open, I used to stick pins into my legs: now, however, I am used to it; and I'm sure I don't take more than fifty pinches of snuff at a sitting."

"Ah! àpropos of snuff: you are near Spain here, and were always a famous smoker. Give me a cigar,—it will take away the musty odour of these piles of papers."

"Impossible, my dear; I don't smoke: my wife cannot bear a cigar."

"His wife, thought I: always his wife; and I remember Juliette, who really grew sick at the smell of a pipe, and Harmodius would smoke, until, at last, the poor thing grew to smoke herself, like a trooper. To compensate, however, as much as possible for the loss of my cigar, Dambergeac drew from his pocket an enormous gold snuff-box, on which figured the self-same head that I had before remarked in plaster, but this time surrounded with a ring of pretty princes and princesses, all nicely painted in miniature. As for the statue of Louis Philippe, that, in the cabinet of an official, is a thing of course; but the snuff-box seemed to indicate a degree of sentimental and personal devotion, such as the old royalists were only supposed to be guilty of.

"What! you are turned decided juste milieu?" said I.

"I am a sous-préfet," answered Harmodius.

"I had nothing to say, but held my tongue, wondering, not at the change which had taken place in the habits, manners, and opinions of my friend, but at my own folly, which led me to fancy that I should find the student of '26 in the functionary of '34. At this moment a domestic appeared.

"Madame is waiting for Monsieur," said he: "the last bell has gone, and mass beginning."

"Mass!" said I, bounding up from my chair. "You at mass, like a decent serious Christian, without crackers in your pocket, and bored keys to whistle through?"— The sous-préfet rose, his countenance was calm, and an indulgent smile played upon his lips, as he said, "My arrondissement is very devout; and not to interfere with the belief of the population is the maxim of every wise politician: I have precise orders from Government on the point, too, and go to eleven o'clock mass every Sunday."

There is a great deal of curious matter for speculation in the accounts here so wittily given by M. de Bernard: but, perhaps, it is still more curious to think of what he has *not* written, and to judge of his characters, not so much by the words in which he describes them, as by the unconscious testimony that the words all together convey. In the first place, our author describes a swindler imitating the manners of a dandy; and many swindlers and dandies be there, doubtless, in London as well as in Paris. But there is about the present swindler, and about Monsieur Dambergeac the student, and Monsieur Dambergeac the sous-préfet, and his friend, a rich store of calm internal *debauch*, which does not, let us hope and pray, exist in England. Hearken to M. de Gustan, and his smirking whispers about the Duchess of San Severino, who *pour son bonheur particulier*, &c. &c. Listen to Monsieur Dambergeac's friend's remonstrances concerning *pauvre Juliette*, who grew sick at the smell of a pipe; to his *naïve* admiration at the fact that the sous-préfet goes to church: and we may set down, as axioms, that religion is so uncommon among the Parisians, as to awaken the surprise of all candid observers; that gallantry is so common as to create no remark, and to be considered as a matter of course. With us, at least, the converse of the proposition prevails: it is the man professing *ir*religion who would be remarked and reprehended in England; and, if the second-named vice exists, at any rate, it adopts the decency of secrecy, and is not made patent and notorious to all the world. A French gentleman thinks no more of proclaiming that he has a mistress than that he has a tailor; and one lives the time of Boccaccio over again, in the thousand and one French novels which depict society in that country.

For instance, here are before us a few specimens (do not, madam, be alarmed, you can skip the sentence if you like) to be found in as many admirable witty tales, by the before-lauded Monsieur de Bernard. He is more remarkable than any other French author, to our notion, for writing like a gentleman: there is ease, grace, and *ton*, in his style, which, if we judge aright, cannot be discovered in Balzac, or Soulié, or Dumas. We have then—*Gerfaut*, a novel : a lovely creature is married to a brave, haughty Alsacian nobleman, who allows her to spend her winters at Paris, he remaining on his *terres*, cultivating, carousing, and hunting the boar. The lovely creature meets the fascinating Gerfaut at Paris; instantly the latter makes love to her; a duel takes place : baron killed ; wife throws herself out of window ; Gerfaut plunges into dissipation ; and so the tale ends.

Next : *La Femme de Quarante Ans,* a capital tale, full of exquisite fun and sparkling satire : La femme de quarante ans has a husband and *three* lovers ; all of whom find out their mutual connexion one starry night : for the lady of forty is of a romantic poetical turn, and has given her three admirers *a star apiece ;* saying to one and the other, " Alphonse, when you pale orb rises in heaven, think of me ; " " Isidore, when that bright planet sparkles in the sky, remember your Caroline," &c.

Un Acte de Vertu, from which we have taken Dambergeac's history, contains him, the husband—a wife—and a brace of lovers ; and a geat deal of fun takes place in the manner in which one lover supplants the other.—Pretty morals truly !

If we examine an author who rejoices in the aristocratic name of le Comte Horace de Viel-Castel, we find, though with infinitely less wit, exactly the same intrigues going on. A noble Count lives in the Faubourg St. Honoré, and has a noble Duchess for a mistress : he introduces her Grace to the Countess, his wife. The Countess, his wife, in order to *ramener* her lord to his conjugal duties, is counselled, by a friend, *to pretend to take a lover:* one is found, who, poor fellow! takes the affair in earnest: climax —duel, death, despair, and what not? In the *Faubourg St. Germain,* another novel by the same writer, which professes to describe the very pink of that society which Napoleon dreaded more than Russia, Prussia, and Austria, there is an old husband, of course; a sentimental young German nobleman, who falls in love with his wife; and the moral of the piece lies in the shewing up of the conduct of the lady, who is reprehended—not for deceiving her husband (poor devil!)—but for being a flirt, *and taking a second lover,* to the utter despair, confusion, and annihilation of the first.

Why, ye gods, do Frenchmen marry at all? Had Père Enfantin (who, it is said, has shaved his ambrosial beard, and is now a clerk in a banking-house) been allowed to carry out his chaste, just, dignified social scheme, what a deal of marital discomfort might have been avoided:— would it not be advisable that a great reformer and lawgiver of our own, Mr. Robert Owen, should be presented at the Tuileries, and there propound his scheme for the regeneration of France?

He might, perhaps, be spared, for our country is not yet sufficiently advanced to give such a philosopher fair play. In London, as yet, there are no blessed *Bureaux de Mariage,* where an old bachelor may have a charming young maiden—for his money; or a widow of seventy may buy a gay young fellow of twenty, for a certain number of bank-billets. If *mariages de convenance* take place here (as they will wherever avarice, and poverty, and desire, and yearning after riches are to be found), at least, thank God, such unions are not arranged upon a regular organized *system*: there is a fiction of attachment with us, and there is a consolation in the deceit ("the homage," according to the old *mot* of Rochefoucauld, "which vice pays to virtue"); for the very falsehood shows that the virtue exists somewhere. We once heard a furious old French colonel inveighing against the chastity of English *demoiselles*: "*Figurez vous*, sir," said he (he had been a prisoner in England), "that these women come down to dinner in low dresses, and walk out alone with the men!"—and, pray Heaven, so may they walk, fancy-free in all sorts of maiden meditations, and suffer no more molestation than that young lady of whom Moore sings, and who (there must have been a famous lord-lieutenant in those days) walked through all Ireland, with rich and rare gems, beauty, and a gold ring on her stick, without meeting or thinking of harm.

Now, whether Monsieur de Viel-Castel has given a true picture of the Faubourg St. Germain, it is impossible for most foreigners to say; but some of his descriptions will not fail to astonish the English reader; and all are filled with that remarkable *naïf* contempt of the institution called marriage, which we have seen in M. de Bernard. The romantic young nobleman of Westphalia arrives at Paris, and is admitted into, what a celebrated female author calls, *la créme de la créme de la haute volée* of Parisian society. He is a youth of about twenty years of age. "No passion had as yet come to move his heart, and give life to his faculties; he was awaiting and fearing the moment of love;

calling for it, and yet trembling at its approach; feeling, in the depths of his soul, that that moment would create a mighty change in his being, and decide, perhaps, by its influence, the whole of his future life."

Is it not remarkable, that a young nobleman, with these ideas, should not pitch upon a *demoiselle*, or a widow, at least? but no, the rogue must have a married woman, bad luck to him; and what his fate is to be, is thus recounted by our author, in the shape of

A FRENCH FASHIONABLE CONVERSATION.

"A lady, with a great deal of esprit, to whom forty years' experience of the great world had given a prodigious perspicacity of judgment, the Duchess of Chalux, arbitress of the opinion to be held on all new comers to the Faubourg Saint Germain, and of their destiny and reception in it;— one of those women, in a word, who make or ruin a man,— said, in speaking of Gerard de Stolberg, whom she received at her own house, and met everywhere, 'This young German will never gain for himself the title of an exquisite, or a man of *bonnes fortunes*, among us. In spite of his calm and politeness, I think I can see in his character some rude and insurmountable difficulties, which time will only increase, and which will prevent him for ever from bending to the exigencies of either profession; but, unless I very much deceive myself, he will, one day, be the hero of a veritable romance.'

"'He, Madame?' answered a young man, of fair complexion and fair hair, one of the most devoted slaves of the fashion:—'He, Madame la Duchesse? why, the man is, at best, but an original, fished out of the Rhine: a dull, heavy creature, as much capable of understanding a woman's heart as I am of speaking bas-breton.'

"'Well, Monsieur de Belport, you will speak bas-breton. Monsieur de Stolberg has not your admirable ease of manner, nor your facility of telling pretty nothings, nor your—in a word, that particular something which makes you the most recherché man of the Faubourg Saint Germain; and even I avow to you, that, were I still young, and a coquette, *and that I took it into my head to have a lover*, I would prefer you.'

"All this was said by the Duchess, with a certain air of raillery, and such a mixture of earnest and malice, that Monsieur de Belport, piqued not a little, could not help saying, as he bowed profoundly, before the Duchess's chair, 'And might I, madam, be permitted to ask the reason of this preference?'

"'*O mon Dieu*, oui,' said the Duchess, always in the same tone; 'because a lover like you would never think of carrying his attachment to the height of passion; and these passions, do you know, have frightened me all my life. One cannot retreat, at will, from the grasp of a passionate lover; one leaves behind one some fragment of one's moral *self*, or the best part of one's physical life. A passion, if it does not kill you, adds cruelly to your years; in a word, it is the very lowest possible taste. And now you understand why I should prefer you, M. de Belport—you, who are reputed to be the leader of the fashion.'

"'Perfectly,' murmured the gentleman, piqued more and more.

"'Gerard de Stolberg *will* be passionate. I don't know what woman will please him, or will be pleased by him (here the Duchess of Chalux spoke more gravely); but his love will be no play, I repeat it to you once more. All this astonishes you, because you, great leaders of the ton that you are, never can fancy that a hero of romance should be found among your number. Gerard de Stolberg—but look, here he comes!'

"M. de Belport rose, and quitted the Duchess, without believing in her prophecy; but he could not avoid smiling as he passed near the *hero of romance.*

"It was because M. de Stolberg had never, in all his life, been a hero of romance, or even an apprentice-hero of romance.

* * * * *

"Gerard de Stolberg was not, as yet, initiated into the thousand secrets in the chronicle of the great world: he knew but superficially the society in which he lived; and, therefore, he devoted his evening to the gathering of all the information which he could acquire from the indiscreet conversations of the people about him. His whole man became ear and memory; so much was Stolberg convinced of the necessity of becoming a diligent student in this new school, where was taught the art of knowing and advancing in the great world. In the recess of a window he learned more, on this one night, than months of investigation would have taught him. The talk of a ball is more indiscreet than the confidential chatter of a company of idle women. No man present at a ball, whether listener or speaker, thinks he has a right to affect any indulgence for his companions, and the most learned in malice will always pass for the most witty.

"'How!' said the Viscount de Mondragé : ' the Duchess of Rivesalte arrives alone to-night, without her inevitable Dormilly!'—And the Viscount, as he spoke, pointed towards a tall and slender young woman, who, gliding rather than walking, met the ladies, by whom she passed, with a graceful and modest salute, and replied to the looks of the men *by brilliant veiled glances, full of coquetry and attack.*

"'Parbleu!' said an elegant personage, standing near the Viscount de Mondragé, ' don't you see Dormilly ranged behind the Duchess, in quality of train-bearer, and hiding, under his long locks and his great screen of mustachios, the blushing consciousness of his good luck?—They call him *the fourth chapter* of the Duchess's memoirs. The little Marquise d'Alberas is ready to die out of spite; but the best of the joke is, that she has only taken poor de Vendre for a lover, in order to vent her spleen on him. Look at him, against the chimney yonder : if the Marchioness do not break at once with him, by quitting him for somebody else, the poor fellow will turn an idiot.'

"' Is he jealous ?' asked a young man, looking as if he did not know what jealousy was, and as if he had no time to be jealous.

" Jealous !—the very incarnation of jealousy ; the second edition, revised, corrected, and considerably enlarged ; as jealous as poor Gressigny, who is dying of it.'

"'What! Gressigny too? why, 'tis growing quite

into fashion: egad! *I* must try and be jealous,' said Monsieur de Beauval. 'But see! here comes the delicious Duchess of Bellefiore,'" &c. &c. &c.

* * * * *

Enough, enough: this kind of fashionable Parisian conversation, which is, says our author, " a prodigious labour of improvising," a " chef-d'œuvre," a " strange and singular thing, in which monotony is unknown," seems to be, if correctly reported, a " strange and singular thing " indeed; but somewhat monotonous, at least, to an English reader, and "prodigious" only, if we may take leave to say so, for the wonderful rascality which all the conversationists betray. Miss Neverout and the Colonel, in Swift's famous dialogue, are a thousand times more entertaining and moral; and, besides, we can laugh *at* those worthies, as well as with them; whereas the "prodigious" French wits are to us quite incomprehensible. Fancy a Duchess, as old as Lady —— herself, and who should begin to tell us "of what she would do if ever she had a mind to take a lover;" and another Duchess, with a fourth lover, tripping modestly among the ladies, and returning the gaze of the men by veiled glances, full of coquetry and attack!—Parbleu, if Monsieur de Viel-Castel should find himself among a society of French Duchesses, and they should tear his eyes out, and send the fashionable Orpheus floating by the Seine, his slaughter might almost be considered as justifiable *Counticide.*

A GAMBLER'S DEATH.

ANYBODY who was at C—— school, some twelve years since, must recollect Jack Attwood: he was the most dashing lad in the place, with more money in his pocket than belonged to the whole fifth form in which we were companions.

When he was about fifteen, Jack suddenly retreated from C——, and presently we heard that he had a commission in a cavalry regiment, and was to have a great fortune from his father, when that old gentleman should die. Jack himself came to confirm these stories a few months after, and paid a visit to his old school chums. He had laid aside his little school-jacket and inky corduroys, and now appeared in such a splendid military suit as won the respect of all of us. His hair was dripping with oil, his hands were covered with rings, he had a dusky down over his upper lip which looked not unlike a mustachio, and a multiplicity of frogs and braiding on his surtout which would have sufficed to lace a field-marshal. When old Swishtail, the usher, passed in his seedy black coat and gaiters, Jack gave him such a look of contempt as set us all a-laughing: in fact, it was his turn to laugh now; for he used to roar very stoutly some months before, when Swishtail was in the custom of belabouring him with his great cane.

Jack's talk was all about the regiment and the fine fellows in it: how he had ridden a steeple-chase with Captain Boldero, and licked him at the last hedge; and how he had very nearly fought a duel with Sir George Grig, about dancing with Lady Mary Slamken at a ball. "I soon made the baronet know what it was to deal with a man of the n—th," said Jack. "Dammee, sir, when I lugged out my barkers, and talked of fighting across the mess-room table, Grig turned as pale as a sheet, or as ———"

"Or as you used to do, Attwood, when Swishtail hauled you up," piped out little Hicks, the foundation-boy.

It was beneath Jack's dignity to thrash anybody, now, but a grown-up baronet; so he let off little Hicks, and passed over the general titter which was raised at his expense. However, he entertained us with his histories about lords and ladies, and so-and-so "of ours," until we thought him one of the greatest men in his Majesty's service, and until the school-bell rung; when, with a heavy heart, we got our books together, and marched in to be whacked by old Swishtail. I promise you he revenged himself on us for Jack's contempt of him. I got that day at least twenty cuts to my share, which ought to have belonged to Cornet Attwood, of the n—th dragoons.

When we came to think more coolly over our quondam schoolfellow's swaggering talk and manner, we were not quite so impressed by his merits as at his first appearance among us. We recollected how he used, in former times, to tell us great stories, which were so monstrously improbable that the smallest boy in the school would scout at them; how often we caught him tripping in facts, and how unblushingly he admitted his little errors in the score of veracity. He and I, though never great friends, had been close companions: I was Jack's form-fellow (we fought with amazing emulation for the *last* place in the class); but still I was rather hurt at the coolness of my old comrade, who had forgotten all our former intimacy, in his steeple-chases with Captain Boldero and his duel with Sir George Grig.

Nothing more was heard of Attwood for some years; a tailor one day came down to C——, who had made clothes for Jack in his school-days, and furnished him with regimentals: he produced a long bill for one hundred and twenty pounds and upwards, and asked where news might be had of his customer. Jack was in India, with his regiment, shooting tigers and jackals, no doubt. Occasionally, from that distant country, some magnificent rumour would reach us of his proceedings. Once I heard that he had been called to a court-martial for unbecoming conduct; another time, that he kept twenty horses, and won the gold plate at the Calcutta races. Presently, however, as the recollections of the fifth form wore away, Jack's image disappeared likewise, and I ceased to ask or think about my college chum.

A year since, as I was smoking my cigar in the "Estaminet du Grand Balcon," an excellent smoking-shop, where the tobacco is unexceptionable, and the Hollands of singular merit, a dark-looking, thick-set man, in a greasy well-cut coat, with a shabby hat, cocked on one side of his dirty face, took the place opposite me, at the little marble table, and called for brandy. I did not much admire the impudence or the appearance of my friend, nor the fixed stare with which he chose to examine me. At last, he thrust a great greasy hand across the table, and said, " Titmarsh, do you forget your old friend Attwood ? "

I confess my recognition of him was not so joyful as on the day ten years earlier, when he had come, bedizened with lace and gold rings, to see us at C—— school: a man in the tenth part of a century learns a deal of worldly wisdom, and his hand, which goes naturally forward to seize the gloved finger of a millionaire, or a milor, draws instinctively back from a dirty fist, encompassed by a ragged wristband and a tattered cuff. But Attwood was in nowise so backward; and the iron squeeze with which he shook my passive paw, proved that he was either very affectionate or very poor. "You, my dear sir, who are reading this history, know very well the great art of shaking hands: recollect how you shook Lord Dash's hand the other day, and how you shook *off* poor Blank, when he came to borrow five pounds of you."

However, the genial influence of the Hollands speedily dissipated anything like coolness between us; and, in the course of an hour's conversation, we became almost as intimate as when we were suffering together under the ferule of old Swishtail. Jack told me that he had quitted the army in disgust; and that his father, who was to leave him a fortune, had died ten thousand pounds in debt: he did not touch upon his own circumstances; but I could read them in his elbows, which were peeping through his old frock. He talked a great deal, however, of runs of luck, good and bad; and related to me an infallible plan for breaking all the play-banks in Europe—a great number of old tricks;—and a vast quantity of gin-punch was consumed on the occasion; so long, in fact, did our conversation continue, that, I confess it with shame, the sentiment, or something stronger, quite got the better of me, and I have, to this day, no sort of notion how our palaver concluded.—Only, on the next morning, I did not possess a certain five-pound note, which, on the previous evening, was in my sketch-book (by far the prettiest drawing by the way in the collection); but there, instead, was a strip of paper, thus inscribed:—

I. O. U.
Five Pounds. JOHN ATTWOOD,
Late of the N—th Dragoons.

I suppose Attwood borrowed the money, from this remarkable and ceremonious acknowledgment on his part: had I been sober, I would just as soon have lent him the nose on my face; for, in my then circumstances, the note was of much more consequence to me.

As I lay, cursing my ill fortune, and thinking how on earth I should manage to subsist for the next two months, Attwood burst into my little garret—his face strangely flushed—singing and shouting as if it had been the night before. "Titmarsh," cried he, "you are my preserver!—my best friend! Look here, and here, and here!" And at every word Mr. Attwood produced a handful of gold, or a glittering heap of five-franc pieces, or a bundle of greasy, dusky bank-notes, more beautiful than either silver or gold:—he had won thirteen thousand francs after leaving me at midnight in my garret. He separated my poor little all, of six pieces, from this shining and imposing collection; and the passion of envy entered my soul: I felt far more anxious now than before, although starvation was then staring me in the face; I hated Attwood for *cheating* me out of all this wealth. Poor fellow! it had been better for him had he never seen a shilling of it.

However, a grand breakfast at the Café Anglais dissipated my chagrin; and I will do my friend the justice to say, that he nobly shared some portion of his good fortune with me. As far as the creature comforts were concerned, I feasted as well as he, and never was particular as to settling my share of the reckoning.

Jack now changed his lodgings; had cards, with Captain Attwood engraved on them, and drove about a prancing cab-horse, as tall as the giraffe at the Jardin des Plantes; he had as many frogs on his coat as in the old days, and frequented all the flash restaurateurs and boarding-houses of the capital. Madame de Saint Laurent, and Madame la Baronne de Vaudrey, and Madame la Comtesse de Don Jouville, ladies of the highest rank, who keep a *société choisie* and condescend to give dinners at five francs a-head, vied with each other in their attentions to Jack. His was the wing of the fowl, and the largest portion of the Charlotte-Russe; his was the place at the écarté table, where the Countess would ease him nightly of a few pieces, declaring that he was the most charming cavalier, la fleur d'Albion. Jack's society, it may be seen, was not very select; nor, in truth, were his inclinations: he was a careless, dare-devil, Macheath kind of fellow, who might be seen daily with a wife on each arm.

It may be supposed, that, with the life he led, his five hundred pounds of winnings would not last him long; nor did they: but, for some time, his luck never deserted him; and his cash, instead of growing lower, seemed always to maintain a certain level:—he played every night.

Of course, such a humble fellow as I, could not hope

for a continued acquaintance and intimacy with Attwood. He grew overbearing and cool, I thought; at any rate I did not admire my situation, as his follower and dependant, and left his grand dinner, for a certain ordinary, where I could partake of five capital dishes for ninepence. Occasionally, however, Attwood favoured me with a visit, or gave me a drive behind his great cab-horse. He had formed a whole host of friends besides. There was Fips, the barrister; heaven knows what he was doing at Paris; and Gortz, the West Indian, who was there on the same business, and Flapper, a medical student,—all these three I met one night at Flapper's rooms, where Jack was invited, and a great " spread " was laid in honour of him.

Jack arrived rather late—he looked pale and agitated; and, though he ate no supper, he drank raw brandy in such a manner as made Flapper's eyes wink: the poor fellow had but three bottles, and Jack bid fair to swallow them all. However, the West Indian generously remedied the evil, and producing a napoleon, we speedily got the change for it in the shape of four bottles of champagne.

Our supper was uproariously harmonious; Fips sung the good " Old English gentleman ; " Jack, the " British grenadiers ; " and your humble servant, when called upon, sang that beautiful ditty, " When the bloom is on the rye," in a manner that drew tears from every eye, except Flapper's, who was asleep, and Jack's, who was singing the " Bay of Biscay O," at the same time. Gortz and Fips were all the time lunging at each other with a pair of single-sticks, the barrister having a very strong notion that he was Richard the Third.

At last Fips hits the West Indian such a blow across his sconce, that the other grew furious; he seized a champagne bottle, which was, providentially, empty, and hurled it across the room at Fips: had that celebrated barrister not bowed his head at the moment, the Queen's Bench would have lost one of its most eloquent practitioners.

Fips stood as straight as he could; his cheek was pale with wrath. "M-m-ister Go-gortz," he said, "I always heard you were a blackguard; now I can pr-pr-peperove it. Flapper, your pistols! every ge-ge-genlmn knows what I mean."

Young Mr. Flapper had a small pair of pocket-pistols, which the tipsy barrister had suddenly remembered, and with which he proposed to sacrifice the West Indian. Gortz was nothing loth, but was quite as valorous as the lawyer.

Attwood, who, in spite of his potations, seemed the soberest man of the party, had much enjoyed the scene, until this sudden demand for the weapons. "Pshaw!" said he, eagerly, "don't give these men the means of murdering each other; sit down, and let us have another song."

But they would not be still; and Flapper forthwith produced his pistol-case, and opened it, in order that the duel might take place on the spot.—There were no pistols there! "I beg your pardon," said Attwood, looking much confused; "I—I took the pistols home with me, to clean them!"

I don't know what there was in his tone, or in the words, but we were sobered all of a sudden. Attwood was conscious of the singular effect produced by him, for he blushed, and endeavoured to speak of other things, but we could not bring our spirits back to the mark again, and soon separated for the night. As we issued into the street, Jack took me aside, and whispered "Have you a napoleon, Titmarsh, in your purse?" Alas! I was not so rich. My reply was, that I was coming to Jack, only in the morning, to borrow a similar sum.

He did not make any reply, but turned away homeward: I never heard him speak another word.

* * * * *

Two mornings after (for none of our party met on the day succeeding the supper), I was awakened by my porter, who brought a pressing letter from Mr. Gortz.

"DEAR T.—

"I WISH you would come over here to breakfast. There's a row about Attwood.

"Yours truly,

SOLOMON GORTZ."

I immediately set forward to Gortz's; he lived in the Rue du Heldes, a few doors from Attwood's new lodging. If the reader is curious to know the house in which the catastrophe of this history took place, he has but to march some twenty doors down from the Boulevard des Italiens, when he will see a fine door, with a naked Cupid shooting at him from the hall, and a Venus beckoning him up the stairs.

11

On arriving at the West Indian's, at about mid-day (it was a Sunday morning), I found that gentleman in his dressing-gown, discussing, in the company of Mr. Fips, a large plate of *bifteck aux pommes.*

"Here's a pretty row!" said Gortz, quoting from his letter;—"Attwood's off—have a bit of beefsteak?"

"What do you mean?" exclaimed I, adopting the familiar phraseology of my acquaintances:—"Attwood off?—has he cut his stick?"

"Not bad," said the feeling and elegant Fips—"not such a bad guess, my boy; but he has not exactly *cut his stick.*"

"What then?"

"*Why, his throat.*" The man's mouth was full of bleeding beef as he uttered this gentlemanly witticism.

I wish I could say that I was myself in the least affected by the news. I did not joke about it like my friend Fips; this was more for propriety's sake than for feeling's: but for my old school acquaintance, the friend of my early days, the merry associate of the last few months, I own, with shame that I had not a tear or a pang. In some German tale, there is an account of a creature, most beautiful and bewitching, whom all men admire and follow; but this charming and fantastic spirit only leads them, one by one, into ruin, and then leaves them. The novelist, who describes her beauty, says that his heroine is a fairy, and *has no heart.* I think the intimacy which is begotten over the wine bottle, is a spirit of this nature; I never knew a good feeling come from it, or an honest friendship made by it; it only entices men, and ruins them; it is only a phantom of friendship and feeling, called up by the delirious blood, and the wicked spells of the wine.

But to drop this strain of moralizing (in which the writer is not too anxious to proceed, for he cuts in it a most pitiful figure), we passed sundry criticisms upon poor Attwood's character, expressed our horror at his death—which sentiment was fully proved by Mr. Fips, who declared that the notion of it made him feel quite faint, and was obliged to drink a large glass of brandy; and, finally, we agreed that we would go and see the poor fellow's corpse, and witness, if necessary, his burial.

Flapper, who had joined us, was the first to propose this visit: he said he did not mind the fifteen francs which Jack owed him for billiards, but he was anxious to *get back his pistol*. Accordingly, we sallied forth, and speedily arrived at the hotel which Attwood inhabited still.

He had occupied, for a time, very fine apartments in this house: and it was only on arriving there that day, that we found he had been gradually driven from his magnificent suite of rooms, *au premier*, to a little chamber in the fifth story:—we mounted, and found him.

It was a little shabby room, with a few articles of rickety furniture, and a bed in an alcove; the light from the one window was falling full upon the bed and the body.

Jack was dressed in a fine lawn shirt; he had kept it, poor fellow, *to die in;* for, in all his drawers and cupboards, there was not a single article of clothing; he had pawned everything by which he could raise a penny—desk, books, dressing-case, and clothes; and not a single halfpenny was found in his possession.*

He was lying as I have drawn him, one hand on his breast, the other falling towards the ground. There was an expression of perfect calm on the face, and no mark of blood to stain the side towards the light. On the other side, however, there was a great pool of black blood, and in it the pistol; it looked more like a toy than a weapon to take away the life of this vigorous young man. In his forehead, at the side, was a small black wound; Jack's life had passed through it; it was little bigger than a mole.

* * * * *

"*Regardez un peu,*" said the landlady, "*Messieurs, il m'a gâté trois matelas, et il me doit quarante quatre francs.*"

* In order to account for these trivial details, the reader must be told that the story is, for the chief part, a fact; and that the little sketch, in this page, was *taken from nature*. The letter was likewise a copy from one found in the manner described.

This was all his epitaph : he had spoiled three mattresses, and owed the landlady four-and-forty francs. In the whole world there was not a soul to love him or lament him. We, his friends, were looking at his body more as an object of curiosity, watching it with a kind of interest with which one follows the fifth act of a tragedy, and leaving it with the same feeling with which, one leaves the theatre when the play is over and the curtain is down.

Beside Jack's bed, on his little "table de nuit," lay the remains of his last meal, and an open letter, which we read. It was from one of his suspicious acquaintances of former days, and ran thus :—

"Où es tu, cher Jack ? *why you not come and see me* —tu me dois de l'argent, entends tu ?—un chapeau, une cachemire, *a box of the Play*. Viens demain soir, je t'attendrai *at eight o'clock*, Passage des Panoramas. *My Sir is at his country*. Adieu à demain.   Fifine."

"Samedi."

*   *   *   *   *   *

I shuddered as I walked through this very Passage des Panoramas, in the evening. The girl was there, pacing to and fro, and looking in the countenance of every passer-by, to recognize Attwood. "Adieu à demain !"—there was a dreadful meaning in the words, which the writer of them little knew. "Adieu à demain !"—the morrow was come, and the soul of the poor suicide was now in the presence of God. I dare not think of his fate ; for, except in the fact of his poverty and desperation, was he worse than any of us, his companions, who had shared his debauches, and marched with him up to the very brink of the grave ?

There is but one more circumstance to relate regarding poor Jack—his burial; it was of a piece with his death.

He was nailed into a paltry coffin, and buried, at the expense of the arrondissement, in a nook of the burial place, beyond the Barrière de l'Etoile. They buried him at six o'clock, of a bitter winter's morning, and it was with difficulty that an English clergyman could be found to read a service over his grave. The three men who have figured in this history acted as Jack's mourners; and as the ceremony was to take place so early in the morning, these men sate up the night through, *and were almost drunk* as they followed his coffin to its resting place.

MORAL.

"When we turned out in our great-coats," said one of them afterwards, "reeking of cigars and brandy-and-water, d——e, sir, we quite frightened the old buck of a parson; he did not much like our company." After the ceremony was concluded, these gentlemen were very happy to get home to a warm and comfortable breakfast, and finished the day royally at Frascati's.

NAPOLEON AND HIS SYSTEM.

ON PRINCE LOUIS NAPOLEON'S WORK.

Any person who recollects the history of the absurd outbreak of Strasburg, in which Prince Louis Napoleon Bonaparte figured, three years ago, must remember that, however silly the revolt was, however foolish its pretext, however doubtful its aim, and inexperienced its leader, there was, nevertheless, a party, and a considerable one in France, that were not unwilling to lend the new projectors their aid. The troops who declared against the Prince, were, it was said, all but willing to declare for him; and it was certain that, in many of the regiments of the army, there existed a strong spirit of disaffection, and an eager wish for the return of the imperial system and family.

As to the good that was to be derived from the change, that is another question. Why the Emperor of the French should be better than the King of the French, or the King of the French better than the King of France and Navarre, it is not our business to inquire; but all the three monarchs have no lack of supporters; republicanism has no lack of supporters; St. Simonianism was followed by a respectable body of admirers; Robespierrism has a select party of friends. If, in a country where so many quacks have had their day, Prince Louis Napoleon thought he might renew the imperial quackery, why should he not? It has recollections with it that must always be dear to a gallant nation; it has certain claptraps in its vocabulary that can never fail to inflame a vain, restless, grasping, disappointed one.

In the first place, and don't let us endeavour to disguise it, they hate us. Not all the protestations of friendship, not all the wisdom of Lord Palmerston, not all the diplomacy of our distinguished plenipotentiary, Mr. Henry Lytton Bulwer, and, let us add, not all the benefit which both countries would derive from the alliance, can make it, in our times at least, permanent and cordial. They hate us. The Carlist organs revile us with a querulous fury that never sleeps; the moderate party, if they admit the utility of our alliance, are continually pointing out our treachery, our insolence, and our monstrous infractions of it; and for the Republicans, as sure as the morning comes, the columns of their journals thunder out volleys of fierce denunciations against our unfortunate country. They live by feeding the natural hatred against England, by keeping old wounds open, by recurring ceaselessly to the history of old quarrels, and as in these we, by God's help, by land and by sea, in old times and late, have had the uppermost, they perpetuate the shame and mortification of the losing party, the bitterness of past defeats, and the eager desire to avenge them. A party which knows how to *exploiter* this hatred will always be popular to a certain extent; and the imperial scheme has this, at least, among its conditions.

Then there is the favourite claptrap of the "natural frontier." The Frenchman yearns to be bounded by the Rhine and the Alps; and next follows the cry, "Let France take her place among nations, and direct, as she ought to do, the affairs of Europe." These are the two chief articles contained in the new imperial programme, if we may credit the journal which has been established to advocate the cause. A natural boundary—stand among the nations—popular development—Russian alliance, and a reduction of *la perfide Albion* to its proper insignificance. As yet we know little more of the plan: and yet such foundations are sufficient to build a party upon, and with such windy weapons a substantial Government is to be overthrown!

In order to give these doctrines, such as they are, a chance of finding favour with his countrymen, Prince Louis has the advantage of being able to refer to a former great professor of them—his uncle Napoleon. His attempt is at once pious and prudent; it exalts the memory of the uncle, and furthers the interests of the nephew, who attempts to show what Napoleon's ideas really were; what good had already resulted from the practice of them; how cruelly they had been thwarted by foreign wars and difficulties; and what vast benefits *would* have resulted from them; ay, and (it is reasonable to conclude) might still, if the French nation would be wise enough to pitch upon a governor that would continue the interrupted scheme. It is, however, to be borne in mind, that the Emperor Napoleon had certain arguments in favour of his opinions for the time being, which his nephew has not employed. On the 13th Vendemiaire, when General Bonaparte believed in the excellence of a Directory, it may be remembered that he aided his opinions by forty pieces of artillery, and by Colonel Murat at the head of his dragoons. There was no resisting such a philosopher; the Directory was established forthwith, and the sacred cause of the minority triumphed. In like manner, when the General was convinced of the weakness of the Directory, and saw fully the necessity of establishing a Consulate, what were his arguments? Moreau, Lannes, Murat, Berthier, Leclerc, Lefebvre—gentle apostles of the truth!—marched to St. Cloud, and there, with fixed bayonets, caused it to prevail. Error vanished in an instant. At once five hundred of its high-priests tumbled out of windows, and lo! three Consuls appeared to guide the destinies of France! How much more expeditious, reasonable, and clinching was this argument of the 18th Brumaire, than any one that can be found in any pamphlet! A fig for your duodecimos and octavos! Talk about points, there are none like those at the end of a bayonet; and the most powerful of styles is a good rattling "article" from a nine-pounder.

At least this is our interpretation of the manner in which were always propagated the *Idées Napoléoniennes*. Not such, however, is Prince Louis's belief; and, if you wish to go along with him in opinion, you will discover that a more liberal, peaceable, prudent Prince never existed: you will read that "the mission of Napoleon" was to be the "*testamentary executor of the revolution;*" and the Prince should have added, the legatee; or, more justly still, as well as the *executor*, he should be called the *executioner*, and then his title would be complete. In Vendemiaire, the military Tartuffe, he threw aside the Revolution's natural heirs, and made her, as it were, *alter her will;* on the 18th of Brumaire he strangled her, and on the 19th seized on her property, and kept it until force deprived him of it. Illustrations, to be sure, are no arguments, but the example is the Prince's, not ours.

In the Prince's eyes, then, his uncle is a god; of all monarchs, the most wise, upright, and merciful. Thirty years ago the opinion had millions of supporters; while millions, again, were ready to avouch the exact contrary. It is curious to think of the former difference of opinion concerning Napoleon; and, in reading his nephew's rapturous encomiums of him, one goes back to the days when we ourselves were as loud and mad in his dispraise. Who does not remember his own personal hatred and horror, twenty-five years ago, for the man whom we used to call the "bloody Corsican upstart and assassin?" What stories did we not believe of him?—what murders, rapes, robberies, not lay to his charge?—we, who were living within a few miles of his territory, and might, by books and newspapers, be made as well acquainted with his merits or demerits as any of his own countrymen.

Then was the age when the *Idées Napoléoniennes* might have passed through many editions; for, while we were thus outrageously bitter, our neighbours were as extravagantly attached to him, by a strange infatuation—adored him like a god, whom we chose to consider as a fiend; and vowed that, under his government, their nation had attained its highest pitch of grandeur and glory. In revenge there existed in England (as is proved by a thousand authentic documents) a monster so hideous, a tyrant so ruthless and bloody, that the world's history cannot shew his parallel. This ruffian's name was, during the early part of the French revolution, Pittetcobourg. Pittetcobourg's emissaries were in every corner of France; Pittetcobourg's gold chinked in the pockets of every traitor in Europe; it menaced the life of the god-like Robespierre; it drove into cellars and fits of delirium even the gentle philanthropist Marat; it fourteen times caused the dagger to be lifted against the bosom of the First Consul, Emperor, and King,—that first, great, glorious, irresistible, cowardly, contemptible, bloody hero and fiend, Bonaparte, before mentioned.

On our side of the Channel we have had leisure, long since, to re-consider our verdict against Napoleon; though, to be sure, we have not changed our opinion about Pittetcobourg. After five-and-thirty years all parties bear witness to his honesty, and speak with affectionate reverence of his patriotism, his genius, and his private virtue. In France, however, or, at least, among certain parties in France, there has been no such modification of opinion. With the Republicans, Pittetcobourg is Pittetcobourg still,—crafty, bloody, seeking whom he may devour; and *perfide Albion* more perfidious than ever. This hatred is the point of union between the Republic and the Empire; it has been fostered ever since, and must be continued by Prince Louis, if he would hope to conciliate both parties.

With regard to the Emperor, then, Prince Louis erects to his memory as fine a monument as his wits can raise. One need not say that the imperial apologist's opinion should be received with the utmost caution; for a man who has such a hero for an uncle may naturally be proud of and partial to him; and when this nephew of the great man would be his heir, likewise, and, bearing his name, step also into his imperial shoes, one may reasonably look for much affectionate panegyric. "The empire was the best of empires," cries the Prince; and possibly it was; undoubtedly, the Prince thinks it was; but he is the very last person who would convince a man with the proper suspicious impartiality. One remembers a certain consultation of politicians which is recorded in the Spelling-book; and the opinion of that patriotic sage who avowed that, for a real blameless constitution, an impenetrable shield for liberty, and cheap defence of nations, there was nothing like leather.

Let us examine some of the Prince's article. If we may be allowed humbly to express an opinion, his leather is not only quite insufficient for those vast public purposes for which he destines it, but is, moreover, and in itself, very *bad leather*. The hides are poor, small, unsound slips of skin; or, to drop this cobbling metaphor, the style is not particularly brilliant, the facts not very startling, and, as for the conclusions, one may differ with almost every one of them. Here is an extract from his first chapter, " on Governments in general:"—

"I speak it with regret, I can see but two Governments, at this day, which fulfil the mission that Providence has confided to them : they are the two colossi at the end of the world; one at the extremity of the old world, the other at the extremity of the new. Whilst our old European centre is as a volcano, consuming itself in its crater, the two nations of the East and the West march, without hesitation, towards perfection ; the one under the will of a single individual, the other under liberty.

"Providence has confided to the United States of North America the task of peopling and civilizing that immense territory which stretches from the Atlantic to the South Sea, and from the North Pole to the Equator. The Government, which is only a simple administration, has only hitherto been called upon to put in practice the old adage, *Laissez faire, laissez passer,* in order to favour that irresistible instinct which pushes the people of America to the west.

"In Russia it is to the imperial dynasty that is owing all the vast progress which, in a century and a half, has rescued that empire from barbarism. The imperial power must contend against all the ancient prejudices of our old Europe : it must centralize, as far as possible, all the powers of the state in the hands of one person, in order to destroy the abuses which the feudal and communal franchises have served to perpetuate. The last alone can hope to receive from it the improvements which it expects.

"But thou, France of Henry IV., of Louis XIV., of Carnot, of Napoleon—thou, who wert always for the west of Europe the source of progress, who possessest in thyself the two great pillars of empire, the genius for the arts of peace, and the genius of war—hast thou no further mission to fulfil ? Wilt thou never cease to waste thy force and energies in intestine struggles ? No ; such cannot be thy destiny : the day will soon come, when, to govern thee, it will be necessary to understand that thy part is to place in all treaties thy sword of Brennus on the side of civilization."

These are the conclusions of the Prince's remarks upon Governments in general ; and it must be supposed that the reader is very little wiser at the end than at the beginning. But two Governments in the world fulfil their mission : the one government, which is no government ; the other, which is a despotism. The duty of France is *in all treaties* to place her sword of Brennus in the scale of civilization. Without quarrelling with the somewhat confused language of the latter proposition, may we ask what, in Heaven's name, is the meaning of all the three ? What is this *épée de Brennus ?* and how is France to use it ? Where is the great source of political truth, from which, flowing pure, we trace American republicanism in one stream, Russian despotism in another ? Vastly prosperous is the great republic, if you will : if dollars and cents constitute happiness, there is plenty for all : but can any one, who has read of the American doings in the late frontier troubles, and the daily disputes on the slave question, praise the *Government* of the States ?—a Government which dares not punish homicide or arson performed before its very eyes, and which the pirates of Texas and the pirates of Canada can brave at their will ? There is no government, but a prosperous anarchy; as the Prince's other favourite government is a prosperous slavery. What, then, is to be the *épée de Brennus* government? Is it to be a mixture of the two? "Society," writes the Prince, axiomatically, "contains in itself two principles—the one of progress and immortality, the other of disease and disorganization." No doubt; and as the one tends towards liberty, so the other is only to be cured by order: and then, with a singular felicity, Prince Louis picks us out a couple of governments, in one of which the common regulating power is as notoriously too weak, as it is in the other too strong, and talks in rapturous terms of the manner in which they fulfil their "providential mission!"

From these considerations on things in general, the Prince conducts us to Napoleon in particular, and enters largely into a discussion of the merits of the imperial system. Our author speaks of the Emperor's advent in the following grandiose way :—

"Napoleon, on arriving at the public stage, saw that his part was to be the *testamentary executor* of the Revolution. The destructive fire of parties was extinct; and when the Revolution, dying, but not vanquished, delegated to Napoleon the accomplishment of her last will, she said to him, 'Establish upon solid bases the principal result of my efforts. Unite divided Frenchmen. Defeat feudal Europe that is leagued against me. Cicatrize my wounds. Enlighten the nations. Execute that in width, which I have had to perform in depth. Be for Europe what I have been for France. And, even if you must water the tree of civilization with your blood—if you must see your projects misunderstood, and your sons without a country, wandering over the face of the earth, never abandon the sacred cause of the French people. Insure its triumph by all the means which genius can discover and humanity approve.'

"This grand mission Napoleon performed to the end. His task was difficult. He had to place upon new principles a society still boiling with hatred and revenge; and to use, for building up, the same instruments which had been employed for pulling down.

"The common lot of every new truth that arises, is to wound rather than to convince—rather than to gain proselytes, to awaken fear. For, oppressed as it long has been, it rushes forward with additional force; having to encounter obstacles, it is compelled to combat them, and overthrow them; until, at length, comprehended and adopted by the generality, it becomes the basis of new social order.

"Liberty will follow the same march as the Christian religion. Armed with death from the ancient society of Rome, it for a long while excited the hatred and fear of the people. At last, by force of martyrdoms and persecutions, the religion of Christ penetrated into the conscience and the soul; it soon had kings and armies at its orders, and Constantine and Charlemagne bore it triumphant throughout Europe. Religion then laid down her arms of war. It laid open to all the principles of peace and order which it contained; it became the prop of Government, as it was the organizing element of society. Thus will it be with liberty. In 1793 it frightened people and sovereigns alike; thus, having clothed itself in a milder garb, *it insinuated itself everywhere in the train of our battalions.* In 1815 all parties adopted its flag, and armed themselves with its moral force—covered themselves with its colours. The adoption was not sincere, and liberty was soon obliged to re-assume its warlike accoutrements. With the contest their fears returned. Let us hope that they will soon cease, and that liberty will soon resume her peaceful standards, to quit them no more.

"The Emperor Napoleon contributed more than any one else towards accelerating the reign of liberty, by saving the moral influence of the revolution, and diminishing the fears which it imposed. Without the Consulate and the Empire, the revolution would have been only a grand drama, leaving grand revolutions but no traces: the revolution would have been drowned in the counter-revolution. The contrary, however, was the case. Napoleon rooted the revolution in France, and introduced, throughout Europe, the principal benefits of the crisis of 1789. To use his own words, 'He purified the revolution,' he confirmed kings, and ennobled people. He purified the revolution in separating the truths which it contained from the passions that, during its delirium, disfigured it. He ennobled the people in giving them the consciousness of their force, and those institutions which raise men in their own eyes. The Emperor may be considered as the Messiah of the new ideas; for, and we must confess it, in the moments immediately succeeding a social revolution, it is not so essential to put rigidly into practice all the propositions resulting from the new theory, but to become master of the regenerative genius, to identify one's self with the sentiments of the people, and boldly to direct them towards the desired point. To accomplish such a task *your fibre should respond to that of the people*, as the Emperor said; you should feel like it, your interests should be so intimately raised with its own, that you should vanquish or fall together."

Let us take breath after these big phrases,—grand round figures of speech,—which, when put together, amount, like certain other combinations of round figures, to exactly 0. We shall not stop to argue the merits and demerits of Prince Louis's notable comparison between the Christian religion and the Imperial-revolutionary system. There are many blunders in the above extract as we read it; blundering metaphors, blundering arguments, and blundering assertions; but this is surely the grandest blunder of all; and one wonders at the blindness of the legislator and historian who can advance such a parallel. And what are we to say of the legacy of the dying revolution to Napoleon? Revolutions do not die, and, on their death-beds, making fine speeches, hand over their property to young officers of artillery. We have all read the history of his rise. The constitution of the year III. was carried. Old men of the Montagne, disguised royalists, Paris sections, *Pittetcobourg*, above all, with his money-bags, thought that here was a fine opportunity for a revolt, and opposed the new constitution in arms: the new constitution had knowledge of a young officer, who would not hesitate to defend its cause, and who effectually beat the majority. The tale may be found

12—2

in every account of the revolution, and the rest of his story need not be told. We know every step that he took: we know how, by doses of cannon-balls promptly administered, he cured the fever of the sections—that fever which another camp-physician (Menou) declined to prescribe for; we know how he abolished the Directory; and how the Consulship came; and then the Empire; and then the disgrace, exile, and lonely death. Has not all this been written by historians in all tongues?—by memoir-writing pages, chamberlains, marshals, lackeys, secretaries, contemporaries, and ladies of honour? Not a word of miracle is there in all this narration; not a word of celestial missions, or political Messiahs. From Napoleon's rise to his fall, the bayonet marches alongside of him: now he points it at the tails of the scampering "five hundred," —now he charges with it across the bloody planks of Arcola, —now he flies before it over the fatal plain of Waterloo.

Unwilling, however, as he may be to grant that there are any spots in the character of his hero's government, the Prince is, nevertheless, obliged to allow that such existed; that the Emperor's manner of rule was a little more abrupt and dictatorial than might possibly be agreeable. For this the Prince has always an answer ready—it is the same poor one that Napoleon uttered a million of times to his companions in exile—the excuse of necessity. He *would* have been very liberal, but that the people were not fit for it; or that the cursed war prevented him—or any other reason why. His first duty, however, says his apologist, was to form a general union of Frenchmen, and he set about his plan in this wise :—

"Let us not forget, that all which Napoleon undertook, in order to create a general fusion, he performed without renouncing the principles of the revolution. He recalled the *émigrés*, without touching upon the law by which their goods had been confiscated and sold as public property. He re-established the Catholic religion at the same time that he proclaimed the liberty of conscience, and endowed equally the ministers of all sects. He caused himself to be consecrated by the Sovereign Pontiff, without conceding to the Pope's demand any of the liberties of the Gallican church. He married a daughter of the Emperor of Austria, without abandoning any of the rights of France to the conquests she had made. He re-established noble titles, without attaching to them any privileges or prerogatives, and these titles were conferred on all ranks, on all services, on all professions. Under the empire all idea of caste was destroyed; no man ever thought of vaunting his pedigree —no man ever was asked how he was born, but what he had done.

"The first quality of a people which aspires to liberal government, is respect to the law. Now, a law has no other power than lies in the interest which each citizen has to defend or to contravene it. In order to make a people respect the law, it was necessary that it should be executed in the interest of all, and should consecrate the principle of equality in all its extension. It was necessary to restore the *prestige* with which the Government had been formerly invested, and to make the principles of the revolution take root in the public manners. At the commencement of a new society, it is the legislator who makes or corrects the manners; later, it is the manners which make the law, or preserve it, from age to age intact."

Some of these fusions are amusing. No man in the empire was asked how he was born, but what he had done; and, accordingly, as a man's actions were sufficient to illustrate him, the Emperor took care to make a host of new title-bearers, princes, dukes, barons, and what not, whose rank has descended to their children. He married a princess of Austria; but, for all that, did not abandon his conquests—perhaps not actually; but he abandoned his allies, and, eventually, his whole kingdom. Who does not recollect his answer to the Poles, at the commencement of the Russian campaign? But for Napoleon's imperial father-in-law, Poland would have been a kingdom, and his race, perhaps, imperial still. Why was he to fetch this princess out of Austria to make heirs for his throne? Why did not the man of the people marry a girl of the people? Why must he have a pope to crown him—half-a-dozen kings for brothers, and a bevy of aides-de-camp dressed out like so many mountebanks from Astley's, with duke's coronets, and grand blue velvet marshals' batons? We have repeatedly his words for it. He wanted to create an aristocracy—another acknowledgment on his part of the Republican dilemma—another apology for the revolutionary blunder. To keep the republic within bounds, a despotism is necessary; to rally round the despotism, an aristocracy must be created; and for what have we been labouring all this while? for what have bastiles been battered down, and kings' heads hurled, as a gage of battle, in the face of armed Europe? To have a Duke of Otranto instead of a

Duke de la Tremuoille, and Emperor Stork in place of King Log. O lame conclusion! Is the blessed revolution which is prophesied for us in England only to end in establishing a Prince Fergus O'Connor, or a Cardinal Wade, or a Duke Daniel Whittle Harvey? Great as those patriots are, we love them better under their simple family names, and scorn titles and coronets.

At present, in France, the delicate matter of titles seems to be better arranged, any gentleman, since the revolution, being free to adopt any one he may fix upon; and it appears that the Crown no longer confers any patents of nobility, but contents itself with saying, as in the case of M. de Pontois, the other day, "*Le Roi trouve convenable* that you take the title of," &c.

To execute the legacy of the revolution, then; to fulfil his providential mission; to keep his place,—in other words, for the simplest are always the best,—to keep his place, and to keep his Government in decent order, the Emperor was obliged to establish a military despotism, to re-establish honours and titles; it was necessary, as the Prince confesses, to restore the old *prestige* of the Government, in order to make the people respect it; and he adds —a truth which one hardly would expect from him,—" At the commencement of a new society, it is the legislator who makes and corrects the manners; later, it is the manners which preserve the laws." Of course, and here is the great risk that all revolutionizing people run—they must tend to despotism; "they must personify themselves in a man," is the Prince's phrase; and, according as is his temperament or disposition—according as he is a Cromwell, a Washington, or a Napoleon—the revolution becomes tyranny or freedom, prospers or falls.

Somewhere in the St. Helena memorials, Napoleon reports a message of his to the Pope. "Tell the Pope," he says to an archbishop, "to remember that I have six hundred thousand armed Frenchmen, *qui marcheront avec moi, pour moi, et comme moi.*" And this is the legacy of the revolution, the advancement of freedom! A hundred volumes of imperial special pleading will not avail against such a speech as this—one so insolent, and, at the same time so humiliating, which gives unwittingly the whole of the Emperor's progress, strength, and weakness. The six hundred thousand armed Frenchmen were used up, and the whole fabric falls; the six hundred thousand are reduced to sixty thousand, and straightway all the rest of the fine imperial scheme vanishes: the miserable senate, so crawling and abject but now, becomes, of a sudden, endowed with a wondrous independence; the miserable sham nobles, sham empress, sham kings, dukes, princes, chamberlains, pack up their plumes and embroideries, pounce upon what money and plate they can lay their hands on, and when the allies appear before Paris, when for courage and manliness there is yet hope, when with fierce marches hastening to the relief of his capital, bursting through ranks upon ranks of the enemy, and crushing or scattering them from the path of his swift and victorious despair, the Emperor at last is at home,—where are the great dignitaries and the lieutenant-generals of the empire? Where is Maria Louisa, the Empress Eagle, with her little callow King of Rome? Is she going to defend her nest and her eaglet? Not she. Empress-queen, lieutenant-general, and court dignitaries, are off on the wings of all the winds—*profligati sunt*, they are away with the money-bags, and Louis Stanislas Xavier rolls into the palace of his fathers.

With regard to Napoleon's excellences as an administrator, a legislator, a constructor of public works, and a skilful financier, his nephew speaks with much diffuse praise, and few persons, we suppose, will be disposed to contradict him. Whether the Emperor composed his famous code, or borrowed it, is of little importance; but he established it, and made the law equal for every man in France, except one. His vast public works and vaster wars were carried on without new loans, or exorbitant taxes; it was only the blood and liberty of the people that were taxed, and we shall want a better advocate than Prince Louis to show us that these were not most unnecessarily and lavishly thrown away. As for the former and material improvements, it is not necessary to confess here that a despotic energy can effect such far more readily than a Government of which the strength is diffused in many conflicting parties. No doubt, if we could create a despotical governing machine, a steam autocrat,—passionless, untiring, and supreme,—we should advance further, and live more at ease than under any other form of government. Ministers might enjoy their pensions, and follow their own devices; Lord John might compose histories or tragedies at his leisure, and Lord Palmerston, instead of racking his brains to write leading articles for Cupid, might crown his locks with flowers, and sing ἔρωτα μοῦνον, his natural Anacreontics; but, alas! not so: if the despotic Government has its good side, Prince Louis Napoleon must acknowledge that it has its bad, and it is for this that the civilized world is compelled to substitute for it something more orderly, and less capricious. Good as the Imperial Government might have been, it must be recollected, too, that since its first fall, both the Emperor and his admirer and would-be successor have had their chance of re-establishing it. "Fly from steeple to steeple" the eagles of the former did actually, and according to promise perch for a while on the towers of Notre Dame. We know the event: if the fate of war declared against the Emperor, the country declared against him too; and, with old Lafayette for a mouthpiece, the representatives of the nation did, in a neat speech, pronounce themselves in permanence, but spoke no more of the Emperor than if he had never been. Thereupon the Emperor proclaimed his son the Emperor Napoleon II. "L'Empereur est mort, vive l'Empereur!" shouted Prince Lucien. Psha! not a soul echoed the words: the play was played, and as for old Lafayette and his "permanent" representatives, a corporal with a hammer nailed up the door of their spouting-club, and once more Louis Stanislas Xavier rolled back to the bosom of his people.

In like manner, Napoleon III. returned from exile, and made his appearance on the frontier. His eagle appeared at Strasburg, and from Strasburg advanced to the capital; but it arrived at Paris with a keeper, and in a postchaise; whence, by the orders of the sovereign, it was removed to the American shores, and there magnanimously let loose. Who knows, however, how soon it may be on the wing again, and what a flight it will take?

THE STORY OF MARY ANCEL.

"Go, my nephew," said old Father Jacob to me, "and complete thy studies at Strasburg: Heaven, surely, hath ordained thee for the ministry in these times of trouble, and my excellent friend Schneider will work out the divine intention."

Schneider was an old college friend of uncle Jacob's, was a Benedictine monk, and a man famous for his learning; as for me, I was at that time my uncle's chorister, clerk, and sacristan; I swept the church, chanted the prayers with my shrill treble, and swung the great copper incense-pot on Sundays and feasts; and I toiled over the Fathers for the other days of the week.

The old gentleman said that my progress was prodigious, and, without vanity, I believe he was right, for I then verily considered that praying was my vocation, and not fighting, as I have found since.

You would hardly conceive (said the Major, swearing a great oath) how devout and how learned I was in those days; I talked Latin faster than my own beautiful *patois* of Alsatian French; I could utterly overthrow, in argument, every Protestant (heretics we called them) parson in the neighbourhood, and there was a confounded sprinkling of these unbelievers in our part of the country. I prayed half-a-dozen times a day; I fasted thrice in a week; and, as for penance, I used to scourge my little sides, till they had no more feeling than a peg-top: such was the godly life I led at my uncle Jacob's in the village of Steinbach.

Our family had long dwelt in this place, and a large farm and a pleasant house were then in the possession of another uncle—uncle Edward. He was the youngest of the three sons of my grandfather; but Jacob, the elder, had shown a decided vocation for the church, from, I believe, the age of three, and now was by no means tired of it at sixty. My father, who was to have inherited the paternal property, was, as I hear, a terrible scamp and scapegrace, quarrelled with his family, and disappeared altogether, living and dying at Paris; so far, we knew through my mother, who came, poor woman, with me, a child of six months, on her bosom, was refused all shelter by my grandfather, but was housed and kindly cared for by my good uncle Jacob.

Here she lived for about seven years, and the old gentleman, when she died, wept over her grave a great deal more than I did, who was then too young to mind anything but toys or sweetmeats.

During this time my grandfather was likewise carried off: he left, as I said, the property to his son Edward, with a small proviso in his will that something should be done for me, his grandson.

Edward was himself a widower, with one daughter, Mary, about three years older than I, and certainly she was the dearest little treasure with which Providence ever blessed a miserly father; by the time she was fifteen, five farmers, three lawyers, twelve Protestant parsons, and a lieutenant of dragoons had made her offers: it must not be denied that she was an heiress as well as a beauty, which, perhaps, had something to do with the love of these gentlemen. However, Mary declared that she intended to live single, turned away her lovers one after another, and devoted herself to the care of her father.

Uncle Jacob was as fond of her as he was of any saint or martyr. As for me, at the mature age of twelve, I had made a kind of divinity of her, and when we sang Ave Maria on Sundays I could not refrain from turning to her, where she knelt, blushing and praying and looking like an angel, as she was. Besides her beauty, Mary had a thousand good qualities; she could play better on the harpsichord, she could dance more lightly, she could make better pickles and puddings, than any girl in Alsace; there was not a want or a fancy of the old hunks, her father, or a wish of mine or my uncle's, that she would not gratify if she could; as for herself, the sweet soul had neither wants nor wishes except to see us happy.

I could talk to you for a year of all the pretty kindnesses that she would do for me; how, when she found me of early mornings among my books, her presence "would cast a light upon the day;" how she used to smooth and fold my little surplice, and embroider me caps and gowns for high feast-days; how she used to bring flowers for the altar: and who could deck it so well as she? But sentiment does not come glibly from under a grizzled moustache, so I will drop it, if you please.

Amongst other favours she shewed me, Mary used to be particularly fond of kissing me: it was a thing I did not so much value in those days, but I found that the more I grew alive to the extent of the benefit, the less she would condescend to confer it on me; till, at last, when I was about fourteen, she discontinued it altogether, of her own wish at least; only sometimes I used to be rude, and take what she had now become so mighty unwilling to give.

I was engaged in a contest of this sort one day with Mary, when, just as I was about to carry off a kiss from her cheek, I was saluted with a staggering slap on my own, which was bestowed by uncle Edward, and sent me reeling some yards down the garden.

The old gentleman, whose tongue was generally as close as his purse, now poured forth a flood of eloquence which quite astonished me. I did not think that so much was to be said on any subject as he managed to utter on one, and that was abuse of me; he stamped, he swore, he screamed; and then, from complimenting me, he turned to Mary, and saluted her in a manner equally forcible and significant: she, who was very much frightened at the commencement of the scene, grew very angry at the coarse words he used, and the wicked motives he imputed to her.

"The child is but fourteen," she said; "he is your own nephew, and a candidate for holy orders:—father, it is a shame that you should thus speak of me, your daughter, or of one of his holy profession."

Mary Ann.

I did not particularly admire this speech myself, but it had an effect on my uncle, and was the cause of the words with which this history commences. The old gentleman persuaded his brother that I must be sent to Strasburg, and there kept until my studies for the church were concluded. I was furnished with a letter to my uncle's old college chum, Professor Schneider, who was to instruct me in theology and Greek.

I was not sorry to see Strasburg, of the wonders of which I had heard so much; but felt very loth as the time drew near when I must quit my pretty cousin, and my good old uncle. Mary and I managed, however, a parting walk, in which a number of tender things were said on both sides. I am told that you Englishmen consider it cowardly to cry; as for me, I wept and roared incessantly: when Mary squeezed me, for the last time, the tears came out of me as if I had been neither more nor less than a great wet sponge. My cousin's eyes were stoically dry; her ladyship had a part to play, and it would have been wrong for her to be in love with a young chit of fourteen—so she carried herself with perfect coolness, as if there was nothing the matter. I should not have known that she cared for me, had it not been for a letter which she wrote me a month afterwards—*then*, nobody was by, and the consequence was that the letter was half washed away with her weeping; if she had used a watering-pot the thing could not have been better done.

Well, I arrived at Strasburg—a dismal, old-fashioned, rickety town in those days—and straightway presented myself and letter at Schneider's door; over it was written—

COMITE DE SALUT PUBLIC.

Would you believe it? I was so ignorant a young fellow, that I had no idea of the meaning of the words; however, I entered the citizen's room without fear, and sate down in his ante-chamber until I could be admitted to see him.

Here I found very few indications of his reverence's profession; the walls were hung round with portraits of Robespierre, Marat, and the like; a great bust of Mirabeau, mutilated, with the word *Traitre* underneath; lists and republican proclamations, tobacco-pipes and fire-arms. At a deal-table, stained with grease and wine, sate a gentleman, with a huge pig-tail dangling down to that part of his person which immediately succeeds his back, and a red nightcap, containing a *tricolor* cockade as large as a pancake. He was smoking a short pipe, reading a little book, and sobbing as if his heart would break. Every now and then he would make brief remarks upon the personages or the incidents of his book, by which I could judge that he was a man of the very keenest sensibilities—"*Ah brigand!*" "*O malheureuse!*" "*O Charlotte, Charlotte!*" The work which this gentleman was perusing is called "The Sorrows of Werter;" it was all the rage in those days, and my friend was only following the fashion. I asked him if I could see Father Schneider? he turned towards me a hideous, pimpled face, which I dream of now at forty years' distance.

"Father who?" said he. "Do you imagine that citizen Schneider has not thrown off the absurd mummery of priesthood? If you were a little older you would go to prison for calling him Father Schneider—many a man has died for less;" and he pointed to a picture of a guillotine, which was hanging in the room.

I was in amazement.

"What is he? Is he not a teacher of Greek, an abbé, a monk, until monasteries were abolished, the learned editor of the songs of 'Anacreon?'"

"He *was* all this," replied my grim friend; "he is now a Member of the Committee of Public Safety, and would think no more of ordering your head off than of drinking this tumbler of beer."

He swallowed, himself, the frothy liquid, and then proceeded to give me the history of the man to whom my uncle had sent me for instruction.

Schneider was born in 1756: was a student at Würzburg, and afterwards entered a convent, where he remained nine years. He here became distinguished for his learning and his talents as a preacher, and became chaplain to Duke Charles of Würtemberg. The doctrines of the Illuminati began about this time to spread in Germany, and Schneider speedily joined the sect. He had been a professor of Greek at Cologne; and being compelled, on account of his irregularity, to give up his chair, he came to Strasburg at the commencement of the French Revolution, and acted for some time a principal part as a revolutionary agent at Strasburg.

["Heaven knows what would have happened to me had I continued long under his tuition!" said the captain. "I owe the preservation of my morals entirely to my entering the army. A man, sir, who is a soldier, has very little time to be wicked; except in the case of a siege and the sack of a town, when a little licence can offend nobody."]

By the time that my friend had concluded Schneider's biography, we had grown tolerably intimate, and I imparted to him (with that experience so remarkable in youth) my whole history—my course of studies, my pleasant country life, the names and qualities of my dear relations, and my occupations in the vestry before religion was abolished by order of the republic. In the course of my speech I recurred so often to the name of my cousin Mary, that the gentleman could not fail to perceive what a tender place she had in my heart.

Then we reverted to "The Sorrows of Werter," and discussed the merits of that sublime performance. Although I had before felt some misgivings about my new acquaintance, my heart now quite yearned towards him. He talked about love and sentiment in a manner which made me recollect that I was in love myself; and you know that, when a man is in that condition, his taste is not very refined, any maudlin trash of prose or verse appearing sublime to him, provided it correspond, in some degree, with his own situation.

"Candid youth!" cried my unknown, "I love to hear thy innocent story, and look on thy guileless face. There is, alas! so much of the contrary in this world, so much terror, and crime, and blood, that we, who mingle with it, are only too glad to forget it. Would that we could shake off our cares as men, and be boys, as thou art, again!"

Here my friend began to weep once more, and fondly shook my hand. I blessed my stars that I had, at the very outset of my career, met with one who was so likely to aid me. What a slanderous world it is, thought I; the people in our village call these republicans wicked and bloody-minded: a lamb could not be more tender than this sentimental bottle-nosed gentleman! The worthy man then gave me to understand that he held a place under Government. I was busy in endeavouring to discover what his situation might be, when the door of the next apartment opened, and Schneider made his appearance.

At first he did not notice me, but he advanced to my new acquaintance, and gave him, to my astonishment, something very like a blow.

"You drunken, talking fool," he said, "you are always after your time. Fourteen people are cooling their heels yonder, waiting until you have finished your beer and your sentiment!"

My friend slunk, muttering, out of the room.

"That fellow," said Schneider, turning to me, "is our public executioner: a capital hand, too, if he would but keep decent time; but the brute is always drunk, and blubbering over 'The Sorrows of Werter!'"

* * * * *

I know not whether it was his old friendship for my uncle, or my proper merits, which won the heart of this the sternest ruffian of Robespierre's crew; but certain it is, that he became strangely attached to me, and kept me constantly about his person. As for the priesthood and the Greek, they were, of course, very soon out of the question.

The Austrians were on our frontier; every day brought us accounts of battles won; and the youth of Strasburg, and of all France, indeed, were bursting with military ardour. As for me, I shared the general mania, and speedily mounted a cockade as large as that of my friend the executioner.

The occupations of this worthy were unremitting. Saint Just, who had come down from Paris to preside over our town, executed the laws and the aristocrats with terrible punctuality; and Schneider used to make country excursions in search of offenders, with this fellow, as a provost-marshal, at his back. In the meantime, having entered my sixteenth year, and being a proper lad of my age, I had joined a regiment of cavalry, and was scampering now after the Austrians who menaced us, and now threatening the Emigrés, who were banded at Coblentz. My love for my dear cousin increased as my whiskers grew; and when I was scarcely seventeen, I thought myself man enough to marry her, and to cut the throat of any one who should venture to say me nay.

I need not tell you that during my absence at Strasburg, great changes had occurred in our little village, and somewhat of the revolutionary rage had penetrated even to that quiet and distant place. The hideous "Fête of the Supreme Being" had been celebrated at Paris; the practice of our ancient religion was forbidden; its professors were most of them in concealment, or in exile, or had expiated, on the scaffold, their crime of Christianity. In our poor village my uncle's church was closed, and he, himself, an inmate in my brother's house, only owing his safety to his great popularity among his former flock, and the influence of Edward Ancel.

The latter had taken in the revolution a somewhat prominent part; that is, he had engaged in many contracts for the army, attended the clubs regularly, corresponded with the authorities of his department, and was loud in his denunciations of the aristocrats in the neighbourhood. But owing, perhaps, to the German origin of the peasantry, and their quiet and rustic lives, the revolutionary fury which prevailed in the cities had hardly reached the country people. The occasional visit of a commissary from Paris or Strasburg, served to keep the flame alive, and to remind the rural swains of the existence of a republic in France.

Now and then, when I could gain a week's leave of absence, I returned to the village, and was received with tolerable politeness by my uncle, and with a warmer feeling by his daughter.

I won't describe to you the progress of our love, or the wrath of my uncle Edward, when he discovered that it still continued. He swore and he stormed; he locked Mary into her chamber, and vowed that he would withdraw the allowance he made me, if ever I ventured near her. His daughter, he said, should never marry a hopeless, penniless subaltern; and Mary declared she would not marry without his consent. What had I to do?—to despair and to leave her. As for my poor uncle Jacob, he had no counsel to give me, and, indeed, no spirit left: his little church was turned into a stable, his surplice torn off his shoulders, and he was only too lucky in keeping *his head* on them. A bright thought struck him: suppose you were to ask the advice of my old friend Schneider regarding this marriage? he has ever been your friend, and may help you now as before.

(Here the Captain paused a little.) You may fancy (continued he) that it was droll advice of a reverend gentleman like uncle Jacob to counsel me in this manner, and to bid me make friends with such a murderous cut-throat as Schneider; but we thought nothing of it in those days; guillotining was as common as dancing, and a man was only thought the better patriot the more severe he might be. I departed forthwith to Strasburg, and requested the vote and interest of the Citizen President of the Committee of Public Safety.

He heard me with a great deal of attention. I described to him most minutely the circumstance, expatiated upon the charms of my dear Mary, and painted her to him from head to foot. Her golden hair and her bright blushing cheeks, her slim waist and her tripping tiny feet; and furthermore, I added that she possessed a fortune which ought, by rights, to be mine, but for the miserly old father. "Curse him for an aristocrat!" concluded I, in my wrath.

As I had been discoursing about Mary's charms, Schneider listened with much complacency and attention: when I spoke about her fortune, his interest redoubled; and when I called her father an aristocrat, the worthy ex-jesuit gave a grin of satisfaction, which was really quite terrible. O fool that I was to trust him so far!

*　　*　　*　　*　　*

The very same evening an officer waited upon me with the following note from Saint Just:—

> "Strasburg, Fifth Year of the Republic, one and
> indivisible, 11 Ventose.

"THE citizen Pierre Ancel is to leave Strasburg within two hours, and to carry the enclosed despatches to the President of the Committee of Public Safety at Paris. The necessary leave of absence from his military duties has been provided. Instant punishment will follow the slightest delay on the road.—Salut et Fraternité."

There was no choice but obedience, and off I sped on my weary way to the capital.

As I was riding out of the Paris gate, I met an equipage which I knew to be that of Schneider. The ruffian smiled at me as I passed, and wished me a *bon voyage*. Behind his chariot came a curious machine, or cart; a great basket, three stout poles, and several planks, all painted red, were lying in this vehicle, on the top of which was seated my friend with the big cockade. It was the *portable guillotine*, which Schneider always carried with him on his travels. The *bourreau* was reading "The Sorrows of Werter," and looked as sentimental as usual.

I will not speak of my voyage, in order to relate to you Schneider's. My story had awakened the wretch's curiosity and avarice, and he was determined that such a prize as I had shown my cousin to be should fall into no hands but his own. No sooner, in fact, had I quitted his room, than he procured the order for my absence, and was on the way to Steinbach as I met him.

The journey is not a very long one; and on the next day my uncle Jacob was surprised by receiving a message that the citizen Schneider was in the village, and was coming to greet his old friend. Old Jacob was in an ecstasy, for he longed to see his college acquaintance, and he hoped, also, that Schneider had come into that part of the country upon the marriage-business of your humble servant. Of course, Mary was summoned to give her best dinner, and wear her best frock; and her father made ready to receive the new state-dignitary.

Schneider's carriage speedily rolled into the court-yard, and Schneider's *cart* followed, as a matter of course. The ex-priest only entered the house; his companion remaining with the horses to dine in private. Here was a most touching meeting between him and Jacob. They talked over their old college pranks and successes; they capped Greek verses, and quoted ancient epigrams upon their tutors, who had been dead since the Seven Years' war. Mary declared it was quite touching to listen to the merry friendly talk of these two old gentlemen.

After the conversation had continued for a time in this strain, Schneider drew up all of a sudden, and said, quietly, that he had come on particular and unpleasant business—hinting about troublesome times, spies, evil reports, and so forth. Then he called uncle Edward aside, and had with him a long and earnest conversation: so Jacob went out and talked with Schneider's *friend;* they speedily became very intimate, for the ruffian detailed all the circumstances of his interview with me. When he returned into the house, some time after this pleasing colloquy, he found the tone of the society strangely altered. Edward Ancel, pale as a sheet, trembling, and crying for mercy; poor

Mary weeping; and Schneider pacing energetically about the apartment, raging about the rights of man, the punishment of traitors, and the one and indivisible republic.

"Jacob," he said, as my uncle entered the room, "I was willing, for the sake of our old friendship, to forget the crimes of your brother. He is a known and dangerous aristocrat; he holds communications with the enemy on the frontier; he is a possessor of great and ill-gotten wealth, of which he has plundered the republic. Do you know," said he, turning to Edward Ancel, "where the least of these crimes, or the mere suspicion of them, would lead you?"

Poor Edward sate trembling in his chair, and answered not a word. He knew full well how quickly, in this dreadful time, punishment followed suspicion; and, though guiltless of all treason with the enemy, perhaps he was aware that, in certain contracts with the Government, he had taken to himself a more than patriotic share of profit.

"Do you know," resumed Schneider, in a voice of thunder, "for what purpose I came hither, and by whom I am accompanied? I am the administrator of the justice of the Republic. The life of yourself and your family is in my hands: yonder man, who follows me, is the executor of the law; he has rid the nation of hundreds of wretches like yourself. A single word from me, and your doom is sealed without hope, and your last hour is come. Ho! Gregoire!" shouted he; "is all ready?"

Gregoire replied from the court, "I can put up the machine in half an hour. Shall I go down to the village and call the troops and the law people?"

"Do you hear him?" said Schneider. "The guillotine is in the court-yard; your name is on my list, and I have witnesses to prove your crime. Have you a word in your defence?"

Not a word came; the old gentleman was dumb; but his daughter, who did not give way to his terror, spoke for him.

"You cannot, sir," said she, "although you say it, *feel* that my father is guilty; you would not have entered our house thus alone if you had thought it. You threaten him in this manner because you have something to ask and to gain from us: what is it, citizen?—tell us how much you value our lives, and what sum we are to pay for our ransom?"

"Sum!" said uncle Jacob; "he does not want money of us: my old friend, my college chum, does not come hither to drive bargains with anybody belonging to Jacob Ancel."

"Oh! no, sir, no, you can't want money of us," shrieked Edward; "we are the poorest people of the village: ruined, Monsieur Schneider, ruined in the cause of the republic."

"Silence, father," said my brave Mary; "this man wants a *price:* he comes, with his worthy friend yonder, to frighten us, not to kill us. If we die, he cannot touch a sou of our money; it is confiscated to the State. Tell us, sir, what is the price of our safety."

Schneider smiled, and bowed with perfect politeness.

"Mademoiselle Marie," he said, "is perfectly correct in her surmise. I do not want the life of this poor drivelling old man: my intentions are much more peaceable, be assured. It rests entirely with this accomplished young lady (whose spirit I like, and whose ready wit I admire), whether the business between us shall be a matter of love or death. I humbly offer myself, citizen Ancel, as a candidate for the hand of your charming daughter. Her goodness, her beauty, and the large fortune which I know you intend to give her, would render her a desirable match for the proudest man in the republic, and, I am sure, would make me the happiest."

"This must be a jest, Monsieur Schneider," said Mary, trembling, and turning deadly pale: "you cannot mean this; you do not know me; you never heard of me until to-day."

"Pardon me, *belle dame*," replied he; "your cousin Pierre has often talked to me of your virtues; indeed, it was by his special suggestion that I made the visit."

"It is false!—it is a base and cowardly lie!" exclaimed she (for the young lady's courage was up).—"Pierre never could have forgotten himself and me so as to offer me to one like you. You come here with a lie on your lips—a lie against my father, to swear his life away, against my dear cousin's honour and love. It is useless now to deny it: father, I love Pierre Ancel; I will marry no other but him—no, though our last penny were paid to this man as the price of our freedom."

Schneider's only reply to this was a call to his friend Gregoire.

"Send down to the village for the *maire* and some *gendarmes;* and tell your people to make ready."

"Shall I put *the machine* up?" shouted he of the sentimental turn.

"You hear him," said Schneider; "Marie Ancel, you may decide the fate of your father. I shall return in a few hours," concluded he, "and will then beg to know your decision."

The advocate of the rights of man then left the apartment, and left the family, as you may imagine, in no very pleasant mood.

Old uncle Jacob, during the few minutes which had elapsed in the enactment of this strange scene, sate staring wildly at Schneider, and holding Mary on his knees: the poor little thing had fled to him for protection, and not to her father, who was kneeling almost senseless at the window, gazing at the executioner and his hideous preparations. The instinct of the poor girl had not failed her; she knew that Jacob was her only protector, if not of her life—Heaven bless him!—of her honour. "Indeed," the old man said, in a stout voice, "this must never be, my dearest child—you must not marry this man. If it be the will of Providence that we fall, we shall have at least the thought to console us that we die innocent. Any man in France, at a time like this, would be a coward and traitor if he feared to meet the fate of the thousand brave and good who have preceded us."

"Who speaks of dying?" said Edward. "You, brother Jacob!—you would not lay that poor girl's head on the scaffold, or mine, your dear brother's. You will not let us die, Mary; you will not, for a small sacrifice, bring your poor old father into danger?"

Mary made no answer. "Perhaps," she said, "there is time for escape: he is to be here but in two hours; in two hours we may be safe, in concealment, or on the frontier." And she rushed to the door of the chamber, as if she would have instantly made the attempt: two *gendarmes* were at the door. "We have orders, Mademoiselle," they said, "to allow no one to leave this apartment until the return of the citizen Schneider."

Alas! all hope of escape was impossible. Mary became quite silent for a while; she would not speak to uncle Jacob; and, in reply to her father's eager questions, she only replied, coldly, that she would answer Schneider when he arrived.

The two dreadful hours passed away only too quickly; and, punctual to his appointment, the ex-monk appeared. Directly he entered, Mary advanced to him, and said, calmly,—

"Sir, I could not deceive you if I said that I freely accepted the offer which you have made me. I will be your wife; but I tell you that I love another; and that it is only to save the lives of those two old men that I yield my person up to you."

Schneider bowed, and said,—

"It is bravely spoken. I like your candour—your beauty. As for the love, excuse me for saying that is a matter of total indifference. I have no doubt, however, that it will come as soon as your feelings in favour of the young gentleman, your cousin, have lost their present fervour. That engaging young man has, at present, another mistress—Glory. He occupies, I believe, the distinguished post of corporal in a regiment which is about to march to—Perpignan, I believe."

It was, in fact, Monsieur Schneider's polite intention to banish me as far as possible from the place of my birth; and he had, accordingly, selected the Spanish frontier as the spot where I was to display my future military talents.

Mary gave no answer to this sneer: she seemed perfectly resigned and calm: she only said,—

"I must make, however, some conditions regarding our proposed marriage, which a gentleman of Monsieur Schneider's gallantry cannot refuse."

"Pray command me," replied the husband elect. "Fair lady, you know I am your slave."

"You occupy a distinguished political rank, citizen representative," said she; "and we in our village are likewise known and beloved. I should be ashamed, I confess, to wed you here; for our people would wonder at the sudden marriage, and imply that it was only by compulsion that I gave you my hand. Let us, then, perform this ceremony at Strasburg, before the public authorities of the city, with the state and solemnity which befits the marriage of one of the chief men of the Republic."

"Be it so, madam," he answered, and gallantly proceeded to embrace his bride.

Mary did not shrink from this ruffian's kiss; nor did she reply when poor old Jacob, who sat sobbing in a corner, burst out, and said,—

"O Mary, Mary, I did not think this of thee!"

"Silence, brother!" hastily said Edward; "my good son-in-law will pardon your ill-humour."

I believe uncle Edward in his heart was pleased at the notion of the marriage; he only cared for money and rank, and was little scrupulous as to the means of obtaining them.

The matter then was finally arranged; and presently, after Schneider had transacted the affairs which brought him into that part of the country, the happy bridal party set forward for Strasburg. Uncles Jacob and Edward occupied the back seat of the old family carriage, and the young bride and bridegroom (he was nearly Jacob's age) were seated majestically in front. Mary has often since talked to me of this dreadful journey. She said she wondered at the scrupulous politeness of Schneider during the route; nay, that at another period she could have listened to and admired the singular talent of this man, his great learning, his fancy, and wit; but her mind was bent upon other things, and the poor girl firmly thought that her last day was come.

In the meantime, by a blessed chance, I had not ridden three leagues from Strasburg, when the officer of a passing troop of a cavalry regiment, looking at the beast on which I was mounted, was pleased to take a fancy to it, and ordered me, in an authoritative tone, to descend, and to give up my steed for the benefit of the Republic. I represented to him, in vain, that I was a soldier, like himself, and the bearer of despatches to Paris. "Fool!" he said; "do you think they would send despatches by a man who can ride at best but ten leagues a-day?" And the honest soldier was so wroth at my supposed duplicity, that he not only confiscated my horse, but my saddle, and the little portmanteau which contained the chief part of my worldly goods and treasure. I had nothing for it but to dismount, and take my way on foot back again to Strasburg. I arrived there in the evening, determining the next morning to make my case known to the citizen St. Just; and though I made my entry without a sou, I don't know what secret exultation I felt at again being able to return.

The ante-chamber of such a great man as St. Just was, in those days, too crowded for an unprotected boy to obtain an early audience; two days passed before I could obtain a sight of the friend of Robespierre. On the third day, as I was still waiting for the interview, I heard a great bustle in the court-yard of the house, and looked out with many others at the spectacle.

A number of men and women, singing epithalamiums, and dressed in some absurd imitation of Roman costume, a troop of soldiers and gendarmerie, and an immense crowd of the *badauds* of Strasburg, were surrounding a carriage which then entered the court of the mayoralty. In this carriage, great God! I saw my dear Mary, and Schneider by her side. The truth instantly came upon me: the reason for Schneider's keen inquiries and my abrupt dismissal; but I could not believe that Mary was false to me. I had only to look in her face, white and rigid as marble, to see that this proposed marriage was not with her consent.

I fell back in the crowd as the procession entered the great room in which I was, and hid my face in my hands: I could not look upon her as the wife of another,—upon her so long loved and truly—the saint of my childhood—the pride and hope of my youth—torn from me for ever, and delivered over to the unholy arms of the murderer who stood before me.

The door of St. Just's private apartment opened, and he took his seat at the table of mayoralty just as Schneider and his cortège arrived before it.

Schneider then said that he came in before the authorities of the Republic to espouse the citoyenne Marie Ancel.

"Is she a minor?" asked St. Just.

"She is a minor, but her father is here to give her away."

"I am here," said uncle Edward, coming eagerly forward and bowing. "Edward Ancel, so please you, citizen representative. The worthy citizen Schneider has done me the honour of marrying into my family."

"But my father has not told you the terms of the marriage," said Mary, interrupting him, in a loud, clear voice.

Here Schneider seized her hand, and endeavoured to prevent her from speaking. Her father turned pale, and cried, "Stop, Mary, stop! For Heaven's sake, remember your poor old father's danger!"

"Sir, may I speak?"

"Let the young woman speak," said St. Just, "if she have a desire to talk." He did not suspect what would be the purport of her story.

"Sir," she said, "two days since the citizen Schneider entered for the first time our house; and you will fancy that it must be a love of very sudden growth which has

14

brought either him or me before you to-day. He had heard from a person who is now, unhappily, not present, of my name, and of the wealth which my family was said to possess; and hence arose this mad design concerning me. He came into our village with supreme power, an executioner at his heels, and the soldiery and authorities of the district entirely under his orders. He threatened my father with death if he refused to give up his daughter; and I, who knew that there was no chance of escape, except here before you, consented to become his wife. My father I know to be innocent, for all his transactions with the State have passed through my hands. Citizen representative, I demand to be freed from this marriage; and I charge Schneider as a traitor to the Republic, as a man who would have murdered an innocent citizen for the sake of private gain."

During the delivery of this little speech, uncle Jacob had been sobbing and panting like a broken-winded horse; and when Mary had done, he rushed up to her and kissed her, and held her tight in his arms. "Bless thee, my child!" he cried, "for having had the courage to speak the truth, and shame thy old father and me, who dared not say a word."

"The girl amazes me," said Schneider, with a look of astonishment. "I never saw her, it is true, till yesterday; but I used no force: her father gave her to me with his free consent, and she yielded as gladly. Speak, Edward Ancel, was it not so?"

"It was, indeed, by my free consent," said Edward, trembling.

"For shame, brother!" cried old Jacob. "Sir, it was by Edward's free consent and my niece's; but the guillotine was in the court-yard! Question Schneider's famulus, the man Gregoire, him who reads 'The Sorrows of Werter.'"

Gregoire stepped forward, and looked hesitatingly at Schneider, as he said, "I know not what took place within doors; but I was ordered to put up the scaffold without; and I was told to get soldiers, and let no one leave the house."

"Citizen St. Just," cried Schneider, "you will not allow the testimony of a ruffian like this, of a foolish girl, and a mad ex-priest, to weigh against the word of one who has done such service to the Republic: it is a base conspiracy to betray me; the whole family is known to favour the interest of the *émigrés*."

"And therefore you would marry a member of the family, and allow the others to escape: you must make a better defence, citizen Schneider," said St. Just, sternly.

Here I came forward, and said that, three days since, I had received an order to quit Strasburg for Paris, immediately after a conversation with Schneider, in which I had asked him his aid in promoting my marriage with my cousin, Mary Ancel; that he had heard from me full accounts regarding her father's wealth; and that he had abruptly caused my dismissal, in order to carry on his scheme against her.

"You are in the uniform of a regiment in this town; who sent you from it?" said St. Just.

I produced the order, signed by himself, and the despatches which Schneider had sent me.

"The signature is mine, but the despatches did not come from my office. Can you prove in any way your conversation with Schneider?"

"Why," said my sentimental friend Gregoire, "for the matter of that, I can answer that the lad was always talking about this young woman: he told me the whole story himself, and many a good laugh I had with citizen Schneider as we talked about it."

"The charge against Edward Ancel must be examined into," said St. Just. "The marriage cannot take place. But, if I had ratified it, Mary Ancel, what would then have been your course?"

Mary felt for a moment in her bosom, and said—"*He would have died to-night—I would have stabbed him with this dagger.*" *

* * * * *

The rain was beating down the streets, and yet they were thronged: all the world was hastening to the market-place, where the worthy Gregoire was about to perform some of the pleasant duties of his office. On this occasion, it was not death that he was to inflict; he was only to expose a criminal, who was to be sent on, afterwards, to Paris. St. Just had ordered that Schneider should stand for six hours in the public *place* of Strasburg, and then be sent on to the capital, to be dealt with as the authorities might think fit.

---

* This reply, and indeed, the whole of the story, is historical. An account, by Charles Nodier, in the *Revue de Paris*, suggested it to the writer.

The people followed with execrations the villain to his place of punishment; and Gregoire grinned as he fixed up to the post the man whose orders he had obeyed so often—who had delivered over to disgrace and punishment so many who merited it not.

Schneider was left for several hours exposed to the mockery and insults of the mob; he was then, according to his sentence, marched on to Paris, where it is probable that he would have escaped death, but for his own fault. He was left for some time in prison, quite unnoticed, perhaps forgotten : day by day fresh victims were carried to the scaffold, and yet the Alsatian tribune remained alive ; at last, by the mediation of one of his friends, a long petition was presented to Robespierre, stating his services and his innocence, and demanding his freedom. The reply to this was an order for his instant execution : the wretch died in the last days of Robespierre's reign. His comrade, St. Just, followed him, as you know ; but Edward Ancel had been released before this, for the action of my brave Mary had created a strong feeling in his favour.

"And Mary ?" said I.

Here a stout and smiling old lady entered the Captain's little room : she was leaning on the arm of a military-looking man of some forty years, and followed by a number of noisy, rosy children.

"This is Mary Ancel," said the Captain, "and I am Captain Pierre, and yonder is the Colonel, my son ; and you see us here assembled in force, for it is the *fête* of little Jacob yonder, whose brothers and sisters have all come from their schools to dance at his birthday."

BEATRICE MERGER.

Beatrice Merger, whose name might figure at the head of one of Mr. Colburn's politest romances—so smooth and

aristocratic does it sound—is no heroine, except of her own simple history; she is not a fashionable French Countess, nor even a victim of the Revolution.

She is a stout, sturdy girl of two-and-twenty, with a face beaming with good nature, and marked dreadfully by small-pox; and a pair of black eyes, which might have done some execution had they been placed in a smoother face. Beatrice's station in society is not very exalted; she is a servant of all-work: she will dress your wife, your dinner, your children; she does beefsteaks and plain work; she makes beds, blacks boots, and waits at table; —such, at least, were the offices which she performed in the fashionable establishment of the writer of this book: perhaps her history may not inaptly occupy a few pages of it.

"My father died," said Beatrice, "about six years since, and left my poor mother with little else but a small cottage and a strip of land, and four children too young to work. It was hard enough in my father's time to supply so many little mouths with food; and how was a poor widowed woman to provide for them now, who had neither the strength nor the opportunity for labour?

"Besides us, to be sure, there was my old aunt; and she would have helped us, but she could not, for the old woman is bed-ridden; so she did nothing but occupy our best room, and grumble from morning till night: Heaven knows! poor old soul, that she had no great reason to be very happy; for you know, sir, that it frets the temper to be sick; and that it is worse still to be sick and hungry too.

"At that time, in the country where we lived (in Picardy, not very far from Boulogne), times were so bad that the best workman could hardly find employ; and when he did, he was happy if he could earn a matter of twelve sous a day. Mother, work as she would, could not gain more than six; and it was a hard job, out of this, to put meat into six bellies, and clothing on six backs. Old aunt Bridget would scold, as she got her portion of black bread; and my little brothers used to cry if theirs did not come in time. I, too, used to cry when I got my share; for mother kept only a little, little piece for herself, and said that she had dined in the fields,—God pardon her for the lie! and bless her, as I am sure He did; for, but for Him, no working man or woman could subsist upon such a wretched morsel as my dear mother took.

"I was a thin, ragged, barefooted girl, then, and sickly and weak for want of food; but I think I felt mother's hunger more than my own: and many and many a bitter night I lay awake, crying, and praying to God to give me means of working for myself and aiding her. And He has, indeed, been good to me," said pious Beatrice, " for He has given me all this !

" Well, time rolled on, and matters grew worse than ever: winter came, and was colder to us than any other winter, for our clothes were thinner and more torn; mother sometimes could find no work, for the fields in which she laboured were hidden under the snow; so that when we wanted them most, we had them least—warmth, work, or food.

"I knew that, do what I would, mother would never let me leave her, because I looked to my little brothers and my old cripple of an aunt; but, still, bread was better for us than all my service; and when I left them, the six would have a slice more; so I determined to bid good-by to nobody, but to go away, and look for work elsewhere. One Sunday, when mother and the little ones were at church, I went in to aunt Bridget, and said, Tell mother, when she comes back, that Beatrice is gone. I spoke quite stoutly, as if I did not care about it.

"'Gone! gone where?' said she. 'You ain't going to leave me alone, you nasty thing; you ain't going to the village to dance, you ragged, barefooted slut: you're all of a piece in this house—your mother, your brothers, and you. I know you've got meat in the kitchen, and you only give me black bread;' and here the old lady began to scream as if her heart would break; but we did not mind it, we were so used to it.

"Aunt, said I, I'm going, and took this very opportunity because you *were* alone: tell mother, I am too old now to eat her bread, and do no work for it: I am going, please God, where work and bread can be found: and so I kissed her: she was so astonished that she could not move or speak; and I walked away through the old room, and the little garden, God knows whither!

"I heard the old woman screaming after me, but I did not stop nor turn round. I don't think I could, for my heart was very full; and if I had gone back again, I should never have had the courage to go away. So I walked a long, long way, until night fell; and I thought of poor mother coming home from mass, and not finding me; and little Pierre shouting out, in his clear voice, for Beatrice to bring him his supper. I think I should like to have died that night, and I thought I should too; for when I was obliged to throw myself on the cold, hard ground, my feet were too torn and weary to bear me any further.

"Just then the moon got up; and do you know I felt a comfort in looking at it, for I knew it was shining on our little cottage, and it seemed like an old friend's face. A little way on, as I saw by the moon, was a village; and I saw, too, that a man was coming towards me; he must have heard me crying, I suppose.

"Was not God good to me? This man was a farmer, who had need of a girl in his house; he made me tell him why I was alone, and I told him the same story I have told you, and he believed me, and took me home. I had walked six long leagues from our village, that day, asking everywhere for work in vain; and here, at bed-time, I found a bed and a supper!

"Here I lived very well for some months; my master was very good and kind to me; but, unluckily, too poor to give me any wages; so that I could save nothing to send to my poor mother. My mistress used to scold; but I was used to that at home, from aunt Bridget; and she beat me sometimes, but I did not mind it; for your hardy country girl is not like your tender town lasses, who cry if a pin pricks them, and give warning to their mistresses at the first hard word. The only drawback to my comfort was, that I had no news of my mother; I could not write to her, nor could she have read my letter, if I had; so there I was, at only six leagues distance from home, as far off as if I had been to Paris or to 'Merica.

"However, in a few months I grew so listless and

homesick, that my mistress said she would keep me no longer; and though I went away as poor as I came, I was still too glad to go back to the old village again, and see dear mother, if it were but for a day. I knew she would share her crust with me, as she had done for so long a time before; and hoped that, now, as I was taller and stronger, I might find work more easily in the neighbourhood.

"You may fancy what a fête it was when I came back; though I'm sure we cried as much as if it had been a funeral. Mother got into a fit, which frightened us all; and as for aunt Bridget, she *skreeled* away for hours together, and did not scold for two days at least. Little Pierre offered me the whole of his supper; poor little man! his slice of bread was no bigger than before I went away.

"Well, I got a little work here, and a little there; but still I was a burden at home, rather than a bread-winner; and, at the closing in of the winter, was very glad to hear of a place at two leagues distance, where work, they said, was to be had. Off I set, one morning, to find it, but missed my way, somehow, until it was night-time before I arrived. Night-time, and snow again; it seemed as if all my journeys were to be made in this bitter weather.

"When I came to the farmer's door, his house was shut up, and his people all a-bed; I knocked for a long while in vain; at last he made his appearance at a window up-stairs, and seemed so frightened, and looked so angry, that I suppose he took me for a thief. I told him how I had come for work. 'Who comes for work at such an hour?' said he: 'Go home, you impudent baggage, and do not disturb honest people out of their sleep.' He banged the window to; and so I was left alone to shift for myself as I might. There was no shed, no cow-house, where I could find a bed; so I got under a cart, on some straw; it was no very warm berth. I could not sleep for the cold; and the hours passed so slowly, that it seemed as if I had been there a week, instead of a night; but still it was not so bad as the first night when I left home, and when the good farmer found me.

"In the morning, before it was light, the farmer's people came out, and saw me crouching under the cart: they told me to get up; but I was so cold that I could not: at last the man himself came, and recognized me as the girl who had disturbed him the night before. When he heard my name, and the purpose for which I came, this good man took me into the house, and put me into one of the beds out of which his sons had just got; and, if I was cold before, you may be sure I was warm and comfortable now: such a bed as this I had never slept in, nor ever did I have such good milk-soup as he gave me out of his own breakfast. Well, he agreed to hire me; and what do you think he gave me?—six sous a day! and let me sleep in the cow-house besides: you may fancy how happy I was now, at the prospect of earning so much money.

"There was an old woman, among the labourers, who used to sell us soup: I got a cupful every day for a halfpenny, with a bit of bread in it; and might eat as much beet-root besides as I liked; not a very wholesome meal, to be sure, but God took care that it should not disagree with me.

" So, every Saturday, when work was over, I had thirty sous to carry home to mother; and tired though I was, I walked merrily the two leagues to our village, to see her again. On the road there was a great wood to pass through, and this frightened me; for if a thief should come and rob me of my whole week's earnings, what could a poor lone girl do to help herself? But I found a remedy for this too, and no thieves ever came near me; I used to begin saying my prayers as I entered the forest, and never stopped until I was safe at home; and safe I always arrived, with my thirty sous in my pocket. Ah! you may be sure, Sunday was a merry day for us all."

* * * * *

This is the whole of Beatrice's history which is worthy of publication; the rest of it only relates to her arrival in Paris, and the various masters and mistresses whom she there had the honour to serve. As soon as she enters the capital, the romance disappears, and the poor girl's sufferings and privations luckily vanish with it. Beatrice has got now warm gowns, and stout shoes, and plenty of good food. She has had her little brother from Picardy; clothed, fed, and educated him: that young gentleman is now a carpenter, and an honour to his profession. Madame Merger is in easy circumstances, and receives, yearly, fifty francs from her daughter. To crown all, Mademoiselle Beatrice herself is a funded proprietor, and consulted the writer of this biography as to the best method of laying out a capital of two hundred francs, which is the present amount of her fortune.

God bless her! she is richer than his Grace the Duke of Devonshire; and, I dare to say, has, in her humble walk, been more virtuous and more happy than all the dukes in the realm.

It is, indeed, for the benefit of dukes and such great people (who, I make no doubt, have long since ordered copies of these Sketches), that poor little Beatrice's story has been indited. Certain it is, that the young woman would never have been immortalized in this way, but for the good which her betters may derive from her example. If your Ladyship will but reflect a little, after boasting of the sums which you spend in charity; the beef and blankets, which you dole out at Christmas; the poonah-painting, which you execute for fancy fairs; the long, long sermons, which you listen to, at St. George's, the whole year through;—your Ladyship, I say, will allow that, although perfectly meritorious in your line, as a patroness of the Church of England, of Almack's, and of the Lying-in Asylum, yours is but a paltry sphere of virtue, a pitiful attempt at benevolence, and that this honest servant-girl puts you to shame! And you, my Lord Bishop; do you, out of your six sous a day, give away five to support your flock and family? Would you drop a single coach-horse (I do not say *a dinner*, for such a notion is monstrous, in one of your Lordship's degree), to feed any one of the starving children of your Lordship's mother—the Church?

I pause for a reply. His Lordship took too much turtle and cold punch for dinner yesterday, and cannot speak just now; but we have, by this ingenious question, silenced him altogether : let the world wag as it will, and poor Christians and curates starve as they may, my Lord's footmen must have their new liveries, and his horses their four feeds a day.

*　　　*　　　*　　　*　　　*

When we recollect his speech about the Catholics—when we remember his last charity sermon,—but I say nothing. Here is a poor benighted superstitious creature, worshipping images, without a rag to her tail, who has as much faith, and humility, and charity, as all the reverend bench.

*　　　*　　　*　　　*　　　*

This angel is without a place; and for this reason (besides the pleasure of composing the above slap at episcopacy)—I have indited her history. If the Bishop is going to Paris, and wants a good honest maid-of-all-work, he can have her, I have no doubt; or if he chooses to give a few pounds to her mother, they can be sent to Mr. Titmarsh, at the publisher's.

Here is Miss Merger's last letter and autograph. The note was evidently composed by an *Ecrivain public :*—

" *Madame,*

" *Ayant apris par ce Monsieur, que vous vous portiez bien, ainsi que Monsieur, ayant su aussi que vous parliez de moi dans votre lettre cette nouvelle m'a fait bien plaisir Je profite de l'occasion pour vous faire passer ce petit billet ou Je voudrais pouvoir m'envelopcr pour aller vous voir* *et pour vous dire que Je suis encore sans place Je m'ennuye toujours de ne pas vous voir ainsi que Minette (*Minette is a cat*) qui semble m'interroger tour a tour et demander ou vous êtes. Je vous envoye aussi la note du linge a blanchir —ah, Madame! Je vais cesser de vous ecrire mais non de vous regretter.*"

Beatrice Merger

The cheap Defence of Nations.

CARICATURES AND LITHOGRAPHY IN PARIS.

FIFTY years ago there lived at Munich a poor fellow, by name Aloys Senefelder, who was in so little repute as an author and artist, that printers and engravers refused to publish his works at their own charges, and so set him upon some plan for doing without their aid. In the first place, Aloys invented a certain kind of ink, which would resist the action of the acid that is usually employed by engravers, and with this he made his experiments upon copper-plates, as long as he could afford to purchase them. He found that to write upon the plates backwards, after the manner of engravers, required much skill and many trials; and he thought that, were he to practise upon any other polished surface—a smooth stone, for instance, the least costly article imaginable—he might spare the expense of the copper until he had sufficient skill to use it.

One day, it is said, that Aloys was called upon to write —rather a humble composition for an author and artist— a washing-bill. He had no paper at hand, and so he wrote out the bill with some of his newly-invented ink upon one of his Kelheim stones. Some time afterwards he thought he would try and take an *impression* of his washing-bill: he did, and succeeded. Such is the story, which the reader most likely knows very well; and having alluded to the origin of the art, we shall not follow the stream through its windings and enlargement after it issued from the little parent rock, or fill our pages with the rest of the pedigree. Senefelder invented Lithography. His invention has not made so much noise and larum in the world as some others, which have an origin quite as humble and unromantic; but it is one to which we owe no small profit, and a great deal of pleasure; and, as such, we are bound to speak of it with all gratitude and respect. The schoolmaster, who is now abroad, has taught us, in our youth, how the cultivation of art " *emollit mores nec sinit esse* "— (it is needless to finish the quotation); and Lithography has been, to our thinking, the very best ally that art ever had; the best friend of the artist, allowing him to produce rapidly-multiplied and authentic copies of his own works (without trusting to the tedious and expensive assistance of the engraver); and the best friend to the people likewise, who have means of purchasing these cheap and beautiful productions, and thus having their ideas " mollified," and their manners " feros " no more.

With ourselves, among whom money is plenty, enterprise so great, and everything matter of commercial speculation, Lithography has not been so much practised as wood or steel engraving; which, by the aid of great original capital and spread of sale, are able more than to compete with the art of drawing on stone. The two former may be called art done by *machinery*. We confess to a prejudice in favour of the honest work of *hand*, in matters of art, and prefer the rough workmanship of the painter to the smooth copies of his performances which are produced, for the most part, on the wood-block or the steel-plate.

The theory will possibly be objected to by many of our readers: the best proof in its favour, we think, is, that the state of art amongst the people in France and Germany, where publishers are not so wealthy or enterprising as with us,* and where Lithography is more practised, is infinitely higher than in England, and the appreciation more correct. As draughtsmen, the French and German painters are incomparably superior to our own; and with art, as with any other commodity, the demand will be found pretty equal to the supply: with us, the general demand is for neatness, prettiness, and what is called *effect* in pictures, and these can be rendered completely, nay, improved, by the engraver's conventional manner of copying the artist's performances. But to copy fine expression and fine drawing, the engraver himself must be a fine artist; and let anybody examine the host of picture-books which appear every Christmas, and say whether, for the most part, painters or engravers possess any artistic merit? We boast, nevertheless, of some of the best engravers and painters in Europe. Here, again, the supply is accounted for by the demand; our highest class is richer than any other aristocracy, quite as well instructed, and can judge and pay for fine pictures

* These countries are, to be sure, inundated with the productions of our market, in the shape of Byron Beauties, reprints from the Keepsakes, Books of Beauty, and such trash; but these are only of late years, and their original schools of art are still flourishing.

and engravings. But these costly productions are for the few, and not for the many, who have not yet certainly arrived at properly appreciating fine art.

Take the standard "Album" for instance — that unfortunate collection of deformed Zuleikas and Medoras (from the Byron Beauties, the Flowers, Gems, Souvenirs, Caskets of Loveliness, Beauty, as they may be called); glaring caricatures of flowers, singly, in groups, in flower-pots, or with hideous deformed little Cupids sporting among them; of what are called "mezzotinto" pencil drawings, "poonah-paintings," and what not. "The Album" is to be found invariably upon the round rosewood brass-inlaid drawing-room table of the middle classes, and with a couple of "Annuals" besides, which flank it on the same table, represents the art of the house; perhaps there is a portrait of the master of the house in the dining-room, grim-glancing from above the mantel-piece; and of the mistress over the piano upstairs; add to these some odious miniatures of the sons and daughters, on each side of the chimney-glass; and here, commonly (we appeal to the reader if this is an overcharged picture), the collection ends. The family goes to the Exhibition once a year, to the National Gallery once in ten years: to the former place they have an inducement to go; there are their own portraits, or the portraits of their friends, or the portraits of public characters; and you will see them infallibly wondering over No. 2645 in the catalogue, representing "The Portrait of a Lady," or of the "First Mayor of Little Pedlington since the passing of the Reform Bill;" or else bustling and squeezing among the miniatures, where lies the chief attraction of the Gallery. England has produced, owing to the effects of this class of admirers of art, two admirable, and five hundred very clever, portrait-painters. How many *artists?* Let the reader count upon his five fingers, and see if, living at the present moment, he can name one for each.

If, from this examination of our own worthy middle classes, we look to the same class in France, what a difference do we find! Humble *cafés* in country towns have their walls covered with pleasing picture papers, representing Les Gloires de l'Armée Française, the Seasons, the Four Quarters of the World, Cupid and Psyche, or some other allegory, landscape or history, rudely painted, as papers for walls usually are; but the figures are all tolerably well drawn; and the common taste, which has caused a demand for such things, is undeniable. In Paris, the manner in which the *cafés* and houses of the *restaurateurs* are ornamented, is, of course, a thousand times richer, and nothing can be more beautiful, or more exquisitely finished and correct, than the designs which adorn many of them. We are not prepared to say what sums were expended upon the painting of Véry's or Véfour's, of the Salle-Musard, or of numberless other places of public resort in the capital. There is many a shopkeeper whose sign is a very tolerable picture; and often have we stopped to admire (the reader will give us credit for having remained *outside*) the excellent workmanship of the grapes and vine-leaves over the door of some very humble, dirty, inodorous shop of a *marchand de vin.*

These, however, serve only to educate the public taste,

and are ornaments, for the most part, much too costly for the people. But the same love of ornament which is shown in their public places of resort, appears in their houses likewise; and every one of our readers who has lived in Paris, in any lodging, magnificent or humble, with any family, however poor, may bear witness how profusely the walls of his smart *salon* in the English quarter, or of his little room *au sixième* in the Pays-Latin, has been decorated with prints of all kinds. In the first, probably, with bad engravings on copper, from the bad and tawdry pictures of the artists of the time of the Empire; in the latter, with gay caricatures of Granville or Monnier; military pieces, such as are dashed off by Raffet, Charlet, Vernet (one can hardly say which of the three designers has the greatest merit, or the most vigorous hand); or clever pictures from the crayon of the Deverias, the admirable Roqueplan, or Decamp. We have named here, we believe, the principal lithographic artists in Paris; and those, as, doubtless, there are many, of our readers who have looked over Monsieur Aubert's portfolios, or gazed at that famous caricature-shop window in the Rue de Coq, or are even acquainted with the exterior of Monsieur Delaporte's little emporium in the Burlington Arcade, need not be told how excellent the productions of all these artists are, in their *genre*. We get, in these engravings, the *loisirs* of men of genius, not the finikin performances of laboured mediocrity, as with us; all these artists are good painters, as well as good designers; a design from them is worth a whole gross of Books of Beauty; and if we might raise a humble supplication to the artists in our own country of similar merit

—to such men as Leslie, Maclise, Herbert, Cattermole, and others—it would be, that they should, after the example of their French brethren, and of the English landscape painters, take chalk in hand, produce their own copies of their own sketches, and never more draw a single Forsaken One, Rejected One, Dejected one, at the entreaty of any publisher, or for the pages of any Book of Beauty, Royalty, or Loveliness, whatever.

Can there be a more pleasing walk, in the whole world, than a stroll through the Gallery of the Louvre, on a *fête-day*: not to look so much at the pictures as at the lookers-on? Thousands of the poorer classes are there: mechanics in their Sunday clothes, smiling *grisettes*, smart, dapper soldiers of the line, with bronzed wondering faces, marching together in little companies of six or seven, and stopping every now and then at Napoleon or Leonidas, as they appear, in proper vulgar heroics, in the pictures of David or Gros. The taste of these people will hardly be approved by the connoisseur, but they have *a* taste for art. Can the same be said of our lower classes, who, if they are inclined to be sociable and amused in their holidays, have no place of resort but the tap-room or tea-garden, and no food for conversation, except such as can be built upon the politics or the police reports of the last Sunday paper? So much has church and state puritanism done for us—so well has it succeeded in materializing and binding down to the earth the imagination of men, for which God has made another world (which certain statesmen take but too little into account)—that fair and beautiful world of heart, in which there *can* be nothing selfish or sordid, of which

Dulness has forgotten the existence, and which Bigotry has endeavoured to shut out from sight—

> " On a banni les démons et les fées,
> Le raisonner tristement s'accrédite :
> On court, helas ! après la verité :
> Ah ! croyez moi, l'erreur a son mérite ! "

We are not putting in a plea, here, for demons and fairies, as Voltaire does in the above exquisite lines ; nor about to expatiate on the beauties of error, for it has none ; but the clank of steam-engines, and the shouts of politicians, and the struggle for gain or bread, and the loud denunciations of stupid bigots, have well nigh smothered poor *Fancy* among us. We boast of our science, and vaunt our superior morality. Does the latter exist ? In spite of all the forms which our policy has invented to secure it—in spite of all the preachers, all the meeting-houses, and all the legislative enactments—if any person will take upon himself the painful labour of purchasing and perusing some of the cheap periodical prints which form the people's library of amusement, and contain what may be presumed to be their standard in matters of imagination and fancy, he will see how false the claim is that we bring forward of superior morality. The aristocracy, who are so eager to maintain, were, of course, not the last to feel, the annoyance of the legislative restrictions on the Sabbath, and eagerly seized upon that happy invention for dissipating the gloom and *ennui* ordered by Act of Parliament to prevail on that day—the Sunday paper. It might be read in a club-room, where the poor could not see how their betters ordained one thing for the vulgar, and another for themselves; or in an easy-chair,

in the study, whither my lord retires every Sunday for his
devotions. It dealt in private scandal and ribaldry, only
the more piquant for its pretty flimsy veil of *double
entendre*. It was a fortune to the publisher, and it
became a necessary to the reader, which he could not do
without, any more than without his snuff-box, his opera-
box, or his *chasse* after coffee. The delightful novelty
could not for any time be kept exclusively for the *haut
ton*; and from my lord it descended to his valet or tradesmen, and from Grosvenor Square it spread all the town
through; so that now the lower classes have their scandal
and ribaldry organs, as well as their betters (the rogues, they
will imitate them!) and, as their tastes are somewhat coarser
than my lord's, and their numbers a thousand to one, why,
of course the prints have increased, and the profligacy has
been diffused in a ratio exactly proportionable to the
demand, until the town is infested with such a number
of monstrous publications of the kind as would have put
Abbé Dubois to the blush, or made Louis XV. cry shame.
Talk of English morality!—the worst licentiousness, in the
worst period of the French monarchy, scarcely equalled the
wickedness of this Sabbath-keeping country of ours.

The reader will be glad, at last, to come to the conclusion that we would fain draw from all these descriptions—
why does this immorality exist? Because the people *must*
be amused, and have not been taught *how;* because the
upper classes, frightened by stupid cant, or absorbed in
material wants, have not as yet learned the refinement
which only the cultivation of art can give; and when their
intellects are uneducated, and their tastes are coarse, the

tastes and amusements of classes still more ignorant must be coarse and vicious likewise, in an increased proportion.

Such discussions and violent attacks upon high and low, Sabbath-bills, politicians, and what not, may appear, perhaps, out of place, in a few pages which purport only to give an account of some French drawings: all we would urge is, that, in France, these prints are made because they are liked and appreciated; with us they are not made, because they are not liked and appreciated:—and the more is the pity. Nothing merely intellectual will be popular among us: we do not love beauty for beauty's sake, as Germans; or wit, for wit's sake, as the French: for abstract art we have no appreciation. We admire H. B.'s caricatures, because they are the caricatures of well-known political characters, not because they are witty; and Boz, because he writes us good palpable stories (if we may use such a word to a story); and Madame Vestris, because she has the most beautifully shaped legs;—the *art* of the designer, the writer, the actress (each admirable in its way,) is a very minor consideration; each might have ten times the wit, and would be quite unsuccessful without their substantial points of popularity.

In France such matters are far better managed, and the love of art is a thousand times more keen; and (from this feeling, surely) how much superiority is there in French *society* over our own; how much better is social happiness understood; how much more manly equality is there between Frenchman and Frenchman, than between rich and poor in our own country, with all our superior wealth, instruction, and political freedom! There is, amongst the humblest, a gaiety, cheerfulness, politeness, and sobriety, to which, in England, no class can shew a parallel : and these, be it remembered, are not only qualities for holidays, but for working-days too, and add to the enjoyment of human life as much as good clothes, good beef, or good wages. If, to our freedom, we could but add a little of their happiness!—it is one, after all, of the cheapest commodities in the world, and in the power of every man (with means of gaining decent bread) who has the will or the skill to use it.

We are not going to trace the history of the rise and progress of art in France; our business, at present, is only to speak of one branch of art in that country—lithographic designs, and those chiefly of a humorous character. A history of French caricature was published in Paris, two or three years back, illustrated by numerous copies of designs, from the time of Henry III. to our own day. We can only speak of this work from memory, having been unable, in London, to procure the sight of a copy; but our impression, at the time we saw the collection, was as unfavourable as could possibly be : nothing could be more meagre than the wit, or poorer than the execution, of the whole set of drawings. Under the Empire, art, as may be imagined, was at a very low ebb; and, aping the Government of the day, and catering to the national taste and vanity, it was a kind of tawdry caricature of the sublime; of which the pictures of David and Girodet, and almost the entire collection now at the Luxembourg Palace, will give pretty fair examples. Swollen, distorted, unnatural, the painting was something like the politics of those days;

with force in it, nevertheless, and something of grandeur, that will exist in spite of taste, and is born of energetic will. A man, disposed to write comparisons of characters, might, for instance, find some striking analogies between Mountebank Murat, with his irresistible bravery and horsemanship, who was a kind of mixture of Duguesclin and Ducrow, and Mountebank David, a fierce, powerful painter and genius, whose idea of beauty and sublimity seemed to have been gained from the bloody melodramas on the Boulevard. Both, however, were great in their way, and were worshipped as gods, in those heathen times of false belief and hero-worship.

As for poor caricature and freedom of the press, they, like the rightful princess in a fairy tale, with the merry fantastic dwarf, her attendant, were entirely in the power of the giant who ruled the land. The Princess Press was so closely watched and guarded (with some little show, nevertheless, of respect for her rank), that she dared not utter a word of her own thoughts; and, for poor Caricature, he was gagged, and put out of the way altogether: imprisoned as completely as ever Asmodeus was in his phial.

How the Press and her attendant fared in succeeding reigns, is well known; their condition was little bettered by the downfall of Napoleon: with the accession of Charles X. they were more oppressed even than before— more than they could bear; for so hard were they pressed, that, as one has seen when sailors are working a capstan, back of a sudden the bars flew, knocking to the earth the men who were endeavouring to work them. The Revolution came, and up sprung Caricature in France; all sorts of fierce epigrams were discharged at the flying monarch, and speedily were prepared, too, for the new one.

About this time, there lived at Paris (if our information be correct) a certain M. Philipon, an indifferent artist (painting was his profession), a tolerable designer, and an admirable wit. M. Philipon designed many caricatures himself, married the sister of an eminent publisher of prints (M. Aubert), and the two, gathering about them a body of wits and artists like themselves, set up journals of their own:—*La Caricature,* first published once a week; and the *Charivari* afterwards, a daily paper, in which a design also appears daily.

At first the caricatures inserted in the *Charivari* were chiefly political; and a most curious contest speedily commenced between the state and M. Philipon's little army in the Galérie Véro-Dodat. Half-a-dozen poor artists on the one side, and his Majesty Louis Philippe, his august family, and the numberless placemen and supporters of the monarchy, on the other; it was something like Thersites girding at Ajax, and piercing through the folds of the *clypei septemplicis* with the poisonous shafts of his scorn. Our French Thersites was not always an honest opponent, it must be confessed; and many an attack was made upon the gigantic enemy, which was cowardly, false, and malignant. But to see the monster writhing under the effects of the arrow—to see his uncouth fury in return, and the blind blows that he dealt at his diminutive opponent!—not one of these told in a hundred; when they *did* tell, it may be imagined that they were fierce enough in all conscience, and served almost to annihilate the adversary.

To speak more plainly, and to drop the metaphor of giant and dwarf, the King of the French suffered so much, his Ministers were so mercilessly ridiculed, his family and his own remarkable figure drawn with such odious and grotesque resemblance, in fanciful attitudes, circumstances, and disguises, so ludicrously mean, and often so appropriate, that the King was obliged to descend into the lists and battle his ridiculous enemy in form. Prosecutions, seizures, fines, regiments of furious legal officials, were first brought into play against poor M. Philipon and his little dauntless troop of malicious artists; some few were bribed out of his ranks; and if they did not, like Gilray in England, turn their weapons upon their old friends, at least laid down their arms, and would fight no more. The bribes, fines, indictments, and loud-tongued *avocats du Roi* made no impression; Philipon repaired the defeat of a fine by some fresh and furious attack upon his great enemy; if his epigrams were more covert, they were no less bitter; if he was beaten a dozen times before a jury, he had eighty or ninety victories to shew in the same field of battle, and every victory and every defeat brought him new sympathy. Every one who was at Paris, a few years since, must recollect the famous "*poire*" which was chalked upon all the walls of the city, and which bore so ludicrous a resemblance to Louis Philippe. The *poire* became an object of prosecution, and M. Philipon appeared before a jury to answer for the crime of inciting to contempt against the King's person, by giving such a ludicrous version of his face. Philipon, for defence, produced a sheet of paper, and drew a *poire*, a real large Burgundy pear: in the lower parts round and capacious, narrower near the stalk, and crowned with two or three careless leaves. "There was no treason at least in *that*," he said to the jury; "could any one object to such a harmless botanical representation?" Then he drew a second pear, exactly like the former, except that one or two lines were scrawled in the midst of it, which bore somehow a ludicrous resemblance to the eyes, nose, and mouth of a celebrated personage; and, lastly, he drew the exact portrait of Louis Philippe; the well-known toupet, the ample whiskers and jowl were there, neither extenuated nor set down in malice. "Can I help it, gentlemen of the jury, then," said he, "if his Majesty's face is like a pear? Say yourselves, respectable citizens, is it, or is it not, like a pear?" Such eloquence could not fail of its effect; the artist was acquitted, and *La Poire* is immortal.

At last came the famous September laws; the freedom of the Press, which, from August, 1830, was to be "*désormais une vérité*," was calmly strangled by the Monarch who had gained his crown for his supposed championship of it; by his Ministers, some of whom had been stout republicans on paper but a few years before; and by the Chamber, which, such is the blessed constitution of French elections, will generally vote, unvote, revote in any way the Government wishes. With a wondrous union, and happy forgetfulness of principle, monarch, ministers, and deputies issued the restriction laws; the Press was sent to prison; as for the poor dear Caricature, it was fairly murdered. No more political satires appear now, and, "through the eye, correct the heart;" no more *poires* ripen on the walls of the metropolis; Philipon's political occupation is gone.

But there is always food for satire; and the French caricaturists, being no longer allowed to hold up to ridicule and reprobation the King and the deputies, have found no lack of subjects for the pencil in the ridicules and rascalities of common life. We have said that public decency is greater amongst the French than amongst us, which, to some of our readers, may appear paradoxical; but we shall not attempt to argue that, in private roguery, our neighbours are not our equals. The *procès* of Gisquet, which has appeared lately in the papers, shews how deep the demoralization must be, and how a Government, based itself on dishonesty (a tyranny, that is, under the title and fiction of a democracy), must practise and admit corruption in its own, and in its agents' dealings with the nation. Accordingly, of cheating contracts, of ministers dabbling with the funds, or extracting underhand profits for the granting of unjust privileges and monopolies,—of grasping, envious, police restrictions, which destroy the freedom, and, with it, the integrity of commerce,—those who like to examine such details may find plenty in French history: the whole French finance system has been a swindle from the days of Louvois, or Law, down to the present time. The Government swindles the public, and the small traders swindle their customers, on the authority and example of the superior powers. Hence the art of roguery, under such high patronage, maintains, in France, a noble front of impudence, and a fine audacious openness, which it does not wear in our country.

Among the various characters of roguery which the French satirists have amused themselves by depicting, there is one of which the *greatness* (using the word in the sense which Mr. Jonathan Wild gave to it) so far exceeds that of all others, embracing, as it does, all in turn, that it has come to be considered the type of roguery in general; and now, just as all the political squibs were made to come of old from the lips of Pasquin, all the reflections on the prevailing cant, knavery, quackery, humbug, are put into the mouth of Monsieur Robert Macaire.

A play was written, some twenty years since, called the "Auberge des Adrets," in which the characters of two robbers escaped from the galleys were introduced—Robert Macaire, the clever rogue above mentioned, and Bertrand, the stupid rogue, his friend, accomplice, butt, and scapegoat, on all occasions of danger. It is needless to describe the play—a witless performance enough, of which the joke was Macaire's exaggerated style of conversation, a farrago of all sorts of high-flown sentiments, such as the French love to indulge in—contrasted with his actions, which were philosophically unscrupulous, and his appearance, which was most picturesquely sordid. The play had been acted, we believe, and forgotten, when a very clever actor, M. Frederick Lemaitre, took upon himself the performance of the character of Robert Macaire, and looked, spoke, and acted it to such admirable perfection, that the whole town rung with applauses of the performance, and the caricaturists delighted to copy his singular figure and costume. M. Robert Macaire appears in a most picturesque green coat, with a variety of rents and patches, a pair of crimson pantaloons ornamented in the same way, enormous whiskers and ringlets, an enormous stock and shirt-frill, as dirty and ragged as stock and shirt-frill can be, the relic of a hat very gaily cocked over one eye, and a patch to take away somewhat from the brightness of the other— these are the principal *pièces* of his costume—a snuff-box like a creaking warming-pan, a handkerchief hanging together by a miracle, and a switch of about the thickness of a man's thigh, formed the ornaments of this exquisite personage. He is a compound of Fielding's "Blueskin" and Goldsmith's "Beau Tibbs." He has the dirt and dandyism of the one, with the ferocity of the other: sometimes he is made to swindle, but where he can get a shilling more, M. Macaire will murder without scruple: he performs one and the other act (or any in the scale between them) with a similar bland imperturbability, and accompanies his actions with such philosophical remarks as may be expected from a person of his talents, his energies, his amiable life and character.

Bertrand is the simple recipient of Macaire's jokes, and makes vicarious atonement for his crimes, acting, in fact, the part which pantaloon performs in the pantomime, who is entirely under the fatal influence of clown. He is quite as much a rogue as that gentleman, but he has not his genius and courage. So, in pantomimes (it may, doubtless, have been remarked by the reader), clown always leaps first, pantaloon following after, more clumsily and timidly than his bold and accomplished friend and guide. Whatever blows are destined for clown, fall, by some means of ill-luck, upon the pate of pantaloon: whenever the clown robs, the stolen articles are sure to be found in his companion's pocket; and thus exactly Robert Macaire and his companion Bertrand are made to go through the world; both swindlers, but the one more accomplished than the other. Both robbing all the world, and Robert robbing his friend, and, in the event of danger, leaving him faithfully in the lurch. There is, in the two characters, some grotesque good for the spectator—a kind of "Beggars' Opera" moral.

Ever since Robert, with his dandified rags and airs, his cane and snuff-box, and Bertrand with torn surtout and all-absorbing pocket, have appeared on the stage, they have been popular with the Parisians; and with these two types of clever and stupid knavery, M. Philipon and his companion Daumier have created a world of pleasant satire upon all the prevailing abuses of the day.

Almost the first figure that these audacious caricaturists dared to depict was a political one: in Macaire's red breeches and tattered coat appeared no less a personage than the King himself—the old *Poire*—in a country of humbugs and swindlers the *facile princeps;* fit to govern, as he is deeper than all the rogues in his dominions. Bertrand was opposite to him, and having listened with delight and reverence to some tale of knavery truly royal, was exclaiming, with a look and voice expressive of the most intense admiration, "AH VIEUX BLAGUEUR! va!"—the word *blague* is untranslatable—it means *French* humbug as distinct from all other; and only those who know the value of an epigram in France, an epigram so wonderfully just, a little word so curiously comprehensive, can fancy the

16—2

kind of rage and rapture with which it was received. It was a blow that shook the whole dynasty. Thersites had there given such a wound to Ajax, as Hector in arms could scarcely have inflicted: a blow sufficient almost to create the madness to which the fabulous hero of Homer and Ovid fell a prey.

Not long, however, was French caricature allowed to attack personages so illustrious: the September laws came, and henceforth no more epigrams were launched against politics; but the caricaturists were compelled to confine their satire to subjects and characters that had nothing to do with the State. The Duke of Orleans was no longer to figure in lithography as the fantastic Prince Rosolin; no longer were multitudes (in chalk) to shelter under the enormous shadow of M. d'Argout's nose: Marshal Lobau's squirt was hung up in peace, and M. Thiers's pigmy figure, and round spectacled face, were no more to appear in print.* Robert Macaire was driven out of the Chambers and the Palace—his remarks were a great deal too appropriate and too severe for the ears of the great men who congregated in those places.

The Chambers and the Palace were shut to him; but the rogue, driven out of his rogue's paradise, saw "that the world was all before him where to choose," and found no lack of opportunities for exercising his wit. There was the Bar, with its roguish practitioners, rascally attorneys, stupid juries, and forsworn judges; there was the Bourse,

---

* Almost all the principal public men had been most ludicrously caricatured in the *Charivari*: those mentioned above were usually depicted with the distinctive attributes mentioned by us.

with all its gambling, swindling, and hoaxing, its cheats and its dupes; the Medical Profession, and the quacks, who ruled it alternately; the Stage, and the cant that was prevalent there; the Fashion, and its thousand follies and extravagancies. Robert Macaire had all these to *exploiter*. Of all the empire, through all the ranks, professions, the lies, crimes, and absurdities of men, he may make sport at will; of all except of a certain class. Like Bluebeard's wife, he may see everything, but is bidden *to beware of the blue chamber*. Robert is more wise than Bluebeard's wife, and knows that it would cost him his head to enter it. Robert, therefore, keeps aloof for the moment. Would there be any use in his martyrdom? Bluebeard cannot live for ever; perhaps, even now, those are on their way (one sees a suspicious cloud of dust or two) that are to destroy him.

In the meantime Robert and his friend have been furnishing the designs that we have before us, and of which, perhaps, the reader will be edified by a brief description. We are not, to be sure, to judge of the French nation by M. Macaire, any more than we are to judge of our own national morals, in the last century, by such a book as the "Beggars' Opera;" but upon the morals and the national manners, works of satire afford a world of light that one would in vain look for in regular books of history. Doctor Smollett would have blushed to devote any considerable portion of his pages to a discussion of the acts and character of Mr. Jonathan Wild, such a figure being hardly admissible among the dignified personages who usually push all others out from the possession of the historical page; but a chapter of that gentleman's memoirs, as they are recorded in that exemplary *recueil*—the "Newgate Calendar;" nay, a canto of the great comic epic (involving many fables, and containing much exaggeration, but still having the seeds of truth) which the satirical poet of those days wrote in celebration of him—we mean Fielding's "History of Jonathan Wild the Great"—does seem to us to give a more curious picture of the manners of those times than any recognised history of them. At the close of his history of George II., Smollett condescends to give a short chapter on Literature and Manners. He speaks of Glover's "Leonidas," Cibber's "Careless Husband," the poems of Mason, Gray, the two Whiteheads, "the nervous style, extensive erudition, and superior sense of a Cooke; the delicate taste, the polished muse, and tender feeling of a Lyttelton." "King," he says, "shone unrivalled in Roman eloquence, the female sex distinguished themselves by their taste and ingenuity. Miss Carte rivalled the celebrated Dacier in learning and critical knowledge; Mrs. Lennox signalized herself by many successful efforts of genius, both in poetry and prose; and Miss Reid excelled the celebrated Rosalba in portrait painting, both in miniature and at large, in oil as well as in crayons. The genius of Cervantes was transferred into the novels of Fielding, who painted the characters and ridiculed the follies of life with equal strength, humour, and propriety. The field of history and biography was cultivated by many writers of ability, among whom we distinguish the copious Guthrie, the circumstantial Ralph, the laborious Carte, the learned and elegant Robertson, and, above all, the ingenious, penetrating, and comprehensive Hume," &c. &c. We will quote no more of the passage. Could a man in the best humour sit down to write a graver satire? Who cares for the tender muse of Lyttelton? Who knows the signal efforts of Mrs. Lennox's genius? Who has seen the admirable performances, in miniature and at large, in oil as well as in crayons, of a Miss Reid? Laborious Carte, and circumstantial Ralph, and copious Guthrie, where are they, their works, and their reputation? Mrs. Lennox's name is just as clean wiped out of the list of worthies as if she had never been born; and Miss Reid, though she was once actual flesh and blood, "rival in miniature and at large" of the celebrated Rosalba, she is as if she had never been at all; her little farthing rushlight of a soul and reputation having burnt out, and left neither wick nor tallow. Death, too, has overtaken copious Guthrie and circumstantial Ralph. Only a few know whereabouts is the grave where lies laborious Carte; and yet, O wondrous power of genius! Fielding's men and women are alive, though History's are not. The progenitors of circumstantial Ralph sent forth, after much labour and pains of making, educating, feeding, clothing, a real man child, a great palpable mass of flesh, bones, and blood (we say nothing about the spirit), which was to move through the world, ponderous, writing histories, and to die, having achieved the title of circumstantial Ralph; and lo! without any of the trouble that the parents of Ralph had undergone, alone, perhaps, in a watch or spunging-house, fuddled, most likely, in the blandest, easiest, and most good-humoured way in the world, Henry

Fielding makes a number of men and women on so many sheets of paper, not only more amusing than Ralph or Miss Reid, but more like flesh and blood, and more alive now than they. Is not Amelia preparing her husband's little supper? Is not Miss Snap chastely preventing the crime of Mr. Firebrand? Is not Parson Adams in the midst of his family, and Mr. Wild taking his last bowl of punch with the Newgate Ordinary? Is not every one of them a real substantial *have*-been personage now?—more real than Reid or Ralph? For our parts, we will not take upon ourselves to say that they do not exist somewhere else; that the actions attributed to them have not really taken place; certain we are that they are more worthy of credence than Ralph, who may or may not have been circumstantial; who may or may not even have existed, a point unworthy of disputation. As for Miss Reid, we will take an affidavit that neither in miniature nor at large did she excel the celebrated Rosalba; and with regard to Mrs. Lennox, we consider her to be a mere figment, like Narcissa, Miss Tabitha Bramble, or any hero or heroine depicted by the historian of "Peregrine Pickle."

In like manner, after viewing nearly ninety portraits of Robert Macaire and his friend Bertrand, all strongly resembling each other, we are inclined to believe in them as historical personages, and to canvass gravely the circumstances of their lives. Why should we not? Have we not their portraits? Are not they sufficient proofs? If not, we must discredit Napoleon (as Archbishop Whately teaches), for about his figure and himself we have no more authentic testimony.

Let the reality of M. Robert Macaire and his friend M. Bertrand be granted, if but to gratify our own fondness for those exquisite characters: we find the worthy pair in the French capital, mingling with all grades of its society, *pars magna* in the intrigues, pleasures, perplexities, rogueries, speculations, which are carried on in Paris, as in our own chief city; for it need not be said that roguery is of no country nor clime, but finds ὡς πανταχοῦ γε πατρὶς ἡ βόσκουσα γῆ, is a citizen of all countries where the quarters are good; among our merry neighbours it finds itself very much at its ease.

Not being endowed, then, with patrimonial wealth, but compelled to exercise their genius to obtain distinction, or even subsistence, we see Messrs. Bertrand and Macaire, by turns, adopting all trades and professions, and exercising each with their own peculiar ingenuity. As public men, we have spoken already of their appearance in one or two important characters, and stated that the Government grew fairly jealous of them, excluding them from office, as the Whigs did Lord Brougham. As private individuals, they are made to distinguish themselves as the founders of journals, *sociétés en commandite* (companies of which the members are irresponsible beyond the amount of their shares), and all sorts of commercial speculations, requiring intelligence and honesty on the part of the directors, confidence and liberal disbursements from the shareholders.

These are, among the French, so numerous, and have been of late years (in the shape of Newspaper Companies, Bitumen Companies, Galvanized-Iron Companies, Railroad Companies, &c.) pursued with such a blind *furor* and lust of gain, by that easily excited and imaginative people, that, as may be imagined, the satirist has found plenty of occasion for remark, and M. Macaire and his friend innumerable opportunities for exercising their talents.

We know nothing of M. Emile de Girardin, except that, in a duel, he shot the best man in France, Armand Carrel; and in Girardin's favour it must be said, that he had no other alternative; but was right in provoking the duel, seeing that the whole Republican party had vowed his destruction, and that he fought and killed their champion, as it were. We know nothing of M. Girardin's private character; but, as far as we can judge from the French public prints, he seems to be the most speculative of speculators, and, of course, a fair butt for the malice of the caricaturists. His one great crime, in the eyes of the French Republicans and Republican newspaper proprietors, was, that Girardin set up a journal, as he called it, "*franchement monarchique,*"—a journal in the pay of the monarchy, that is,—and a journal that cost only forty francs by the year. The *National* costs twice as much; the *Charivari* itself costs half as much again; and though all newspapers, of all parties, concurred in "snubbing" poor M. Girardin and his journal, the Republican prints were by far the most bitter against him, thundering daily accusations and personalities; whether the abuse was well or ill founded, we know not. Hence arose the duel with Carrel; after the termination of which, Girardin put by his pistol, and vowed, very properly, to assist in the shedding of no more blood. Girardin had been the originator of numerous other speculations besides the journal : the capital of these, like that of the journal, was raised by shares, and the shareholders, by some fatality, have found themselves wofully in the lurch ; while Girardin carries on the war gaily, is, or was, a member of the Chamber of Deputies, has money, goes to Court, and possesses a certain kind of reputation. He invented, we believe, the "Institution Agronome de Coetbo,"* the "Physionotype," the "Journal des Connoissances Utiles," the "Panthéon Littéraire," and the system of "Primes" —premiums, that is—to be given, by lottery, to certain subscribers in these institutions. Could Robert Macaire see such things going on, and have no hand in them?

Accordingly, Messrs. Macaire and Bertrand are made the heroes of many speculations of the kind. In almost the first print of our collection, Robert discourses to Bertrand of his projects. "Bertrand," says the disinterested admirer of talent and enterprise, "J'adore l'industrie. Si tu veux nous créons une banque, mais là, une vraie banque : capital cent millions de millions, cent milliards de milliards d'actions. Nous enfonçons la banque de France, les banquiers, les banquistes ; nous enfonçons tout le monde." "Oui," says Bertrand, very calm and stupid, "mais les gendarmes?" "Que tu es bête, Bertrand : est-ce qu'on arrête un millionnaire?" Such is the key to M. Macaire's philosophy ; and a wise creed too, as times go.

Acting on these principles, Robert appears soon after ; he has not created a bank, but a journal. He sits in a

* It is not necessary to enter into descriptions of these various inventions.

chair of state, and discourses to a shareholder. Bertrand, calm and stupid as before, stands humbly behind. "Sir," says the editor of LA BLAGUE, journal quotidienne, "our profits arise from a new combination. The journal costs twenty francs; we sell it for twenty-three and a half. A million subscribers make three millions and a half of profits; there are my figures; contradict me by figures, or I will bring an action for libel." The reader may fancy the scene takes place in England, where many such a swindling prospectus has obtained credit ere now. At Plate 33, Robert is still a journalist; he brings to the editor of a paper an article of his composition, a violent attack on a law. "My dear M. Macaire," says the editor, "this must be changed; we must *praise* this law." "Bon, bon!" says our versatile Macaire. "Je vais rétoucher ça, et je vous fais en faveur de la loi *un article mousseux*."

Can such things be? Is it possible that French journalists can so forget themselves? The rogues! they should come to England and learn consistency. The honesty of the Press in England is like the air we breathe, without it we die. No, no! in France, the satire may do very well; but for England it is too monstrous. Call the press stupid, call it vulgar, call it violent,—but honest it *is*. Who ever heard of a journal changing its politics? *O tempora! O mores!* as Robert Macaire says, this would be carrying the joke too far.

When he has done with newspapers, Robert Macaire begins to distinguish himself on 'Change,* as a creator of

* We have given a description of a genteel Macaire in the account of M. de Bernard's novels.

companies, a vendor of shares, or a dabbler in foreign stock. "Buy my coal-mine shares," shouts Robert; "gold mines, silver mines, diamond mines, 'sont de la pot-bouille de la ratatouille en comparaison de ma houille.'" "Look," says he, on another occasion, to a very timid, open-countenanced client, "you have a property to sell! I have found the very man, a rich capitalist, a fellow whose bills are better than bank-notes." His client sells; the bills are taken in payment, and signed by that respectable capitalist, Monsieur de Saint Bertrand. At Plate 81, we find him inditing a circular letter to all the world, running thus:—"Sir,—I regret to say that your application for shares in the Consolidated European Incombustible Blacking Association cannot be complied with, as all the shares of the C. E. I. B. A. were disposed of on the day they were issued. I have, nevertheless, registered your name, and in case a second series should be put forth, I shall have the honour of immediately giving you notice. I am, sir, yours &c., the Director, Robert Macaire."—"Print 300,000 of these," he says to Bertrand, "and poison all France with them." As usual, the stupid Bertrand remonstrates— "But we have not sold a single share; you have not a penny in your pocket, and "——"Bertrand, you are an ass; do as I bid you."

Will this satire apply anywhere in England? Have we any Consolidated European Blacking Associations amongst us? Have we penniless directors issuing El Dorado prospectuses, and jockeying their shares through the market? For information on this head, we must refer the reader to the newspapers; or if he be connected with the city, and acquainted with commercial men, he will be able to say whether *all* the persons whose names figure at the head of announcements of projected companies are as rich as Rothschild, or quite as honest as heart could desire.

When Macaire has sufficiently *exploité* the Bourse, whether as a gambler in the public funds or other companies, he sagely perceives that it is time to turn to some other profession, and, providing himself with a black gown, proposes blandly to Bertrand to set up—a new religion. "Mon ami," says the repentant sinner, "le temps de la commandite va passer, *mais les badauds ne passeront pas,* (O rare sentence! it should be written in letters of gold!) *occupons nous de ce qui est éternel.* Si nous fassions une réligion?" On which M. Bertrand remarks, "A religion! what the devil—a religion is not an easy thing to make." But Macaire's receipt is easy. "Get a gown, take a shop," he says, "borrow some chairs, preach about Napoleon, or the discovery of America, or Molière—and there's a religion for you."

We have quoted this sentence more for the contrast it offers with our own manners, than for its merits. After the noble paragraph, "Les badauds ne passeront pas, occupons nous de ce qui est éternel," one would have expected better satire upon cant than the words that follow. We are not in a condition to say whether the subjects chosen are those that had been selected by Père Enfantin, or Chatel, or Lacordaire; but the words are curious, we think, for the very reason that the satire is so poor. The fact is, there is no religion in Paris; even clever M. Philipon, who satirizes everything, and must know, therefore, some little about the subject which he ridicules, has nothing to say, but, " Preach a sermon, and that makes a religion; anything will do." If *anything* will do, it is clear that the religious commodity is not in much demand. Tartuffe had better things to say about hypocrisy in his time; but, then, Faith was alive: now, there is no satirizing religious cant in France, for its contrary, true religion, has disappeared altogether; and having no substance, can cast no shadow. If a satirist would lash the religious hypocrites in *England* now—the High-Church hypocrites, the Low-Church hypocrites, the promiscuous Dissenting hypocrites, the No-Popery hypocrites—he would have ample subject enough. In France, the religious hypocrites went out with the Bourbons. Those who remain pious in that country (or, rather, we should say, in the capital, for of that we speak,) are unaffectedly so, for they have no worldly benefit to hope for from their piety; the great majority have no religion at all, and do not scoff at the few, for scoffing is the minority's weapon, and is passed always to the weaker side, whatever that may be. Thus H. B. caricatures the Ministers: if by any accident that body of men should be dismissed from their situations, and be succeeded by H. B.'s friends, the Tories,—what must the poor artist do? He must pine away and die, if he be not converted; he cannot always be paying compliments; for caricature has a spice of Goethe's Devil in it, and is " der Geist der stets verneint," the Spirit that is always denying.

With one or two of the French writers and painters of caricatures, the King tried the experiment of bribery;

which succeeded occasionally in buying off the enemy, and bringing him from the republican to the royal camp; but when there, the deserter was never of any use. Figaro, when so treated, grew fat and desponding, and lost all his sprightly *verve;* and Nemesis became as gentle as a Quakeress. But these instances of "ratting" were not many. Some few poets were bought over; but, among men following the profession of the press, a change of politics is an infringement of the point of honour, and a man must *fight* as well as apostatize. A very curious table might be made, signalizing the difference of the moral standard between us and the French. Why is the grossness and indelicacy, publicly permitted in England, unknown in France, where private morality is certainly at a lower ebb? Why is the point of private honour now more rigidly maintained among the French? Why is it, as it should be, a moral disgrace for a Frenchman to go into debt, and no disgrace for him to cheat his customer? Why is there more honesty and less—more propriety and less?—and how are we to account for the particular vices or virtues which belong to each nation in its turn?

The above is the Reverend M. Macaire's solitary exploit as a spiritual swindler: as *Maître* Macaire in the courts of law, as *avocat, avoué*—in a humbler capacity even, as a prisoner at the bar, he distinguishes himself greatly, as may be imagined. On one occasion we find the learned gentleman humanely visiting an unfortunate *détenu*—no other person, in fact, than his friend M. Bertrand, who has fallen into some trouble, and is awaiting the sentence of the law. He begins—

"Mon cher Bertrand, donne moi cent écus, je te fais acquitter d'emblée."

"J'ai pas d'argent."

"Hé bien, donne moi cent francs."

"Pas le sou."

"Tu n'as pas dix francs?"

"Pas un liard."

"Alors donne moi tes bottes, je plaiderai la circonstance attenuante."

The manner in which Maître Macaire soars from the *cent écus* (a high point already) to the sublime of the boots, is in the best comic style. In another instance he pleads before a judge, and, mistaking his client, pleads for defendant, instead of plaintiff. "The infamy of the plaintiff's character, my *luds*, renders his testimony on such a charge as this wholly unavailing." "M. Macaire, M. Macaire," cries the attorney, in a fright, "you are for the plaintiff!" "This, my lords, is what the defendant *will say*. This is the line of defence which the opposite party intend to pursue; as if slanders like these could weigh with an enlightened jury, or injure the spotless reputation of my client!" In this story and expedient M. Macaire has been indebted to the English bar. If there be an occupation for the English satirist in the exposing of the cant and knavery of the pretenders to religion, what room is there for him to lash the infamies of the law! On this point the French are babes in iniquity compared to us—a counsel prostituting himself for money is a matter with us so stale, that it is hardly food for satire: which, to be popular, must find some much more complicated and interesting knavery whereon to exercise its skill.

M. Macaire is more skilful in love than in law, and appears once or twice in a very amiable light while under the influence of the tender passion. We find him at the head of one of those useful establishments unknown in our country—a Bureau de Mariage: half a dozen of such places are daily advertised in the Journals: and "une veuve de trente ans ayant une fortune de deux cent mille francs," or, "une demoiselle de quinze ans, jolie, d'une famille très distinguée, qui possède trente mille livres de rentes,"—continually, in this kind-hearted way, are offering themselves to the public: sometimes it is a gentleman, with a "physique agréable,—des talens de société"—and a place under Government, who makes a sacrifice of himself in a similar manner. In our little historical gallery we find this philanthropic anti-Malthusian at the head of an establishment of this kind, introducing a very meek, simple-looking bachelor to some distinguished ladies of his *connoissance.* "Let me present you, sir, to Madame de St. Bertrand (it is our old friend), veuve de la grand armée, et Mdlle Eloa de Wormspire—ces dames brûlent de l'envie de faire votre connoissance; je les ai invitées à dîner chez vous ce soir, vous nous menerez à l'opéra, et nous ferons une petite partie d'écarté. Tenez vous bien, M. Gobard! ces dames ont des projets sur vous!"

Happy Gobard! happy system, which can thus bring the pure and loving together, and acts as the best ally of Hymen! The announcement of the rank and titles of Madame de St. Bertrand—"veuve de la grande armée"—is very happy. "*La grande armée*" has been a father to more orphans, and a husband to more widows, than it ever made. Mistresses of *cafés*, old governesses, keepers of boarding-houses, genteel beggars, and ladies of lower rank still, have this favourite pedigree. They have all had *malheurs* (what kind it is needless to particularize), they are all connected with the *grand homme*, and their fathers were all colonels. This title exactly answers to the "clergyman's daughter" in England—as, "A young lady, the daughter of a clergyman, is desirous to teach," &c.; "A clergyman's widow receives into her house a few select," and so forth. "Appeal to the benevolent. By a series of unheard-of calamities, a young lady, daughter of a clergyman in the west of England, has been plunged," &c. &c. The difference is curious, as indicating the standard of respectability.

The male beggar of fashion is not so well known among us as in Paris, where street-doors are open; six or eight families live in a house; and the gentleman who earns his livelihood by this profession can make half-a-dozen visits without the trouble of knocking from house to house, and the pain of being observed by the whole street, while the footman is examining him from the area. Some few may be seen in England about the inns of court, where the locality is favourable (where, however, the owners of the chambers are not proverbially soft of heart, so that the harvest must be poor); but Paris is full of such adventurers,—fat, smooth-tongued, and well-dressed, with gloves and gilt-headed canes, who would be insulted almost by the offer of silver, and expect your gold as their right.

17—2

Among these, of course, our friend Robert plays his part; and an excellent engraving represents him, snuff-box in hand, advancing to an old gentleman, whom, by his poodle, his powdered head, and his drivelling, stupid look, one knows to be a Carlist of the old régime. "I beg pardon," says Robert; "is it really yourself to whom I have the honour of speaking?"—"It is." "Do you take snuff?" —"I thank you." "Sir, I have had misfortunes—I want assistance. I am a Vendéan of illustrious birth. You know the family of *Macairbec*—we are of Brest. My grandfather served the King in his galleys; my father and I belong, also, to the marine. Unfortunate suits at law have plunged us into difficulties, and I do not hesitate to ask you for the succour of ten francs."—"Sir, I never give to those I don't know."—"Right, sir, perfectly right. Perhaps you will have the kindness to *lend* me ten francs?"

The adventures of Doctor Macaire need not be described, because the different degrees in quackery which are taken by that learned physician, are all well known in England, where we have the advantage of many higher degrees in the science, which our neighbours know nothing about. We have not Hahnemann, but we have his disciples; we have not Broussais, but we have the College of Health; and surely a dose of Morrison's pills is a sublimer discovery than a draught of hot water. We had St. John Long, too, —where is his science?—and we are credibly informed that some important cures have been effected by the inspired dignitaries of "the church" in Newman Street; which, if it continue to practise, will sadly interfere with the profits of the regular physicians, and where the miracles of the Abbé Paris are about to be acted over again.

In speaking of M. Macaire and his adventures, we have managed so entirely to convince ourselves of the reality of the personage, that we have quite forgotten to speak of Messrs. Philipon and Daumier, who are, the one the inventor, the other the designer, of the Macaire Picture Gallery. As works of *esprit*, these drawings are not more remarkable than they are as works of art, and we never recollect to have seen a series of sketches possessing more extraordinary cleverness and variety. The countenance and figure of Macaire, and the dear stupid Bertrand, are preserved, of course, with great fidelity throughout; but the admirable way in which each fresh character is conceived, the grotesque appropriateness of Robert's every successive attitude and gesticulation, and the variety of Bertrand's postures of invariable repose, the exquisite fitness of all the other characters, who act their little part and disappear from the scene, cannot be described on paper, or too highly lauded. The figures are very carelessly drawn; but, if the reader can understand us, all the attitudes and limbs are perfectly *conceived*, and wonderfully natural and various. After pondering over these drawings for some hours, as we have been while compiling this notice of them, we have grown to believe that the personages are real, and the scenes remain imprinted on the brain as if we had absolutely been present at their acting. Perhaps the clever way in which the plates are coloured, and the excellent effect which is put into each, may add to this illusion. Now, in looking, for instance, at H. B.'s slim vapoury figures, they have struck us as excellent *likenesses* of men and women, but no more; the bodies want spirit, action, and individuality. George Cruikshank, as a humorist, has quite as much genius, but he does not know the art of "effect" so well as Monsieur Daumier; and, if we might venture to give a word of advice to another humorous designer, whose works are extensively circulated — the illustrator of *Pickwick*, and *Nicholas Nickleby*,—it would be to study well these caricatures of of Monsieur Daumier; who, though he executes very carelessly, knows very well what he would express, indicates perfectly the attitude and identity of his figure, and is quite aware, beforehand, of the effect which he intends to produce. The one we should fancy to be a practised artist, taking his ease; the other, a young one, somewhat bewildered: a very clever one, however, who, if he would think more, and exaggerate less, would add not a little to his reputation.

Having pursued, all through these remarks, the comparison between English art and French art, English and French humour, manners, and morals, perhaps we should endeavour, also, to write an analytical essay on English cant or humbug, as distinguished from French. It might be shown that the latter was more picturesque and startling, the former more substantial and positive. It has none of the poetic flights of the French genius, but advances steadily, and gains more ground in the end than its sprightlier compeer. But such a discussion would carry us through the whole range of French and English history, and the reader has probably read quite enough of the subject in this and the foregoing pages.

We shall, therefore, say no more of French and English caricatures generally, or of Mr. Macaire's particular accomplishments and adventures. They are far better understood by examining the original pictures, by which Philipon and Daumier have illustrated them, than by translations first into print and afterwards into English. They form a very curious and instructive commentary upon the present state of society in Paris, and a hundred years hence, when the whole of this struggling, noisy, busy, merry race shall have exchanged their pleasures or occupations for a quiet coffin (and a tawdry lying epitaph) at Montmartre, or Père la Chaise; when the follies here recorded shall have been superseded by new ones, and the fools now so active shall have given up the inheritance of the world to their children; the latter will, at least, have the advantage of knowing, intimately and exactly, the manners of life and being of their grandsires, and calling up, when they so choose it, our ghosts from the grave, to live, love, quarrel, swindle, suffer, and struggle on blindly as of yore. And when the amused speculator shall have laughed sufficiently at the immensity of our follies, and the paltriness of our aims, smiled at our exploded superstitions, wondered how this man should be considered great, who is now clean forgotten (as copious Guthrie before mentioned); how this should have been thought a patriot who is but a knave spouting commonplace; or how that should have been dubbed a philosopher who is but a dull fool, blinking solemn, and pretending to see in the dark; when he shall have examined all these at his leisure, smiling in a pleasant contempt and good-humoured superiority, and thanking Heaven for his increased lights, he will shut the book, and be a fool as his fathers were before him.

It runs in the blood. Well hast thou said, O ragged Macaire,—"Le jour va passer, MAIS LES BADAUDS NE PASSERONT PAS."

LITTLE POINSINET.

About the year 1760, there lived, at Paris, a little fellow, who was the darling of all the wags of his acquaintance. Nature seemed, in the formation of this little man, to have amused herself, by giving loose to half a hundred of her most comical caprices. He had some wit and drollery of his own, which sometimes rendered his sallies very amusing; but, where his friends laughed with him once, they laughed at him a thousand times, for he had a fund of absurdity in himself that was more pleasant than all the wit in the world. He was as proud as a peacock, as wicked as an ape, and as silly as a goose. He did not possess one single grain of common sense; but, in revenge, his pretensions were enormous, his ignorance vast, and his credulity more extensive still. From his youth upwards, he had read nothing but the new novels, and the verses in the almanacs, which helped him not a little in making, what he called, poetry of his own; for, of course, our little hero was a poet. All the common usages of life, all the ways of the world, and all the customs of society, seemed to be quite unknown to him; add to these good qualities, a magnificent conceit, a cowardice inconceivable, and a face so irresistibly comic, that every one who first beheld it was compelled to burst out a laughing, and you will have some notion of this strange little gentleman. He was very proud of his voice, and uttered all his sentences in the richest tragic tone. He was little better than a dwarf; but he elevated his eyebrows, held up his neck, walked on the tips of his toes, and gave himself the airs of a giant. He had a little pair of bandy legs, which seemed much too short to support anything like a human body; but, by the help of these crooked supporters, he thought he could dance like a Grace; and, indeed, fancied all the graces possible were to be found in his person. His goggle eyes were always rolling about wildly, as if in correspondence with the disorder of his little brain; and his countenance thus wore an expression of perpetual wonder. With such happy natural gifts, he not only fell into all traps that were laid for him, but seemed almost to go out of his way to seek them; although, to be sure, his friends did not give him much trouble in that search, for they prepared hoaxes for him incessantly.

One day the wags introduced him to a company of ladies, who, though not countesses and princesses exactly, took, nevertheless, those titles upon themselves for the nonce; and were all, for the same reason, violently smitten with Master Poinsinet's person. One of them, the lady of the house, was especially tender; and, seating him by her side at supper, so plied him with smiles, ogles, and champagne, that our litte hero grew crazed with ecstasy, and wild with love. In the midst of his happiness, a cruel knock was heard below, accompanied by quick loud talking, swearing, and shuffling of feet: you would have thought a regiment was at the door. "Oh, heavens!" cried the marchioness, starting up, and giving to the hand of Poinsinet one parting squeeze; "fly—fly, my Poinsinet: 'tis the colonel—my husband!" At this, each gentleman of the party rose, and, drawing his rapier, vowed to cut his way through the colonel and all his *mousquetaires*, or die, if need be, by the side of Poinsinet.

The little fellow was obliged to lug out his sword too, and went shuddering down stairs, heartily repenting of his passion for marchionesses. When the party arrived in the street, they found, sure enough, a dreadful company of *mousquetaires*, as they seemed, ready to oppose their passage. Swords crossed,—torches blazed; and, with the most dreadful shouts and imprecations, the contending parties rushed upon one another; the friends of Poinsinet surrounding and supporting that little warrior, as the French knights did King Francis at Pavia, otherwise the poor fellow certainly would have fallen down in the gutter from fright.

But the combat was suddenly interrupted; for the neighbours, who knew nothing of the trick going on, and thought the brawl was real, had been screaming with all their might for the police, who began about this time to arrive. Directly they appeared, friends and enemies of Poinsinet at once took to their heels; and, in *this* part of the transaction, at least, our hero himself showed that he was equal to the longest-legged grenadier that ever ran away.

When, at last, those little bandy legs of his had borne

him safely to his lodgings, all Poinsinet's friends crowded round him, to congratulate him on his escape and his valour.

"Egad, how he pinked that great red-haired fellow!" said one.

"No; did I?" said Poinsinet.

"Did you? Psha! don't try to play the modest, and humbug *us;* you know you did. I suppose you will say, next, that you were not for three minutes point to point with Cartentierce himself, the most dreadful swordsman of the army."

"Why, you see," says Poinsinet, quite delighted, "it was so dark that I did not know with whom I was engaged; although, *corbleu*, I *did for* one or two of the fellows." And after a little more of such conversation, during which he was fully persuaded that he had done for a dozen of the enemy, at least, Poinsinet went to bed, his little person trembling with fright and pleasure; and he fell asleep, and dreamed of rescuing ladies, and destroying monsters, like a second Amadis de Gaule.

When he awoke in the morning, he found a party of his friends in his room: one was examining his coat and waistcoat; another was casting many curious glances at his inexpressibles. "Look here!" said this gentleman, holding up the garment to the light; "one—two—three gashes! I am hanged if the cowards did not aim at Poinsinet's legs! There are four holes in the sword arm of his coat, and seven have gone right through coat and waistcoat. Good Heaven! Poinsinet, have you had a surgeon to your wounds?"

"Wounds!" said the little man, springing up, "I

don't know—that is, I hope—that is—oh Lord! oh Lord! I hope I'm not wounded!" and, after a proper examination, he discovered he was not.

"Thank Heaven! thank Heaven!" said one of the wags (who, indeed, during the slumbers of Poinsinet had been occupied in making these very holes through the garments of that individual), "if you have escaped, it is by a miracle. Alas! alas! all your enemies have not been so lucky."

"How! is anybody wounded?" said Poinsinet.

"My dearest friend, prepare yourself; that unhappy man who came to revenge his menaced honour—that gallant officer—that injured husband, Colonel Count de Cartentierce ——"

"Well?"

"Is NO MORE! he died this morning, pierced through with nineteen wounds from your hand, and calling upon his country to revenge his murder."

When this awful sentence was pronounced, all the auditory gave a pathetic and simultaneous sob; and as for Poinsinet, he sank back on his bed with a howl of terror, which would have melted a Visigoth to tears, or to laughter. As soon as his terror and remorse had, in some degree, subsided, his comrades spoke to him of the necessity of making his escape; and, huddling on his clothes, and bidding them all a tender adieu, he set off, incontinently, without his breakfast, for England, America, or Russia, not knowing exactly which.

One of his companions agreed to accompany him on a part of this journey,—that is, as far as the barrier of St.

Denis, which is, as everybody knows, on the high road to Dover; and there, being tolerably secure, they entered a tavern for breakfast; which meal, the last that he ever was to take, perhaps, in his native city, Poinsinet was just about to discuss, when, behold! a gentleman entered the apartment where Poinsinet and his friend were seated, and, drawing from his pocket a paper, with "AU NOM DU ROY" flourished on the top, read from it, or rather from Poinsinet's own figure, his exact *signalement*, laid his hand on his shoulder, and arrested him in the name of the King, and of the provost-marshal of Paris. "I arrest you, sir," said he, gravely, "with regret; you have slain, with seventeen wounds, in single combat, Colonel Count de Cartentierce, one of his Majesty's household; and, as his murderer, you fall under the immediate authority of the provost-marshal, and die without trial or benefit of clergy."

You may fancy how the poor little man's appetite fell when he heard this speech. "In the provost-marshal's hands?" said his friend: "then it *is* all over, indeed! When does my poor friend suffer, sir?"

"At half-past six o'clock, the day after to-morrow," said the officer, sitting down, and helping himself to wine. "But, stop," said he, suddenly; "sure I can't mistake? Yes—no—yes, it is. My dear friend, my dear Durand! don't you recollect your old schoolfellow, Antoine?" And herewith the officer flung himself into the arms of Durand, Poinsinet's comrade, and they performed a most affecting scene of friendship.

"This may be of some service to you," whispered Durand to Poinsinet; and, after some further parley, he

asked the officer when he was bound to deliver up his prisoner; and, hearing that he was not called upon to appear at the Marshalsea before six o'clock at night, Monsieur Durand prevailed upon Monsieur Antoine to wait until that hour, and in the meantime, to allow his prisoner to walk about the town in his company. This request was, with a little difficulty, granted; and poor Poinsinet begged to be carried to the houses of his various friends, and bid them farewell. Some were aware of the trick that had been played upon him; others were not; but the poor little man's credulity was so great, that it was impossible to undeceive him; and he went from house to house bewailing his fate, and followed by the complaisant marshal's officer.

The news of his death he received with much more meekness than could have been expected; but what he could not reconcile to himself was, the idea of dissection afterwards. "What can they want with me?" cried the poor wretch, in an unusual fit of candour. "I am very small, and ugly; it would be different if I were a tall, fine-looking fellow." But he was given to understand that beauty made very little difference to the surgeons, who, on the contrary, would, on certain occasions, prefer a deformed man to a handsome one; for science was much advanced by the study of such monstrosities. With this reason Poinsinet was obliged to be content; and so paid his rounds of visits, and repeated his dismal adieus.

The officer of the provost-marshal, however amusing Poinsinet's woes might have been, began, by this time, to grow very weary of them, and gave him more than one opportunity to escape. He would stop at shop-windows, loiter round corners; and look up in the sky, but all in vain: Poinsinet would not escape, do what the other would. At length, luckily, about dinner-time, the officer met one of Poinsinet's friends and his own; and the three agreed to dine at a tavern, as they had breakfasted; and here the officer, who vowed that he had been up for five weeks incessantly, fell suddenly asleep, in the profoundest fatigue; and Poinsinet was persuaded, after much hesitation on his part, to take leave of him.

And now, this danger overcome, another was to be avoided. Beyond a doubt, the police were after him, and how was he to avoid them? He must be disguised, of course; and one of his friends, a tall, gaunt, lawyer's clerk, agreed to provide him with habits.

So little Poinsinet dressed himself out in the clerk's dingy black suit, of which the knee-breeches hung down to his heels, and the waist of the coat reached to the calves of his legs; and, furthermore, he blacked his eyebrows, and wore a huge black periwig, in which his friend vowed that no one could recognise him. But the most painful incident, with regard to the periwig, was, that Poinsinet, whose solitary beauty—if beauty it might be called—was a head of copious, curling, yellow hair, was compelled to snip off every one of his golden locks, and to rub the bristles with a black dye; "for if your wig were to come off," said the lawyer, "and your fair hair to tumble over your shoulders, every man would know, or at least suspect you." So off the locks were cut, and in his black suit and periwig little Poinsinet went abroad.

His friends had their cue; and when he appeared

amongst them, not one seemed to know him. He was taken into companies where his character was discussed before him, and his wonderful escape spoken of. At last he was introduced to the very officer of the provost-marshal who had taken him into custody, and who told him that he had been dismissed the provost's service, in consequence of the escape of the prisoner. Now, for the first time, poor Poinsinet thought himself tolerably safe, and blest his kind friends who had procured for him such a complete disguise. How this affair ended I know not,—whether some new lie was coined, to account for his release, or whether he was simply told that he had been hoaxed: it mattered little; for the little man was quite as ready to be hoaxed the next day.

Poinsinet was one day invited to dine with one of the servants of the Tuileries; and, before his arrival, a person in company had been decorated with a knot of lace and a gold key, such as chamberlains wear; he was introduced to Poinsinet as the Count de Truchses, chamberlain to the King of Prussia. After dinner the conversation fell upon the Count's visit to Paris; when his Excellency, with a mysterious air, vowed that he had only come for pleasure. "It is mighty well," said a third person, "and, of course, we can't cross-question your lordship too closely;" but, at the same time, it was hinted to Poinsinet that a person of such consequence did not travel for *nothing*, with which opinion Poinsinet solemnly agreed; and, indeed, it was borne out by a subsequent declaration of the Count, who condescended, at last, to tell the company, in confidence, that he *had* a mission, and a most important one—to find, namely, among the literary men of France, a governor for the Prince Royal of Prussia. The company seemed astonished that the King had not made choice of Voltaire or D'Alembert, and mentioned a dozen other distinguished men who might be competent to this important duty: but the Count, as may be imagined, found objections to every one of them; and, at last, one of the guests said, that, if his Prussian Majesty was not particular as to age, he knew a person more fitted for the place than any other who could be found,—his honourable friend, M. Poinsinet, was the individual to whom he alluded.

"Good heavens!" cried the Count, "is it possible that the celebrated Poinsinet would take such a place? I would give the world to see him!" And you may fancy how Poinsinet simpered and blushed when the introduction immediately took place.

The Count protested to him that the King would be charmed to know him; and added, that one of his operas (for it must be told that our little friend was a vaudeville-maker by trade) had been acted seven-and-twenty times at the theatre at Potsdam. His Excellency then detailed to him all the honours and privileges which the governor of the Prince Royal might expect; and all the guests encouraged the little man's vanity, by asking him for his protection and favour. In a short time our hero grew so inflated with pride and vanity, that he was for patronizing the chamberlain himself, who proceeded to inform him that he was furnished with all the necessary powers by his sovereign, who had specially enjoined him to confer upon the future governor of his son the royal order of the Black Eagle.

Poinsinet, delighted, was ordered to kneel down; and the Count produced a large yellow riband, which he hung over his shoulder, and which was, he declared, the grand cordon of the order. You must fancy Poinsinet's face, and excessive delight at this; for as for describing them, nobody can. For four-and-twenty hours the happy chevalier paraded through Paris with this flaring yellow riband; and he was not undeceived until his friends had another trick in store for him.

He dined one day in the company of a man who understood a little of the noble art of conjuring, and performed some clever tricks on the cards. Poinsinet's organ of wonder was enormous; he looked on with the gravity and awe of a child, and thought the man's tricks sheer miracles. It wanted no more to set his companions to work.

"Who is this wonderful man?" said he to his neighbour.

"Why," said the other, mysteriously, "one hardly knows who he is; or, at least, one does not like to say to such an indiscreet fellow as you are." Poinsinet at once swore to be secret. "Well, then," said his friend, "you will hear that man—that wonderful man—called by a name which is not his; his real name is Acosta; he is a Portuguese Jew, a Rosicrucian, and cabalist of the first order, and compelled to leave Lisbon for fear of the Inquisition. He performs here, as you see, some extraordinary things, occasionally; but the master of the house, who loves him excessively, would not, for the world, that his name should be made public."

"Ah, bah!" said Poinsinet, who affected the *bel esprit*;

"you don't mean to say that you believe in magic, and cabalas, and such trash?"

"Do I not? You shall judge for yourself;" and, accordingly, Poinsinet was presented to the magician, who pretended to take a vast liking for him, and declared that he saw in him certain marks which would infallibly lead him to great eminence in the magic art, if he chose to study it.

Dinner was served, and Poinsinet placed by the side of the miracle-worker, who became very confidential with him, and promised him—ay, before dinner was over—a remarkable instance of his power. Nobody, on this occasion, ventured to cut a single joke against poor Poinsinet; nor could he fancy that any trick was intended against him, for the demeanour of the society towards him was perfectly grave and respectful, and the conversation serious. On a sudden, however, somebody exclaimed, "Where is Poinsinet? Did any one see him leave the room?"

All the company exclaimed how singular the disappearance was; and Poinsinet himself, growing alarmed, turned round to his neighbour, and was about to explain.

"Hush!" said the magician, in a whisper; "I told you that you should see what I could do. *I have made you invisible;* be quiet, and you shall see some more tricks that I shall play with these fellows."

Poinsinet remained then silent, and listened to his neighbours, who agreed, at last, that he was a quiet, orderly personage, and had left the table early, being unwilling to drink too much. Presently they ceased to talk about him, and resumed their conversation upon other matters.

At first it was very quiet and grave, but the master of the house brought back the talk to the subject of Poinsinet, and uttered all sorts of abuse concerning him. He begged the gentleman, who had introduced such a little scamp into his house, to bring him thither no more: whereupon the other took up, warmly, Poinsinet's defence; declared that he was a man of the greatest merit, frequenting the best society, and remarkable for his talents as well as his virtues.

"Ah!" said Poinsinet to the magician, quite charmed at what he heard, "how ever shall I thank you, my dear sir, for thus showing me who my true friends are?"

The magician promised him still further favours in prospect; and told him to look out now, for he was about to throw all the company into a temporary fit of madness, which, no doubt, would be very amusing.

In consequence, all the company, who had heard every syllable of the conversation, began to perform the most extraordinary antics, much to the delight of Poinsinet. One asked a nonsensical question, and the other delivered an answer not at all to the purpose. If a man asked for a drink, they poured him out a pepper-box or a napkin: they took a pinch of snuff, and swore it was excellent wine; and vowed that the bread was the most delicious mutton ever tasted. The little man was delighted.

"Ah!" said he, "these fellows are prettily punished for their rascally backbiting of me!"

"Gentlemen," said the host, "I shall now give you some celebrated champagne," and he poured out to each a glass of water.

"Good Heavens!" said one, spitting it out, with the

most horrible grimace, " where did you get this detestable claret ? "

" Ah, faugh ! " said a second, " I never tasted such vile corked burgundy in all my days ! " and he threw the glass of water into Poinsinet's face, as did half-a-dozen of the other guests, drenching the poor wretch to the skin. To complete this pleasant illusion, two of the guests fell to boxing across Poinsinet, who received a number of the blows, and received them with the patience of a fakir, feeling himself more flattered by the precious privilege of beholding this scene invisible, than hurt by the blows and buffets which the mad company bestowed upon him.

The fame of this adventure spread quickly over Paris, and all the world longed to have at their houses the representation of *Poinsinet the Invisible.* The servants and the whole company used to be put up to the trick; and Poinsinet, who believed in his invisibility as much as he did in his existence, went about with his friend and protector the magician. People, of course, never pretended to see him, and would very often not talk of him at all for some time, but hold sober conversation about any thing else in the world. When dinner was served, of course there was no cover laid for Poinsinet, who carried about a little stool, on which he sate by the side of the magician, and always ate off his plate. Everybody was astonished at the magician's appetite and at the quantity of wine he drank; as for little Poinsinet, he never once suspected any trick, and had such a confidence in his magician, that, I do believe, if the latter had told him to fling himself out of window, he would have done so, without the slightest trepidation.

Among other mystifications in which the Portuguese enchanter plunged him, was one which used to afford always a good deal of amusement. He informed Poinsinet, with great mystery, that *he was not himself;* he was not, that is to say, that ugly, deformed little monster, called Poinsinet; but that his birth was most illustrious, and his real name *Polycarte*. He was, in fact, the son of a celebrated magician; but other magicians, enemies of his father, had changed him in his cradle, altering his features into their present hideous shape, in order that a silly old fellow, called Poinsinet, might take him to be his own son, which little monster the magician had likewise spirited away.

The poor wretch was sadly cast down at this; for he tried to fancy that his person was agreeable to the ladies, of whom he was one of the warmest little admirers possible; and to console him somewhat, the magician told him that his real shape was exquisitely beautiful, and as soon as he should appear in it, all the beauties in Paris would be at his feet. But how to regain it? "Oh, for one minute of that beauty!" cried the little man; "what would he not give to appear under that enchanting form!" The magician hereupon waved his stick over his head, pronounced some awful magical words, and twisted him round three times; at the third twist, the men in company seemed struck with astonishment and envy, the ladies clasped their hands, and some of them kissed his. Everybody declared his beauty to be supernatural.

Poinsinet, enchanted, rushed to a glass. "Fool!" said the magician; "do you suppose that *you* can see the change? My power to render you invisible, beautiful, or ten times more hideous even than you are, extends only to others, not to you. You may look a thousand times in the glass, and you will only see those deformed limbs and disgusting features with which devilish malice has disguised you." Poor little Poinsinet looked, and came back in tears. "But," resumed the magician,—"ha, ha, ha!—*I* know *a* way in which to disappoint the machinations of these fiendish magi."

"O my benefactor!—my great master!—for Heaven's sake tell it!" gasped Poinsinet.

"Look you—it is this. A prey to enchantment and demoniac art all your life long, you have lived until your present age perfectly satisfied; nay, absolutely vain of a person the most singularly hideous that ever walked the earth!"

"*Is* it?" whispered Poinsinet. "Indeed, and indeed, I didn't think it so bad!"

"He acknowledges it! he acknowledges it!" roared the magician. "Wretch, dotard, owl, mole, miserable buzzard! I have no reason to tell thee now that thy form is monstrous, that children cry, that cowards turn pale, that teeming matrons shudder to behold it. It is not thy fault that thou art thus ungainly; but wherefore so blind? wherefore so conceited of thyself? I tell thee, Poinsinet, that over every fresh instance of thy vanity the hostile enchanters rejoice and triumph. As long as thou art blindly satisfied with thyself; as long as thou pretendest, in thy present odious shape, to win the love of aught above a negress; nay, further still, until thou hast learned to regard that face, as others do, with the most intolerable horror and disgust, to abuse it when thou seest it, to despise it, in short, and treat that miserable disguise in which the enchanters have wrapped thee with the strongest hatred and scorn, so long art thou destined to wear it."

Such speeches as these, continually repeated, caused Poinsinet to be fully convinced of his ugliness; he used to go about in companies, and take every opportunity of inveighing against himself; he made verses and epigrams against himself; he talked about "that dwarf, Poinsinet;" "that buffoon, Poinsinet;" "that conceited, humpbacked Poinsinet;" and he would spend hours before the glass, abusing his own face as he saw it reflected there, and vowing that he grew handsomer at every fresh epithet that he uttered.

Of course the wags, from time to time, used to give him every possible encouragement, and declared that, since this exercise, his person was amazingly improved. The ladies, too, began to be so excessively fond of him, that the little fellow was obliged to caution them at last—for the good, as he said, of society; he recommended them to draw lots, for he could not gratify them all; but promised, when his metamorphosis was complete, that the one chosen should become the happy Mrs. Poinsinet; or to speak more correctly, Mrs. Polycarte.

I am sorry to say, however, that, on the score of gallantry, Poinsinet was never quite convinced of the hideousness of his appearance. He had a number of adventures, accordingly, with the ladies, but, strange to say, the husbands or fathers were always interrupting him. On one occasion he was made to pass the night in a slipper-bath full of water; where, although he had all his clothes on, he declared that he nearly caught his death of cold. Another night, in revenge, the poor fellow

—— " dans le simple appareil
D'une beauté, qu'on vient d'arracher au sommeil,"

spent a number of hours contemplating the beauty of the moon on the tiles. These adventures are pretty numerous in the memoirs of M. Poinsinet; but the fact is, that people in France were a great deal more philosophical in those days than the English are now, so that Poinsinet's loves must be passed over, as not being to our taste. His magician was a great diver, and told Poinsinet the most wonderful tales of his two minutes' absence under water. These two minutes, he said, lasted through a year, at least, which he spent in the company of a naiad, more beautiful than Venus, in a palace more splendid than even Versailles. Fired by the description, Poinsinet used to dip, and dip, but he never was known to make any mermaid acquaintances, although he fully believed that one day he should find such.

The invisible joke was brought to an end by Poinsinet's too great reliance on it; for being, as we have said, of a very tender and sanguine disposition, he one day fell in love with a lady in whose company he dined, and whom he actually proposed to embrace; but the fair lady, in the hurry of the moment, forgot to act up to the joke; and instead of receiving Poinsinet's salute with calmness, grew indignant, called him an impudent little scoundrel, and

lent him a sound box on the ear. With this slap the
invisibility of Poinsinet disappeared, the gnomes and genii
left him, and he settled down into common life again, and
was hoaxed only by vulgar means.

A vast number of pages might be filled with narratives
of the tricks that were played upon him; but they resemble
each other a good deal, as may be imagined, and the
chief point remarkable about them is the wondrous faith
of Poinsinet. After being introduced to the Prussian
ambassador at the Tuileries, he was presented to the
Turkish envoy at the Place Vendôme, who received him in
state, surrounded by the officers of his establishment, all
dressed in the smartest dresses that the wardrobe of the
Opéra Comique could furnish.

As the greatest honour that could be done to him,
Poinsinet was invited to eat, and a tray was produced, on
which was a delicate dish prepared in the Turkish manner.
This consisted of a reasonable quantity of mustard, salt,
cinnamon and ginger, nutmegs and cloves, with a couple
of tablespoonfuls of cayenne pepper, to give the whole a
flavour; and Poinsinet's countenance may be imagined
when he introduced into his mouth a quantity of this
exquisite compound.

"The best of the joke was," says the author who
records so many of the pitiless tricks practised upon poor
Poinsinet, "that the little man used to laugh at them
afterwards himself with perfect good humour; and lived
in the daily hope that, from being the sufferer, he should
become the agent in these hoaxes, and do to others as he
had been done by." Passing, therefore, one day, on the

Pont Neuf, with a friend, who had been one of the greatest performers, the latter said to him, "Poinsinet, my good fellow, thou hast suffered enough, and thy sufferings have made thee so wise and cunning, that thou art worthy of entering among the initiated, and hoaxing in thy turn." Poinsinet was charmed; he asked when he should be initiated, and how? It was told him that a moment would suffice, and that the ceremony might be performed on the spot. At this news, and according to order, Poinsinet flung himself straightway on his knees in the kennel; and the other, drawing his sword, solemnly initiated him into the sacred order of jokers. From that day the little man believed himself received into the society; and to this having brought him, let us bid him a respectful adieu.

THE DEVIL'S WAGER.

It was the hour of the night when there be none stirring save churchyard ghosts—when all doors are closed except the gates of graves, and all eyes shut but the eyes of wicked men.

When there is no sound on the earth except the ticking of the grasshopper, or the croaking of obscene frogs in the poole.

And no light except that of the blinking starres, and the wicked and devilish wills-o'-the-wisp, as they gambol among the marshes, and lead good men astraye.

When there is nothing moving in heaven except the owle, as he flappeth along lazily; or the magician, as he rides on his infernal broomsticke, whistling through the aire like the arrowes of a Yorkshire archere.

It was at this hour (namely, at twelve o'clock of the night), that two beings went winging through the black clouds, and holding converse with each other.

Now the first was Mercurius, the messenger, not of gods (as the heathens feigned), but of dæmons; and the second, with whom he held company, was the soul of Sir Roger de Rollo, the brave knight. Sir Roger was Count of Chauchigny, in Champagne; Seigneur of Santerre; Villacerf and aultre lieux. But the great die as well as the humble; and nothing remained of brave Roger, now, but his coffin and his deathless soul.

And Mercurius, in order to keep fast the soul, his companion, had bound him round the neck with his tail; which, when the soul was stubborn, he would draw so tight as to strangle him well nigh, sticking into him the barbed point thereof; whereat the poor soul, Sir Rollo, would groan and roar lustily.

Now they two had come, together, from the gates of purgatorie, being bound to those regions of fire and flame where poor sinners fry and roast in sæcula sæculorum.

"It is hard," said the poor Sir Rollo, as they went gliding through the clouds, "that I should thus be condemned for ever, and all for want of a single ave."

"How, Sir Soul," said the dæmon, "you were on earth so wicked, that not one, or a million of aves, could suffice to keep from hell-flame a creature like thee; but, cheer up and be merry; thou wilt be but a subject of our lord the Devil, as am I; and, perhaps, thou wilt be advanced to posts of honour, as am I also :" and to show his authoritie, he lashed with his tail the ribbes of the wretched Rollo.

"Nevertheless, sinner as I am, one more ave would have saved me; for my sister, who was abbess of St. Mary of Chauchigny, did so prevail, by her prayer and good works, for my lost and wretched soul, that every day I felt the pains of purgatory decrease; the pitchforks which, on my first entry, had never ceased to vex and torment my poor carcass, were now not applied above once a week; the roasting had ceased, the boiling had discontinued; only a certain warmth was kept up, to remind me of my situation.

"A gentle stewe," said the dæmon.

"Yea, truly, I was but in a stew, and all from the effects of the prayers of my blessed sister. But yesterday, he who watched me in purgatory told me, that yet another prayer from my sister, and my bonds should be unloosed, and I, who am now a devil, should have been a blessed angel."

"And the other ave?" said the dæmon.

"She died, sir—my sister died—death choked her in the middle of the prayer." And hereat the wretched spirit began to weepe and whine piteously; his salt tears falling over his beard, and scalding the tail of Mercurius the devil.

"It is, in truth, a hard case," said the dæmon; but I know of no remedy save patience, and for that you will have an excellent opportunity in your lodgings below."

"But I have relations," said the Earl; "my kinsman

Randal, who has inherited my lands, will he not say a prayer for his uncle?"

"Thou didst hate and oppress him when living."

"It is true; but an ave is not much; his sister, my niece, Matilda——"

"You shut her in a convent, and hanged her lover."

"Had I not reason? besides, has she not others?"

"A dozen, without doubt."

"And my brother, the prior?"

"A liege subject of my lord the Devil: he never opens his mouth, except to utter an oath, or to swallow a cup of wine."

"And yet, if but one of these would but say an ave for me, I should be saved."

"Aves with them are raræ aves," replied Mercurius, wagging his tail right waggishly; "and, what is more, I will lay thee any wager that not one of these will say a prayer to save thee."

"I would wager willingly," responded he of Chauchigny; "but what has a poor soul like me to stake?"

"Every evening, after the day's roasting, my lord Satan giveth a cup of cold water to his servants; I will bet thee thy water for a year, that none of the three will pray for thee."

"Done!" said Rollo.

"Done!" said the dæmon; "and here, if I mistake not, is thy castle of Chauchigny."

Indeed, it was true. The soul, on looking down, perceived the tall towers, the courts, the stables, and the fair gardens of the castle. Although it was past midnight, there was a blaze of light in the banqueting-hall, and a lamp burning in the open window of the Lady Matilda.

"With whom shall we begin?" said the dæmon: "with the Baron or the lady?"

"With the lady, if you will."

"Be it so; her window is open, let us enter."

So they descended, and entered silently into Matilda's chamber.

* * * * *

The young lady's eyes were fixed so intently on a little clock, that it was no wonder that she did not perceive the entrance of her two visitors. Her fair cheek rested on her white arm, and her white arm on the cushion of a great chair in which she sat, pleasantly supported by sweet thoughts and swan's down; a lute was at her side, and a book of prayers lay under the table (for piety is always modest). Like the amorous Alexander, she sighed and looked (at the clock)—and sighed for ten minutes or more, when she softly breathed the word "Edward!"

At this the soul of the Baron was wroth. "The jade is at her old pranks," said he to the devil; and then, addressing Matilda: "I pray thee, sweet niece, turn thy thoughts for a moment from that villanous page, Edward, and give them to thine affectionate uncle."

When she heard the voice, and saw the awful apparition of her uncle (for a year's sojourn in purgatory had not increased the comeliness of his appearance), she started, screamed, and of course fainted.

But the devil Mercurius soon restored her to herself.

"What's o'clock?" said she, as soon as she had recovered from her fit: "is he come?"

"Not thy lover, Maude, but thine uncle—that is, his soul. For the love of Heaven, listen to me: I have been frying in purgatory for a year past, and should have been in heaven but for the want of a single ave."

"I will say it for thee to-morrow, uncle."

"To-night, or never."

"Well, to-night be it:" and she requested the devil Mercurius to give her the prayer-book from under the table; but he had no sooner touched the holy book than he dropped it with a shriek and a yell. "It was hotter," he said, "than his master, Sir Lucifer's, own particular pitchfork." And the lady was forced to begin her ave without the aid of her missal.

At the commencement of her devotions the dæmon retired, and carried with him the anxious soul of poor Sir Roger de Rollo.

The lady knelt down—she sighed deeply; she looked again at the clock, and began—

"Ave Maria."

When a lute was heard under the window, and a sweet voice singing—

"Hark!" said Matilda.

> Now the toils of day are over,
> And the sun hath sunk to rest,
> Seeking, like a fiery lover,
> The bosom of the blushing west—
>
> The faithful night keeps watch and ward,
> Raising the moon, her silver shield,
> And summoning the stars to guard
> The slumbers of my fair Mathilde!

"For mercy's sake!" said Sir Rollo, "the ave first, and next the song."

So Matilda again dutifully betook her to her devotions, and began—

"Ave Maria, Gratiâ Plena!" but the music began again, and the prayer ceased of course.

> The faithful night! Now all things lie
> Hid by her mantle dark and dim,
> In pious hope I hither hie,
> And humbly chaunt mine ev'ning hymn.
>
> Thou art my prayer, my saint, my shrine!
> (For never holy pilgrim kneel'd,
> Or wept at feet more pure than thine).
> My virgin love, my sweet Mathilde!

"Virgin love!" said the Baron; "upon my soul, this is too bad!" and he thought of the lady's lover whom he had caused to be hanged.

But *she* only thought of him who stood singing at her window.

"Niece Matilda!" cried Sir Roger, agonisedly, "wilt thou listen to the lies of an impudent page, whilst thine uncle is waiting but a dozen words to make him happy?"

At this Matilda grew angry: "Edward is neither impudent nor a liar, Sir Uncle, and I will listen to the end of the song."

"Come away," said Mercurius, "he hath yet got wield, field, sealed, congealed, and a dozen other rhymes beside; and after the song will come the supper."

So the poor soul was obliged to go; while the lady listened, and the page sung away till morning.

* * * * * *

"My virtues have been my ruin," said poor Sir Rollo, as he and Mercurius slunk silently out of the window. "Had I hanged that knave Edward, as I did the page his predecessor, my niece would have sung mine ave, I should have been by this time an angel in heaven."

"He is reserved for wiser purposes," responded the devil: "he will assassinate your successor, the lady Mathilde's brother; and, in consequence, will be hanged. In the love of the lady he will be succeeded by a gardener, who will be replaced by a monk, who will give way to an ostler, who will be deposed by a Jew pedlar, who shall, finally, yield to a noble earl, the future husband of the fair Mathilde. So that, you see, instead of having one poor soul a-frying, we may now look forward to a goodly harvest for our lord the Devil."

The soul of the Baron began to think that his companion knew too much for one who would make fair bets; but there was no help for it; he would not, and he could not, cry off: and he prayed inwardly that the brother might be found more pious than the sister.

But there seemed little chance of this. As they crossed the court, lackeys, with smoking dishes and full jugs, passed and repassed continually, although it was long past midnight. On entering the hall, they found Sir Randal at the head of a vast table, surrounded by a fiercer and more motley collection of individuals than had congregated there even in the time of Sir Rollo. The lord of the castle had signified that "it was his royal pleasure to be drunk," and the gentlemen of his train had obsequiously followed their master. Mercurius was delighted with the scene, and

relaxed his usually rigid countenance into a bland and benevolent smile, which became him wonderfully.

The entrance of Sir Roger, who had been dead about a year, and a person with hoofs, horns, and a tail, rather disturbed the hilarity of the company. Sir Randal dropped his cup of wine; and Father Peter, the confessor, incontinently paused in the midst of a profane song, with which he was amusing the society.

"Holy Mother!" cried he, "it is Sir Roger."

"Alive!" screamed Sir Randal.

"No, my lord," Mercurius said; "Sir Roger is dead, but cometh on a matter of business; and I have the honour to act as his counsellor and attendant."

"Nephew," said Sir Roger, "the dæmon saith justly; I am come on a trifling affair, in which thy service is essential."

"I will do anything, uncle, in my power."

"Thou canst give me life, if thou wilt?" But Sir Randal looked very blank at this proposition. "I mean life spiritual, Randal," said Sir Roger; and thereupon he explained to him the nature of the wager.

Whilst he was telling his story, his companion Mercurius was playing all sorts of antics in the hall; and, by his wit and fun, became so popular with this godless crew, that they lost all the fear which his first appearance had given them. The friar was wonderfully taken with him, and used his utmost eloquence and endeavours to convert the devil; the knights stopped drinking to listen to the argument; the men-at-arms forbore brawling; and the wicked little pages crowded round the two strange disputants, to hear their edifying discourse. The ghostly man, however, had little chance in the controversy, and certainly little learning to carry it on. Sir Randal interrupted him. "Father Peter," said he, "our kinsman is condemned for ever, for want of a single ave: wilt thou say it for him?" "Willingly, my lord," said the monk, "with my book;" and, accordingly, he produced his missal to read, without which aid it appeared that the holy father could not manage the desired prayer. But the crafty Mercurius had, by his devilish art, inserted a song in the place of the ave, so that Father Peter, instead of chaunting an hymn, sang the following irreverent ditty:—

> Some love the matin-chimes, which tell
>   The hour of prayer to sinner;
> But better far's the mid-day bell,
>   Which speaks the hour of dinner;
> For when I see a smoking fish,
>   Or capon drown'd in gravy,
> Or noble haunch on silver dish,
>   Full glad I sing mine ave.
>
> My pulpit is an alehouse bench,
>   Whereon I sit so jolly;
> A smiling rosy country wench
>   My saint and patron holy.
> I kiss her cheek so red and sleek,
>   I press her ringlets wavy,
> And in her willing ear I speak
>   A most religious ave.
>
> And if I'm blind, yet heaven is kind,
>   And holy saints forgiving;
> For sure he leads a right good life
>   Who thus admires good living.
> Above, they say, our flesh is air,
>   Our blood celestial ichor:
> O grant! 'mid all the changes there,
>   They may not change our liquor!

And with this pious wish the holy confessor tumbled under the table in an agony of devout drunkenness; whilst the knights, the men-at-arms, and the wicked little pages, rang out the last verse with a most melodious and emphatic glee. "I am sorry, fair uncle," hiccupped Sir Randal, "that, in the matter of the ave, we could not oblige thee in a more orthodox manner; but the holy father has failed, and there is not another man in the hall who hath an idea of a prayer."

"It is my own fault," said Sir Rollo, "for I hanged the last confessor." And he wished his nephew a surly good-night, as he prepared to quit the room.

"*Au revoir*, gentlemen," said the devil Mercurius; and once more fixed his tail round the neck of his disappointed companion.

* * * * *

The spirit of poor Rollo was sadly cast down; the devil, on the contrary, was in high good humour. He wagged his tail with the most satisfied air in the world, and cut a hundred jokes at the expense of his poor associate. On they sped, cleaving swiftly through the cold night winds, frightening the birds that were roosting in the woods, and the owls who were watching in the towers.

In the twinkling of an eye, as it is known, devils can fly hundreds of miles: so that almost the same beat of the clock which left these two in Champagne, found them hovering over Paris. They dropped into the court of the Lazarist Convent, and winded their way, through passage and cloister, until they reached the door of the prior's cell.

Now the prior, Rollo's brother, was a wicked and

malignant sorcerer; his time was spent in conjuring devils and doing wicked deeds, instead of fasting, scourging, and singing holy psalms: this Mercurius knew; and he, therefore, was fully at ease as to the final result of his wager with poor Sir Roger.

"You seem to be well acquainted with the road," said the knight.

"I have reason," answered Mercurius, "having, for a long period, had the acquaintance of his reverence, your brother; but you have little chance with him."

"And why?" said Sir Rollo.

"He is under a bond to my master, never to say a prayer, or else his soul and his body are forfeited at once."

"Why, thou false and traitorous devil!" said the enraged knight; "and thou knewest this when we made our wager?"

"Undoubtedly: do you suppose I would have done so had there been any chance of losing?"

And with this they arrived at Father Ignatius's door.

"Thy cursed presence threw a spell on my niece, and stopped the tongue of my nephew's chaplain; I do believe that had I seen either of them alone, my wager had been won."

"Certainly; therefore I took good care to go with thee: however, thou mayest see the prior alone, if thou wilt; and lo! his door is open. I will stand without for five minutes, when it will be time to commence our journey."

It was the poor Baron's last chance: and he entered his brother's room more for the five minutes' respite than from any hope of success.

Father Ignatius, the prior, was absorbed in magic calculations: he stood in the middle of a circle of skulls, with no garment except his long white beard, which reached to his knees; he was waving a silver rod, and muttering imprecations in some horrible tongue.

But Sir Rollo came forward and interrupted his incantation. "I am," said he, "the shade of thy brother Roger de Rollo; and have come, from pure brotherly love, to warn thee of thy fate."

"Whence camest thou?"

"From the abode of the blessed in Paradise," replied Sir Roger, who was inspired with a sudden thought; "it was but five minutes ago that the Patron Saint of thy church told me of thy danger, and of thy wicked compact with the fiend. 'Go,' said he, 'to thy miserable brother, and tell him that there is but one way by which he may escape from paying the awful forfeit of his bond.'"

"And how may that be?" said the prior; "the false fiend hath deceived me; I have given him my soul, but have received no worldly benefit in return. Brother! dear brother! how may I escape?"

"I will tell thee. As soon as I heard the voice of blessed St. Mary Lazarus (the worthy Earl had, at a pinch, coined the name of a saint), I left the clouds, where, with other angels, I was seated, and sped hither to save thee. 'Thy brother,' said the Saint, 'hath but one day more to live, when he will become for all eternity the subject of Satan; if he would escape, he must boldly break his bond, by saying an ave.'"

"It is the express condition of the agreement," said

the unhappy monk, "I must say no prayer, or that instant I become Satan's, body and soul."

"It is the express condition of the Saint," answered Roger, fiercely: "pray, brother, pray, or thou art lost for ever."

So the foolish monk knelt down, and devoutly sung out an ave. "Amen!" said Sir Roger devoutly.

"Amen!" said Mercurius, as, suddenly coming behind, he seized Ignatius by his long beard, and flew up with him to the top of the church-steeple.

The monk roared, and screamed, and swore against his brother; but it was of no avail: Sir Roger smiled kindly on him, and said, "Do not fret, brother; it must have come to this in a year or two."

And he flew alongside of Mercurius to the steeple-top: *but this time the devil had not his tail round his neck.* "I will let thee off thy bet," said he to the dæmon; for he could afford, now, to be generous.

"I believe, my lord," said the dæmon, politely, "that our ways separate here." Sir Roger sailed gaily upwards; while Mercurius, having bound the miserable monk faster than ever, he sunk downwards to earth, and, perhaps, lower. Ignatius was heard roaring and screaming as the devil dashed him against the iron spikes and buttresses of the church.

* * * * * *

The moral of this story will be given in the second edition.

MADAME SAND AND THE NEW APOCALYPSE.

I don't know an impression more curious than that which is formed in a foreigner's mind, who has been absent from this place for two or three years, returns to it, and beholds the change which has taken place, in the meantime, in French fashions and ways of thinking. Two years ago, for instance, when I left the capital, I left the young gentlemen of France with their hair brushed *en toupet* in front, and the toes of their boots round; now the boot toes are pointed, and the hair combed flat, and, parted in the middle, falls in ringlets on the fashionable shoulders; and, in like manner, with books as with boots, the fashion has changed considerably, and it is not a little curious to contrast the old modes with the new. Absurd as was the literary dandyism of those days, it is not a whit less absurd now: only the manner is changed, and our versatile Frenchmen have passed from one caricature to another.

The revolution may be called a caricature of freedom, as the empire was of glory; and what they borrow from foreigners undergoes the same process. They take top-boots and mackintoshes from across the water, and caricature our fashions; they read a little, very little, Shakspeare, and caricature our poetry: and while in David's time art and religion were only a caricature of Heathenism; now, on the contrary, these two commodities are imported from Germany; and distorted caricatures originally, are still farther distorted on passing the frontier.

I trust in Heaven that German art and religion will take no hold in our country (where there is a fund of roast beef, that will expel any such humbug in the end); but these sprightly Frenchmen have relished the mystical doctrines mightily; and having watched the Germans, with their sanctified looks, and quaint imitations of the old times, and mysterious transcendental talk, are aping many of their fashions, as well and solemnly as they can : not very solemnly, God wot; for I think one should always prepare to grin when a Frenchman looks particularly grave, being sure that there is something false and ridiculous lurking under the owl-like solemnity.

When last in Paris, we were in the midst of what was called a Catholic reaction. Artists talked of faith in poems and pictures; churches were built here and there; old missals were copied and purchased; and numberless portraits of saints, with as much gilding about them as ever was used in the fifteenth century, appeared in churches, ladies' boudoirs, and picture-shops. One or two fashionable preachers rose, and were eagerly followed; the very youth of the schools gave up their pipes and billiards for some time, and flocked in crowds to Notre Dame, to sit under

the feet of Lacordaire. I went to visit the church of Notre Dame de Lorrette, yesterday, which was finished in the heat of this Catholic rage, and was not a little struck by the similarity of the place to the worship celebrated in it, and the admirable manner in which the architect has caused his work to express the public feeling of the moment. It is a pretty little bijou of a church : it is supported by sham marble pillars ; it has a gaudy ceiling of blue and gold, which will look very well for some time ; and is filled with gaudy pictures and carvings, in the very pink of the mode. The congregation did not offer a bad illustration of the present state of Catholic reaction. Two or three stray people were at prayers ; there was no service ; a few countrymen and idlers were staring about at the pictures ; and the Swiss, the paid guardian of the place, was comfortably and appropriately asleep on his bench at the door. I am inclined to think the famous reaction is over : the students have taken to their Sunday pipes and billiards again ; and one or two cafés have been established, within the last year, that are ten times handsomer than Notre Dame de Lorrette.

However, if the immortal Görres and the German mystics have had their day, there is the immortal Göthe, and the Pantheists ; and I incline to think that the fashion has set very strongly in their favour. Voltaire and the Encyclopædians are voted, now, *barbares*, and there is no term of reprobation strong enough for heartless Humes and Helvetiuses, who lived but to destroy, and who only thought to doubt. Wretched as Voltaire's sneers and puns are, I think there is something more manly and earnest even in them, than in the present muddy French transcendentalism. Pantheism is the word now; one and all have begun to *éprouver* the *besoin* of a religious sentiment; and we are deluged with a host of gods accordingly. Monsieur de Balzac feels himself to be inspired; Victor Hugo is a god; Madame Sand is a god; that tawdry man of genius, Jules Janin, who writes theatrical reviews for the "Débats," has divine intimations; and there is scarce a beggarly, beardless scribbler of poems and prose, but tells you, in his preface, of the *sainteté* of the *sacerdoce littéraire;* or a dirty student, sucking tobacco and beer, and reeling home with a grisette from the chaumière, who is not convinced of the necessity of a new "Messianism," and will hiccup, to such as will listen, chapters of his own drunken Apocalypse. Surely, the negatives of the old days were far less dangerous than the assertions of the present; and you may fancy what a religion that must be, which has such high priests.

There is no reason to trouble the reader with details of the lives of many of these prophets and expounders of new revelations. Madame Sand, for instance, I do not know personally, and can only speak of her from report. True or false, the history, at any rate, is not very edifying; and so may be passed over: but, as a certain great philosopher told us, in very humble and simple words, that we are not to expect to gather grapes from thorns, or figs from thistles, we may, at least, demand, in all persons assuming the character of moralist or philosopher — order, soberness, and regularity of life; for we are apt to distrust the intellect that we fancy can be swayed by circumstance or passion; and we know how circumstance and passion *will* sway the intellect: how mortified vanity will form excuses for itself; and how temper turns angrily upon conscience, that reproves it. How often have we called our judge our enemy, because he has given sentence against us!—How often have we called the right wrong, because the right condemns us! And in the lives of many of the bitter foes of the Christian doctrine, can we find no personal reason for their hostility? The men in Athens said it was out of regard for religion that they murdered Socrates; but we have had time, since then, to re-consider the verdict; and Socrates' character is pretty pure now, in spite of the sentence and the jury of those days.

The Parisian philosophers will attempt to explain to you the changes through which Madame Sand's mind has passed,—the initiatory trials, labours, and sufferings which she has had to go through,—before she reached her present happy state of mental illumination. She teaches her wisdom in parables, that are, mostly, a couple of volumes long; and began, first, by an eloquent attack on marriage, in the charming novel of "Indiana." "Pity," cried she, "for the poor woman who, united to a being whose brute force makes him her superior, should venture to break the bondage which is imposed on her, and allow her heart to be free."

In support of this claim of pity, she writes two volumes of the most exquisite prose. What a tender, suffering creature is Indiana; how little her husband appreciates that gentleness which he is crushing by his tyranny and brutal scorn; how natural it is that, in the absence of his sympathy, she, poor, clinging, confiding creature, should seek elsewhere for shelter; how cautious should we be, to call criminal—to visit with too heavy a censure—an act which is one of the natural impulses of a tender heart, that seeks but for a worthy object of love. But why attempt to tell the tale of beautiful Indiana? Madame Sand has written it so well, that not the hardest-hearted husband in Christendom can fail to be touched by her sorrows, though he may refuse to listen to her argument. Let us grant, for argument's sake, that the laws of marriage, especially the French laws of marriage, press very cruelly upon unfortunate women.

But if one wants to have a question of this, or any nature, honestly argued, it is better, surely, to apply to an indifferent person for an umpire. For instance, the stealing of pocket-handkerchiefs or snuff-boxes may or may not be vicious; but if we, who have not the wit, or will not take the trouble to decide the question ourselves, want to hear the real rights of the matter, we should not, surely, apply to a pickpocket to know what he thought on the point. It might naturally be presumed that he would be rather a prejudiced person—particularly as his reasoning, if successful, might get him *out of gaol*. This is a homely illustration, no doubt; all we would urge by it is, that Madame Sand having, according to the French newspapers, had a stern husband; and also having, according to the newspapers, sought "sympathy" elsewhere, her arguments may be considered to be somewhat partial, and received with some little caution.

And tell us who have been the social reformers?—the

haters, that is, of the present system, according to which we live, love, marry, have children, educate them, and endow them—*are they pure themselves?* I do believe not one; and directly a man begins to quarrel with the world and its ways, and to lift up, as he calls it, the voice of his despair, and preach passionately to mankind about this tyranny of faith, customs, laws; if we examine what the personal character of the preacher is, we begin pretty clearly to understand the value of the doctrine. Any one can see why Rousseau should be such a whimpering reformer, and Byron such a free and easy misanthropist, and why our accomplished Madame Sand, who has a genius and eloquence inferior to neither, should take the present condition of mankind (French-kind) so much to heart, and labour so hotly to set it right.

After "Indiana" (which, we presume, contains the lady's notions upon wives and husbands) came "Valentine," which may be said to exhibit her doctrine, in regard of young men and maidens, to whom the author would accord, as we fancy, the same tender licence. "Valentine" was followed by "Lelia," a wonderful book indeed, gorgeous in eloquence, and rich in magnificent poetry; a regular topsyturvyfication of morality, a thieves' and prostitutes' apotheosis. This book has received some late enlargements and emendations by the writer; it contains her notions on morals, which, as we have said, are so peculiar, that, alas! they can only be mentioned here, not particularized: but, of "Spiridion," we may write a few pages, as it is her religious manifesto.

In this work, the lady asserts her pantheistical doctrine,

and openly attacks the received Christian creed. She declares it to be useless now, and unfitted to the exigencies and the degree of culture of the actual world; and, though it would be hardly worth while to combat her opinions in due form, it is, at least, worth while to notice them, not merely from the extraordinary eloquence and genius of the woman herself, but because they express the opinions of a great number of people besides: for she not only produces her own thoughts, but imitates those of others very eagerly; and one finds in her writings so much similarity with others, or, in others, so much resemblance to her, that the book before us may pass for the expressions of the sentiments of a certain French party.

"Dieu est mort," says another writer of the same class, and of great genius too.—"Dieu est mort," writes Mr. Henry Heine, speaking of the Christian God; and he adds, in a daring figure of speech,—"N'entendez vous pas sonner la Clochette?—on porte les sacremens à un Dieu qui se meurt!" Another of the pantheist poetical philosophers, Mr. Edgar Quinet, has a poem, in which Christ and the Virgin Mary are made to die similarly, and the former is classed with Prometheus. This book of "Spiridion" is a continuation of the theme, and, perhaps, you will listen to some of the author's expositions of it.

It must be confessed that the controversialists of the present day have an eminent advantage over their predecessors in the days of folios; it required some learning then to write a book, and some time, at least—for the very labour of writing out a thousand such vast pages would demand a considerable period. But now, in the age of duodecimos, the system is reformed altogether: a male or female controversialist draws upon his imagination, and not his learning; makes a story instead of an argument, and, in the course of 150 pages (where the preacher has it all his own way) will prove or disprove you anything. And, to our shame be it said, we Protestants have set the example of this kind of proselytism — those detestable mixtures of truth, lies, false-sentiment, false-reasoning, bad grammar, correct and genuine philanthropy and piety —I mean our religious tracts, which any woman or man, be he ever so silly, can take upon himself to write, and sell for a penny, as if religious instruction were the easiest thing in the world. We, I say, have set the example in this kind of composition, and all the sects of the earth will, doubtless, speedily follow it. I can point you out blasphemies in famous pious tracts that are as dreadful as those above mentioned; but this is no place for such discussions, and we had better return to Madame Sand. As Mrs. Sherwood expounds, by means of many touching histories and anecdotes of little boys and girls, her notions of church history, church catechism, church doctrine;—as the author of "Father Clement, a Roman Catholic Story," demolishes the stately structure of eighteen centuries, the mighty and beautiful Roman Catholic faith, in whose bosom repose so many saints and sages,—by the means of a three-and-sixpenny duodecimo volume, which tumbles over the vast fabric, as David's pebble stone did Goliah; —as, again, the Roman Catholic author of "Geraldine" falls foul of Luther and Calvin, and drowns the awful echoes of their tremendous protest by the sounds of her little half-crown trumpet; in like manner, by means of pretty sentimental tales, and cheap apologues, Mrs. Sand proclaims *her* truth—that we need a new Messiah, and that the Christian religion is no more! O awful, awful name of God! Light unbearable! Mystery unfathomable! Vastness immeasurable!—Who are these who come forward to explain the mystery, and gaze unblinking into the depths of the light, and measure the immeasurable vastness to a hair? O name, that God's people of old did fear to utter! O light, that God's prophet would have perished had he seen! Who are these that are now so familiar with it?—Women, truly; for the most part weak women—weak in intellect, weak, mayhap, in spelling and grammar, but marvellously strong in faith:—women, who step down to the people with stately step and voice of authority, and deliver their twopenny tablets, as if there were some Divine authority for the wretched nonsense recorded there!

With regard to the spelling and grammar, our Parisian Pythoness stands, in the goodly fellowship, remarkable. Her style is a noble, and, as far as a foreigner can judge, a strange tongue, beautifully rich and pure. She has a very exuberant imagination, and, with it, a very chaste style of expression. She never scarcely indulges in declamation, as other modern prophets do, and yet her sentences are exquisitely melodious and full. She seldom runs a thought to death (after the manner of some prophets, who, when they catch a little one, toy with it until they kill it), but she leaves you at the end of one of her brief, rich, melancholy sentences, with plenty of food for future cogitation. I can't express to you the charm of them; they seem to me like the sound of country bells—provoking I don't know what vein of musing and meditation, and falling sweetly and sadly on the ear.

This wonderful power of language must have been felt by most people who read Madame Sand's first books, *Valentine* and *Indiana:* in *Spiridion*, it is greater, I think, than ever; and for those who are not afraid of the matter of the novel, the manner will be found most delightful. The author's intention, I presume, is to describe, in a parable, her notions of the downfall of the Catholic church; and, indeed, of the whole Christian scheme: she places her hero in a monastery in Italy, where, among the characters about him, and the events which occur, the particular tenets of Madame Dudevant's doctrine are not inaptly laid down. Innocent, faithful, tender-hearted, a young monk, by name Angel, finds himself, when he has pronounced his vows, an object of aversion and hatred to the godly men whose lives he so much respects, and whose love he would make any sacrifice to win. After enduring much, he flings himself at the feet of his confessor, and begs for his sympathy and counsel; but the confessor spurns him away, and accuses him, fiercely, of some unknown and terrible crime—bids him never return to the confessional until contrition has touched his heart, and the stains which sully his spirit are, by sincere repentance, washed away.

"Thus speaking," says Angel, "Father Hegesippus tore away his robe, which I was holding in my supplicating hands. In a sort of wildness I still grasped it tighter; he pushed me fiercely from him, and I fell with my face towards the ground. He quitted me, closing violently after him the door of the sacristy, in which this scene had passed. I was left alone in the darkness. Either from the violence of my fall, or the excess of my grief, a vein had burst in my throat, and a hæmorrhage ensued. I had not the force to rise; I felt my senses rapidly sinking, and, presently, I lay stretched on the pavement, unconscious, and bathed in my blood."

[Now the wonderful part of the story begins.]

"I know not how much time I passed in this way. As I came to myself I felt an agreeable coolness. It seemed as if some harmonious air was playing round about me, stirring gently in my hair, and drying the drops of perspiration on my brow. It seemed to approach, and then again to withdraw, breathing now softly and sweetly in the distance, and now returning, as if to give me strength and courage to rise.

"I would not, however, do so as yet; for I felt myself, as I lay, under the influence of a pleasure quite new to me; and listened, in a kind of peaceful aberration, to the gentle murmurs of the summer wind, as it breathed on me through the closed window blinds above me. Then I fancied I heard a voice that spoke to me from the end of the sacristy: it whispered so low that I could not catch the words. I remained motionless, and gave it my whole attention. At last I heard, distinctly, the following sentence:—'*Spirit of Truth, raise up these victims of ignorance and imposture.*' 'Father Hegesippus,' said I, in a weak voice, 'is that you who are returning to me? But no one answered.

I lifted myself on my hands and knees, I listened again, but I heard nothing. I got up completely, and looked about me: I had fallen so near to the only door in this little room, that none, after the departure of the confessor, could have entered it without passing over me; besides, the door was shut, and only opened from the inside by a strong lock of the ancient shape. I touched it, and assured myself that it was closed. I was seized with terror, and, for some moments, did not dare to move. Leaning against the door, I looked round, and endeavoured to see into the gloom in which the angles of the room were enveloped. A pale light, which came from an upper window, half closed, was seen to be trembling in the midst of the apartment. The wind beat the shutter to and fro, and enlarged or diminished the space through which the light issued. The objects which were in this half light—the praying-desk, surmounted by its skull—a few books lying on the benches—a surplice hanging against the wall—seemed to move with the shadow of the foliage that the air agitated behind the window. When I thought I was alone, I felt ashamed of my former timidity; I made the sign of the cross, and was about to move forward in order to open the shutter altogether, but a deep sigh came from the praying-desk, and kept me nailed to my place. And yet I saw the desk distinctly enough to be sure that no person was near it. Then I had an idea which gave me courage. Some person, I thought, is behind the shutter, and has been saying his prayers outside without thinking of me. But who would be so bold as to express such wishes and utter such a prayer as I had just heard?

"Curiosity, the only passion and amusement permitted in a cloister, now entirely possessed me, and I advanced towards the window. But I had not made a step when a black shadow, as it seemed to me, detaching itself from the praying desk, traversed the room, directing itself towards the window, and passed swiftly by me. The movement was so rapid that I had not time to avoid what seemed a body advancing towards me, and my fright was so great, that I thought I should faint a second time. But I felt nothing, and, as if the shadow had passed through me, I saw it suddenly disappear to my left.

"I rushed to the window, I pushed back the blind with precipitation, and looked round the sacristy: I was there, entirely alone. I looked into the garden—it was deserted, and the mid-day wind was wandering among the flowers. I took courage, I examined all the corners of the room; I looked behind the praying-desk, which was very large, and I shook all the sacerdotal vestments which were hanging on the walls; everything was in its natural condition, and could give me no explanation of what had just occurred. The sight of all the blood I had lost, led me to fancy that my brain had, probably, been weakened by the hæmorrhage, and that I had been a prey to some delusion. I retired to my cell, and remained shut up there until the next day."

I don't know whether the reader has been as much struck with the above mysterious scene as the writer has; but the fancy of it strikes me as very fine; and the natural *supernaturalness* is kept up in the best style. The shutter swaying to and fro, the fitful *light appearing* over the furniture of the room, and giving it an air of strange motion—the awful shadow which passed through the body of the timid young novice—are surely very finely painted. "I rushed to the shutter, and flung it back: there was no one in the sacristy. I looked into the garden; it was deserted, and the mid-day wind was roaming among the flowers." The dreariness is wonderfully described: only the poor pale boy looking eagerly out from the window of the sacristy, and the hot mid-day wind walking in the solitary garden. How skilfully is each of these little strokes dashed in, and how well do all together combine to make a picture! But we must have a little more about Spiridion's wonderful visitant.

* * * * *

"As I entered into the garden, I stept a little on one side, to make way for a person whom I saw before me. He was a young man of surprising beauty, and attired in a foreign costume. Although dressed in the large black robe which the superiors of our order wear, he had, underneath, a short jacket of fine cloth, fastened round the waist by a leathern belt, and a buckle of silver, after the manner of the old German students. Like them, he wore, instead of the sandals of our monks, short tight boots; and over the collar of his shirt, which fell on his shoulders, and was as white as snow, hung, in rich golden curls, the most beautiful hair I ever saw. He was tall, and his elegant posture seemed to reveal to me that he was in the habit of commanding. With much respect, and yet uncertain, I half saluted him. He did not return my salute; but he smiled on me with so benevolent an air, and at the same time, his eyes severe and blue, looked towards me with an expression of such compassionate tenderness, that his features have never since then passed away from my recollection. I stopped, hoping he would speak to me, and persuading myself, from the majesty of his aspect, that he had the power to protect me; but the monk, who was walking behind me, and who did not seem to remark him in the least, forced him brutally to step aside from the walk, and pushed me so rudely as almost to cause me to fall. Not wishing to engage in a quarrel with this coarse monk, I moved away; but, after having taken a few steps in the garden, I looked back, and saw the unknown still gazing on me with looks of the tenderest solicitude. The sun shone full upon him, and made his hair look radiant. He sighed, and lifted his fine eyes to heaven, as if to invoke its justice in my favour, and to call it to bear witness to my misery; he turned slowly towards the sanctuary, entered into the quire, and was lost, presently, in the shade. I longed to return, spite of the monk, to follow this noble stranger, and to tell him my afflictions; but who was he, that I imagined he would listen to them, and cause them to cease? I felt, even while his softness drew me towards him, that he still inspired me with a kind of fear; for I saw in his physiognomy as much austerity as sweetness."

* * * * *

Who was he?—we shall see that. He was somebody very mysterious indeed; but our author has taken care, after the manner of her sex, to make a very pretty fellow of him, and to dress him in the most becoming costumes possible.

* * * * *

The individual in tight boots and a rolling collar, with the copious golden locks, and the solemn blue eyes, who had just gazed on Spiridion, and inspired him with such a feeling of tender awe, is a much more important personage than the reader might suppose at first sight. This beautiful, mysterious, dandy ghost, whose costume, with a true woman's coquetry, Madame Dudevant has so rejoiced to describe—is her religious type, a mystical representation of Faith struggling up towards Truth, through superstition, doubt, fear, reason,—in tight inexpressibles, with "a belt such as is worn by the old German students." You will pardon me for treating such an awful person as this somewhat lightly; but there is always, I think, such a dash of the ridiculous in the French sublime, that the critic should try and do justice to both, or he may fail in giving a fair account of either. This character of Hebronius, the type of Mrs. Sand's convictions—if convictions they may be called—or, at least, the allegory under which her doubts are represented, is, in parts, very finely drawn; contains many passages of truth, very deep and touching, by the side of others so entirely absurd and unreasonable, that the reader's feelings are continually swaying between admiration and something very like contempt—always in a kind of wonder at the strange mixture before him. But let us hear Madame Sand:—

"Peter Hebronius," says our author, "was not originally so named. His real name was Samuel. He was a

Jew, and born in a little village in the neighbourhood of Innsprück. His family, which possessed a considerable fortune, left him, in his early youth, completely free to his own pursuits. From infancy he had shown that these were serious. He loved to be alone; and passed his days, and sometimes his nights, wandering among the mountains and valleys in the neighbourhood of his birth-place. He would often sit by the brink of torrents, listening to the voice of their waters, and endeavouring to penetrate the meaning which Nature had hidden in those sounds. As he advanced in years, his inquiries became more curious and more grave. It was necessary that he should receive a solid education, and his parents sent him to study in the German universities. Luther had been dead only a century, and his words and his memory still lived in the enthusiasm of his disciples. The new faith was strengthening the conquests it had made; the Reformers were as ardent as in the first days, but their ardour was more enlightened and more measured. Proselytism was still carried on with zeal, and new converts were made every day. In listening to the morality and to the dogmas which Lutheranism had taken from Catholicism, Samuel was filled with admiration. His bold and sincere spirit instantly compared the doctrines which were now submitted to him, with those in the belief of which he had been bred; and, enlightened by the comparison, was not slow to acknowledge the inferiority of Judaism. He said to himself, that a religion made for a single people, to the exclusion of all others,—which only offered a barbarous justice for rule of conduct,—which neither rendered the present intelligible or satisfactory, and left the future uncertain,—could not be that of noble souls and lofty intellects ; and that he could not be the God of truth who had dictated, in the midst of thunder, his vacillating will, and had called to the performance of his narrow wishes the slaves of a vulgar terror. Always conversant with himself, Samuel, who had spoken what he thought, now performed what he had spoken ; and, a year after his arrival in Germany, solemnly abjured Judaism, and entered into the bosom of the reformed Church. As he did not wish to do things by halves, and desired as much as was in him to put off the old man and lead a new life, he changed his name of Samuel to that of Peter. Some time passed, during which he strengthened and instructed himself in his new religion. Very soon he arrives at the point of searching for objections to refute, and adversaries to overthrow. Bold and enterprising, he went at once to the strongest, and Bossuet was the first Catholic author that he set himself to read. He commenced with a kind of disdain ; believing that the faith which he had just embraced contained the pure truth, he despised all the attacks which could be made against it, and laughed already at the irresistible arguments which he was to find in the works of the Eagle of Meaux. But his mistrust and irony soon gave place to wonder first, and then to admiration : he thought that the cause pleaded by such an advocate must, at least, be respectable ; and, by a natural transition, came to think that great geniuses would only devote themselves to that which was great. He then studied Catholicism with the same ardour and impartiality which he had bestowed on Lutheranism. He went into France to gain instruction from the professors of the Mother Church, as he had from the Doctors of the reformed creed in Germany. He saw Arnauld, Fenelon, that second Gregory of Nazianzen, and Bossuet himself. Guided by these masters, whose virtues made him appreciate their talents the more, he rapidly penetrated to the depth of the mysteries of the Catholic doctrine and morality. He found, in this religion, all that had for him constituted the grandeur and beauty of Protestantism,—the dogmas of the Unity and Eternity of God, which the two religions had borrowed from Judaism; and, what seemed the natural consequence of the last doctrine—a doctrine, however, to which the Jews had not arrived—the doctrine of the immortality of the soul; free will in this life; in the next, recompence for the good, and punishment for the evil. He found, more pure, perhaps, and more elevated in Catholicism than in Protestantism, that sublime morality which preaches equality to man, fraternity, love, charity, renouncement of self, devotion to your neighbour: Catholicism, in a word, seemed to possess that vast formula, and that vigorous unity, which Lutheranism wanted. The latter had, indeed, in its favour, the liberty of inquiry, which is also a want of the human mind; and had proclaimed the authority of individual reason: but it had so lost that which is the necessary basis and vital condition of all revealed religion—the principle of infallibility; because nothing can live except in virtue of the laws that presided at its birth; and, in consequence, one revelation cannot be continued and confirmed without another. Now, infallibility is nothing but revelation continued by God, or the Word, in the person of his vicars. * * *

"At last, after much reflection, Hebronius acknowledged himself entirely and sincerely convinced, and received baptism from the hands of Bossuet. He added the name of Spiridion to that of Peter, to signify that he had been twice enlightened by the Spirit. Resolved thenceforward to consecrate his life to the worship of the new God who had called him to Him, and to the study of His doctrines, he passed into Italy, and, with the aid of a large fortune, which one of his uncles, a Catholic like himself, had left to him, he built this convent, where we now are."

* * * * *

A friend of mine, who has just come from Italy, says that he has there left Messrs. Sp——r, P——l, and W. Dr——d, who were the lights of the great church in Newman-street, who were themselves apostles, and declared and believed that every word of nonsense which fell from their lips was a direct spiritual intervention. These gentlemen have become Puseyites already, and are, my friend states, in the high way to Catholicism. Madame Sand herself was a Catholic some time since: having been converted to that faith along with M. N——, of the Academy of Music; Mr. L——, the pianoforte player; and one or two other chosen individuals, by the famous Abbé de la M——. Abbé de la M—— (so told me, in the Diligence, a priest, who read his breviary and gossiped alternately very curiously and pleasantly) is himself an *âme perdue:* the man spoke of his brother clergyman with actual horror;

and it certainly appears that the Abbé's works of conversion have not prospered ; for Madame Sand, having brought her hero (and herself, as we may presume) to the point of Catholicism, proceeds directly to dispose of that as she has done of Judaism and Protestantism, and will not leave, of the whole fabric of Christianity, a single stone standing.

I think the fate of our English Newman-street apostles, and of M. de la M——, the mad priest, and his congregation of mad converts, should be a warning to such of us as are inclined to dabble in religious speculations ; for, in them, as in all others, our flighty brains soon lose themselves, and we find our reason speedily lying prostrated at the mercy of our passions ; and I think that Madame Sand's novel of Spiridion may do a vast deal of good, and bears a good moral with it ; though not such an one, perhaps, as our fair philosopher intended. For anything he learned, Samuel-Peter-Spiridion-Hebronius might have remained a Jew from the beginning to the end. Wherefore be in such a hurry to set up new faiths ? Wherefore, Madame Sand, try and be so preternaturally wise ? Wherefore be so eager to jump out of one religion, for the purpose of jumping into another ? See what good this philosophical friskiness has done you, and on what sort of ground you are come at last. You are so wonderfully sagacious, that you flounder in mud at every step ; so amazingly clear-sighted, that your eyes cannot see an inch before you, having put out, with that extinguishing genius of yours, every one of the lights that are sufficient for the conduct of common men. And for what ? Let our friend Spiridion speak for himself. After setting up his convent, and filling it with monks, who entertain an immense respect for his wealth and genius, Father Hebronius, unanimously elected prior, gives himself up to further studies, and leaves his monks to themselves. Industrious and sober as they were, originally, they grow quickly intemperate and idle; and Hebronius, who does not appear among his flock until he has freed himself of the Catholic religion, as he has of the Jewish and the Protestant, sees, with dismay, the evil condition of his disciples, and regrets, too late, the precipitancy by which he renounced, then and for ever, Christianity. "But, as he had no new religion to adopt in its place, and as, grown more prudent and calm, he did not wish to accuse himself unnecessarily, once more, of inconstancy and apostasy, he still maintained all the exterior forms of the worship which inwardly he had abjured. But it was not enough for him to have quitted error, it was necessary to discover truth. But Hebronius had well looked round to discover it; he could not find anything that resembled it. Then commenced for him a series of sufferings, unknown and terrible. Placed face to face with doubt, this sincere and religious spirit was frightened at its own solitude; and as it had no other desire nor aim on earth than truth, and nothing else here below interested it, he lived absorbed in his own sad contemplations, looking ceaselessly into the vague that surrounded him like an ocean without bounds, and seeing the horizon retreat and retreat as ever he wished to near it. Lost in this immense uncertainty, he felt as if attacked by vertigo, and his thoughts whirled within his brain. Then, fatigued with his vain toils and hopeless endeavours, he would sink down depressed, unmanned, life-wearied, only living in the sensation of that silent grief which he felt and could not comprehend."

It is a pity that this hapless Spiridion, so eager in his passage from one creed to another, and so loud in his profession of the truth, wherever he fancied that he had found it, had not waited a little, before he avowed himself either Catholic or Protestant, and implicated others in errors and follies which might, at least, have been confined to his own bosom, and there have lain comparatively harmless. In what a pretty state, for instance, will Messrs. Dr——d and P——l have left their Newman-street congregation, who are still plunged in their old superstitions, from which their spiritual pastors and masters have been set free! In what a state, too, do Mrs. Sand and her brother and sister philosophers, Templars, Saint Simonians, Fourierites, Lerouxites, or whatever the sect may be, leave the unfortunate people who have listened to their doctrines, and who have not the opportunity, or the fiery versatility of belief, which carries their teachers from one creed to another, leaving only exploded lies and useless recantations behind them! I wish the State would make a law that one individual should not be allowed to preach more than one doctrine in his life; or, at any rate, should be soundly corrected for every change of creed. How many charlatans would have been silenced,—how much conceit would have been kept within bounds,—how many fools, who are dazzled by fine sentences, and made drunk by declamation, would have remained quiet and sober, in that quiet and sober way of faith which their fathers held before them. However, the reader will be glad to learn that, after all his doubts and sorrows, Spiridion does discover the truth (*the* truth, what a wise Spiridion !), and some discretion with it; for, having found among his monks, who are dissolute, superstitious—and all hate him—one only being, Fulgentius, who is loving, candid, and pious, he says to him,—"If you were like myself, if the first want of your nature were, like mine, to know, I would, without hesitation, lay bare to you my entire thoughts. I would make you drink the cup of truth, which I myself have filled with so many tears, at the risk of intoxicating you with the draught. But it is not so, alas ! you are made to love rather than to know, and your heart is stronger than your intellect. You are attached to Catholicism,—I believe so, at least,—by bonds of sentiment which you could not break without pain, and which, if you were to break, the truth which I could lay bare to you in return would not repay you for what you had sacrificed. Instead of exalting, it would crush you, very likely. It is a food too strong for ordinary men, and which, when it does not revivify, smothers. I will not, then, reveal to you this doctrine, which is the triumph of my life, and the consolation of my last days; because it might, perhaps, be for you only a cause of mourning and despair. * * * Of all the works which my long studies have produced, there is one alone which I have not given to the flames; for it alone is complete. In that you will find me entire, and there LIES THE TRUTH. And, as the sage has said you must not bury your treasures in a well, I will not confide mine to the brutal stupidity of these monks. But as this volume should only pass into hands worthy to touch it, and be laid open for eyes that are capable of comprehending its mysteries, I shall exact from the reader one condition, which, at the same time, shall be a proof: I shall carry it with me to the tomb, in order that he who one day shall read it, may have courage enough to brave the vain terrors of the grave, in searching for it amid the dust of my sepulchre. As soon as I am dead, therefore, place this writing on my breast. * * * Ah! when the time comes for reading it, I think my withered heart will spring up again, as the frozen grass at the return of the sun, and that, from the midst of its infinite transformations, my spirit will enter into immediate communication with thine!"

* * * * *

Does not the reader long to be at this precious manuscript, which contains THE TRUTH; and ought he not to be very much obliged to Mrs. Sand, for being so good as to print it for him? We leave all the story aside:—how Fulgentius had not the spirit to read the manuscript, but left the secret to Alexis; how Alexis, a stern, old, philosophical, unbelieving monk, as ever was, tried in vain to lift up the gravestone, but was taken with fever, and obliged to forego the discovery; and how, finally, Angel, his disciple, a youth amiable and innocent as his name, was the destined person who brought the long-buried treasure to light. Trembling and delighted, the pair read this tremendous MANUSCRIPT OF SPIRIDION.

Will it be believed, that of all the dull, vague, windy documents that mortal ever set eyes on, this is the dullest?

If this be absolute truth, *à quoi bon* search for it, since we have long, long had the jewel in our possession, or since, at least, it has been held up as such by every sham philosopher who has had a mind to pass off his wares on the public? Hear Spiridion :—

"How much have I wept, how much have I suffered, how much have I prayed, how much have I laboured, before I understood the cause and the aim of my passage on this earth! After many incertitudes, after much remorse, after many scruples, *I have comprehended that I was a martyr!*—But why my martyrdom? said I; what crime did I commit before I was born, thus to be condemned to labour and groaning, from the hour when I first saw the day up to that when I am about to enter into the night of the tomb?

"At last, by dint of imploring God—by dint of inquiry into the history of man, a ray of the truth has descended on my brow, and the shadows of the past have melted from before my eyes. I have lifted a corner of the curtain: I have seen enough to know that my life, like that of the rest of the human race, has been a series of necessary errors, yet, to speak more correctly, of incomplete truths, conducting, more or less, slowly and directly, to absolute truth and ideal perfection. But when will they rise on the face of the earth—when will they issue from the bosom of the Divinity—those generations who shall salute the august countenance of Truth, and proclaim the reign of the ideal on earth? I see well how humanity marches, but I neither can see its cradle nor its apotheosis. Man seems to me a transitory race, between the beast and the angel ; but I know how many centuries have been required, that he might pass from the *state of brute to the state of man,* and *I cannot tell how many ages are necessary that he may pass from the state of man to the state of angel!*

"Yet I hope, and I feel within me, at the approach of death, that which warns me that great destinies await humanity. In this life all is over for me. Much have I striven, to advance but little: I have laboured without ceasing, and have done almost nothing. Yet, after pains immeasurable, I die content, for I know that I have done all I could, and am sure that the little I have done will not be lost.

"What, then, have I done? this wilt thou demand of me, man of a future age, who will seek for truth in the testaments of the past. Thou who wilt be no more Catholic —no more Christian, thou wilt ask of the poor monk, lying in the dust, an account of his life and death. Thou wouldst know wherefore were his vows, why his austerities, his labours, his retreat, his prayers?

"You who turn back to me, in order that I may guide you on your road, and that you may arrive more quickly at the goal which it has not been my lot to attain, pause, yet, for a moment, and look upon the past history of humanity. You will see that its fate has been ever to choose between the least of two evils, and ever to commit great faults in order to avoid others still greater. You will see * * * on one side, the heathen mythology, that debased the spirit, in its efforts to deify the flesh ; on the other, the austere Christian principle, that debased the flesh too much, in order to raise the worship of the spirit. You will see, afterwards, how the religion of Christ embodies itself in a church, and raises itself a generous democratic power against the tyranny of princes. Later still, you will see how that power has attained its end, and passed beyond it. You will see it, having chained and conquered princes, league itself with them, in order to oppress the people, and seize on temporal power. Schism, then, raises up against it the standard of revolt, and preaches the bold and legitimate principle of liberty of conscience: but, also, you will see how this liberty of conscience brings religious anarchy in its train; or, worse still, religious indifference and disgust. And if your soul, shattered in the tempestuous changes which you behold humanity undergoing, would strike out for itself a passage through the rocks, amidst which, like a frail bark, lies tossing trembling truth, you will be embarrassed to choose between the new philosophers—who, in preaching tolerance, destroy religious and social unity—and the last Christians, who, to preserve society, that is, religion and philosophy, are obliged to brave the principle of toleration. Man of truth! to whom I address, at once, my instruction and my justification, at the time when you shall live, the science of truth, no doubt, will have advanced a step. Think, then, of all your fathers have suffered, as, bending beneath the weight of their ignorance and uncertainty, they have traversed the desert across which, with so much pain, they have conducted thee! And if the pride of thy young learning shall make thee contemplate the petty strifes in which our life has been consumed, pause and tremble, as you think of that which is still unknown to yourself, and of the judgment that your descendants will pass on you.

Think of this, and learn to respect all those who, seeking their way in all sincerity, have wandered from the path, frightened by the storm, and sorely tried by the severe hand of the All-Powerful. Think of this, and prostrate yourself; for all these, even the most mistaken among them, are saints and martyrs.

"Without their conquests and their defeats, thou wert in darkness still. Yes, their failures, their errors even, have a right to your respect; for man is weak. * * Weep, then, for us obscure travellers—unknown victims, who, by our mortal sufferings and unheard-of labours, have prepared the way before you. Pity me, who, having passionately loved justice, and perseveringly sought for truth, only opened my eyes to shut them again for ever, and saw that I had been in vain endeavouring to support a ruin, to take refuge in a vault of which the foundations were worn away." * * *

The rest of the book of Spiridion is made up of a history of the rise, progress, and (what our philosopher is pleased to call) decay of Christianity—of an assertion, that the "doctrine of Christ is incomplete;" that "Christ may, nevertheless, take his place in the Pantheon of divine men!" and of a long, disgusting, absurd, and impious vision, in which the Saviour, Moses, David, and Elijah are represented, and in which Christ is made to say—"*We are all Messiahs*, when we wish to bring the reign of truth upon earth; we are all Christs, when we suffer for it!"

And this is the ultimatum, the supreme secret, the absolute truth! and it has been published by Mrs. Sand, for so many napoleons per sheet, in the *Revue des Deux*

Mondes;" and the Deux Mondes are to abide by it for the future. After having attained it, are we a whit wiser? "Man is between an angel and a beast: I don't know how long it is since he was a brute—I can't say how long it will be before he is an angel." Think of people living by their wits, and living by such a wit as this! Think of the state of mental debauch and disease which must have been passed through, ere such words could be written, and could be popular!

When a man leaves our dismal, smoky, London atmosphere, and breathes, instead of coal-smoke and yellow fog, this bright, clear, French air, he is quite intoxicated by it at first, and feels a glow in his blood, and a joy in his spirits, which scarcely thrice in a year, and then only at a distance from London, he can attain in England. Is the intoxication, I wonder, permanent among the natives? and may we not account for the ten thousand frantic freaks of these people by the peculiar influence of French air and sun? The philosophers are from night to morning drunk, the politicians are drunk, the literary men reel and stagger from one absurdity to another, and how shall we understand their vagaries? Let us suppose, charitably, that Madame Sand had inhaled a more than ordinary quantity of this laughing gas when she wrote for us this precious manuscript of *Spiridion*. That great destinies are in prospect for the human race, we may fancy, without her ladyship's word for it: but more liberal than she, and having a little retrospective charity, as well as that easy prospective benevolence which Mrs. Sand adopts, let us try and think there is some hope for our fathers (who were nearer brutality than ourselves, according to the Sandean creed), or else there is a very poor chance for us, who, great philosophers as we are, are yet, alas! far removed from that angelic consummation which all must wish for so devoutly. She cannot say—is it not extraordinary?—how many centuries have been necessary before man could pass from the brutal state to his present condition, or how many ages will be required ere we may pass from the state of man to the state of angel! What the deuce is the use of chronology or philosophy?—We were beasts, and we can't tell when our tails dropped off: we shall be angels; but when our wings are to begin to sprout, who knows? In the meantime, O man of genius, follow our counsel: lead an easy life, don't stick at trifles; never mind about *duty*, it is only made for slaves; if the world reproach you, reproach the world in return, you have a good loud tongue in your head : if your strait-laced morals injure your mental respiration, fling off the old-fashioned stays, and leave your free limbs to rise and fall as Nature pleases; and when you have grown pretty sick of your liberty, and yet unfit to return to restraint, curse the world, and scorn it, and be miserable, like my Lord Byron and other philosophers of his kidney; or else mount a step higher, and, with conceit still more monstrous, and mental vision still more wretchedly debauched and weak, begin suddenly to find yourself afflicted with a maudlin compassion for the human race, and a desire to set them right after your own fashion. There is the quarrelsome stage of drunkenness, when a man can as yet walk and speak, when he can call names, and fling plates and wine-glasses at his neighbour's head with a pretty good aim; after this comes the pathetic stage, when the patient becomes wondrous philanthropic, and weeps wildly, as he lies in the gutter, and fancies he is at home in bed—where he ought to be: but this is an allegory.

I don't wish to carry this any farther, or to say a word in defence of the doctrine which Mrs. Dudevant has found "incomplete;"—here, at least, is not the place for discussing its merits, any more than Mrs. Sand's book was the place for exposing, forsooth, its errors: our business is only with the day and the new novels, and the clever or silly people who write them. Oh! if they but knew their places, and would keep to them, and drop their absurd philosophical jargon! Not all the big words in the world can make Mrs. Sand talk like a philosopher: when will she go back to her old trade, of which she was the very ablest practitioner in France?

I should have been glad to give some extracts from the dramatic and descriptive parts of the novel, that cannot, in point of style and beauty, be praised too highly. One must suffice,—it is the descent of Alexis to seek that unlucky manuscript, *Spiridion*.

"It seemed to me," he begins, "that the descent was eternal; and that I was burying myself in the depths of Erebus: at last, I reached a level place,—and I heard a mournful voice deliver these words, as it were, to the secret centre of the earth—'*He will mount that ascent no more!*' —Immediately I heard arise towards me, from the depth of invisible abysses, a myriad of formidable voices united in a strange chant—'*Let us destroy him! Let him be destroyed!*

What does he here among the dead ? Let him be delivered back to torture ! Let him be given again to life !'

"Then a feeble light began to pierce the darkness, and I perceived that I stood on the lowest step of a staircase, vast as the foot of a mountain. Behind me were thousands of steps of lurid iron ; before me, nothing but a void—an abyss, and ether; the blue gloom of midnight beneath my feet, as above my head. I became delirious, and quitting that staircase, which methought it was impossible for me to reascend, I sprung forth into the void with an execration. But, immediately, when I had uttered the curse, the void began to be filled with forms and colours, and I presently perceived that I was in a vast gallery, along which I advanced, trembling. There was still darkness round me ; but the hollows of the vaults gleamed with a red light, and showed me the strange and hideous forms of their building. * * * I did not distinguish the nearest objects ; but those towards which I advanced assumed an appearance more and more ominous, and my terror increased with every step I took. The enormous pillars which supported the vault, and the tracery thereof itself, were figures of men, of supernatural stature, delivered to tortures without a name. Some hung by their feet, and, locked in the coils of monstrous serpents, clenched their teeth in the marble of the pavement ; others, fastened by their waists, were dragged upwards, these by their feet, those by their heads, towards capitals, where other figures stooped towards them, eager to torment them. Other pillars, again, represented a struggling mass of figures devouring one another ; each of which only offered a trunk severed to the knees or

to the shoulders, the fierce heads whereof retained life
enough to seize and devour that which was near them.
There were some who, half hanging down, agonized themselves by attempting, with their upper limbs, to flay the
lower moiety of their bodies, which drooped from the
columns, or were attached to the pedestals; and others,
who, in their fight with each other, were dragged along by
morsels of flesh,—grasping which, they clung to each other
with a countenance of unspeakable hate and agony. Along,
or rather in place of, the frieze, there were on either side a
range of unclean beings, wearing the human form, but of a
loathsome ugliness, busied in tearing human corpses to
pieces—in feasting upon their limbs and entrails. From
the vault, instead of bosses and pendants, hung the crushed
and wounded forms of children; as if to escape these eaters
of man's flesh, they would throw themselves downwards,
and be dashed to pieces on the pavement. * * * The
silence and motionlessness of the whole added to its awful-
ness. I became so faint with terror, that I stopped, and
would fain have returned. But at that moment I heard,
from the depths of the gloom through which I had passed,
confused noises, like those of a multitude on its march.
And the sounds soon became more distinct, and the clamour
fiercer, and the steps came hurrying on tumultuously—at
every new burst nearer, more violent, more threatening. I
thought that I was pursued by this disorderly crowd; and
I strove to advance, hurrying into the midst of those dismal
sculptures. Then it seemed as if those figures began to
heave,—and to sweat blood,—and their beady eyes to move
in their sockets. At once I beheld that they were all

looking upon me, that they were all leaning towards me,— some with frightful derision, others with furious aversion. Every arm was raised against me, and they made as though they would crush me with the quivering limbs they had torn one from the other." * * *

It is, indeed, a pity that the poor fellow gave himself the trouble to go down into damp, unwholesome graves, for the purpose of fetching up a few trumpery sheets of manuscript; and if the public has been rather tired with their contents, and is disposed to ask why Mrs. Sand's religious or irreligious notions are to be brought forward to people who are quite satisfied with their own, we can only say that this lady is the representative of a vast class of her countrymen, whom the wits and philosophers of the eighteenth century have brought to this condition. The leaves of the Diderot and Rousseau tree have produced this goodly fruit: here it is, ripe, bursting, and ready to fall;— and how to fall? Heaven send that it may drop easily, for all can see that the time is come.

THE CASE OF PEYTEL:

IN A LETTER TO EDWARD BRIEFLESS, ESQUIRE, OF PUMP-COURT, TEMPLE.

———◆———

Paris, November, 1839.

MY DEAR BRIEFLESS,—Two months since, when the act of accusation first appeared, containing the sum of the charges against Sebastian Peytel, all Paris was in a fervour on the subject. The man's trial speedily followed, and kept for three days the public interest wound up to a painful point. He was found guilty of double murder at the beginning of September; and, since that time, what with Maroto's disaffection, and Turkish news, we have had leisure to forget Monsieur Peytel, and to occupy ourselves with τι νέον. Perhaps Monsieur de Balzac helped to smother what little sparks of interest might still have remained for the murderous notary. Balzac put forward a letter in his favour, so very long, so very dull, so very pompous, promising so much, and performing so little, that the Parisian public gave up Peytel and his case altogether; nor was it until to-day that some small feeling was raised concerning him, when the newspapers brought the account how Peytel's head had been cut off, at Bourg.

He had gone through the usual miserable ceremonies and delays which attend what is called, in this country, the march of justice. He had made his appeal to the Court of Cassation, which had taken time to consider the verdict of the Provincial Court, and had confirmed it. He had made his appeal for mercy; his poor sister coming up all the way from Bourg (a sad journey, poor thing!) to have an interview with the King, who had refused to see her. Last Monday morning, at nine o'clock, an hour before Peytel's breakfast, the Greffier of Assize Court, in company with the Curé of Bourg, waited on him, and informed him that he had only three hours to live. At twelve o'clock, Peytel's head was off his body: an executioner from Lyons had come over the night before, to assist the professional throat-cutter of Bourg.

I am not going to entertain you with any sentimental lamentations for this scoundrel's fate, or to declare my belief in his innocence, as Monsieur de Balzac has done. As far as moral conviction can go, the man's guilt is pretty clearly brought home to him. But any man who has read the *Causes Célébres*, knows that men have been convicted and executed upon evidence ten times more powerful than that which was brought against Peytel. His own account of his horrible case may be true; there is nothing adduced in the evidence which is strong enough to overthrow it. It is a serious privilege, God knows, that society takes upon itself, at any time, to deprive one of God's creatures of existence. But when the slightest doubt remains, what a tremendous risk does it incur! In England, thank Heaven, the law is more wise and more merciful: an English jury would never have taken a man's blood upon such testimony; an English judge and crown-advocate would never have acted as these Frenchmen have done; the latter inflaming the public mind by exaggerated appeals to their passions; the former seeking, in every way, to draw confessions from the prisoner, to perplex and confound him, to do away, by fierce cross-questioning and bitter remarks from the bench, with any effect that his testimony might have on the jury. I don't mean to say that judges and lawyers have been more violent and inquisitorial against the unhappy Peytel than against any one else; it is the fashion of the country: a man is guilty until he proves himself to be innocent; and to batter down his defence, if he have any, there are the lawyers, with all their horrible ingenuity, and their captivating passionate eloquence. It is hard thus to set the skilful and tried champions of the law against men unused to this kind of combat; nay, give a man all the legal aid that he can purchase or procure, still, by this plan, you take him at a cruel, unmanly disadvantage: he has to fight against the law, clogged with the dreadful weight of his presupposed guilt. Thank God that, in England, things are not managed so.

However, I am not about to entertain you with ignorant disquisitions about the law. Peytel's case may, nevertheless, interest you; for the tale is a very stirring and mysterious one; and you may see how easy a thing it is for a man's life to be talked away in France, if ever he should happen to fall under the suspicion of a crime. The French "Acte d'accusation" begins in the following manner :—

"Of all the events which, in these latter times, have afflicted the department of the Ain, there is none which has caused a more profound and lively sensation than the tragical death of the lady, Felicité Alcazar, wife of Sebastian Benedict Peytel, notary, at Belley. At the end of October, 1838, Madame Peytel quitted that town, with her husband, and their servant, Louis Rey, in order to pass a few days at Macon : at midnight, the inhabitants of Belley were suddenly awakened by the arrival of Monsieur Peytel, by his cries, and by the signs which he exhibited of the most lively agitation : he implored the succours of all the physicians in the town ; knocked violently at their doors ; rung at the bells of their houses with a sort of frenzy, and announced that his wife, stretched out, and dying, in his carriage, had just been shot, on the Lyons road, by his domestic, whose life Peytel himself had taken.

"At this recital a number of persons assembled, and what a spectacle was presented to their eyes.

"A young woman lay at the bottom of a carriage; deprived of life ; her whole body was wet, and seemed as if it had just been plunged into the water. She appeared to be severely wounded in the face ; and her garments, which were raised up, in spite of the cold and rainy weather, left the upper part of her knees almost entirely exposed. At the sight of this half-naked and inanimate body, all the spectators were affected. People said that the first duty to pay to a dying woman was, to preserve her from the cold, to cover her. A physician examined the body; he declared that all remedies were useless; that Madame Peytel was dead and cold.

"The entreaties of Peytel were redoubled; he demanded fresh succours, and, giving no heed to the fatal assurance which had just been given him, required that all the physicians in the place should be sent for. A scene so strange and so melancholy; the incoherent account given by Peytel of the murder of his wife; his extraordinary movements; and the avowal which he continued to make, that he had despatched the murderer, Rey, with strokes of his hammer, excited the attention of Lieutenant Wolf, commandant of gendarmes: that officer gave orders for the immediate arrest of Peytel; but the latter threw himself into the arms of a friend, who interceded for him, and begged the police not immediately to seize upon his person.

"The corpse of Madame Peytel was transported to her apartment; the bleeding body of the domestic was, likewise, brought from the road, where it lay; and Peytel, asked to explain the circumstance, did so." * * *

Now, as there is little reason to tell the reader, when an English counsel has to prosecute a prisoner on the part of the Crown for a capital offence, he produces the articles of his accusation in the most moderate terms, and especially warns the jury to give the accused person the benefit of every possible doubt that the evidence may give, or may leave. See how these things are managed in France, and how differently the French counsel for the Crown sets about his work.

He first prepares his act of accusation, the opening of which we have just read; it is published six days before the trial, so that an unimpassioned, unprejudiced jury has ample time to study it, and to form its opinions accordingly, and to go into court with a happy, just prepossession against the prisoner.

Read the first part of the Peytel act of accusation; it is as turgid and declamatory as a bad romance; and as inflated as a newspaper document, by an unlimited penny-a-liner:—" The department of the Ain is in a dreadful state of excitement; the inhabitants of Belley come trooping from their beds,—and what a sight do they behold;—a young woman at the bottom of a carriage, *toute ruisselante*, just out of a river; her garments, in spite of the cold and rain, raised, so as to leave the upper part of her knee entirely exposed, at which all the beholders were affected, and cried, that the *first duty* was to cover her from the cold." This settles the case at once; the first duty of a man is to cover the legs of the sufferer; the second to call for help. The eloquent " Substitut du Procureur du Roi " has prejudged the case, in the course of a few sentences. He is putting his readers, among whom his future jury is to be found, into a proper state of mind; he works on them with pathetic description, just as a romance writer would: the rain pours in torrents; it is a dreary evening in November; the young creature's situation is neatly described; the distrust which entered into the breast of the keen old officer of gendarmes strongly painted, the suspicions which might, or might not, have been entertained by the inhabitants, eloquently argued. How did the advocate know that the people had such? did all the bystanders say aloud, "I suspect that this is a case of murder by Monsieur Peytel, and that his story about the domestic is all deception?" or did they go off to the mayor, and register their suspicion? or was the advocate there to hear them? Not he; but he paints you the whole scene, as though it had existed, and gives full accounts of suspicions, as if they had been facts, positive, patent, staring, that everybody could see and swear to.

Having thus primed his audience, and prepared them for the testimony of the accused party, "Now," says he, with a fine show of justice, "let us hear Monsieur Peytel;" and that worthy's narrative is given as follows:—

"He said that he had left Macon on the 31st October, at eleven o'clock in the morning, in order to return to Belley, with his wife and servant. The latter drove, or led, an open car; he himself was driving his wife in a four-wheeled carriage, drawn by one horse: they reached Bourg at five o'clock in the evening; left it at seven, to sleep at Pont d'Ain, where they did not arrive before midnight. During the journey, Peytel thought he remarked that Rey had slackened his horse's pace. When they alighted at the inn, Peytel bade him deposit in his chamber 7,500 francs, which he carried with him; but the domestic refused to do so, saying that the inn gates were secure, and there was no danger. Peytel was, therefore, obliged to carry his money upstairs himself. The next day, the 1st November, they set out on their journey again, at nine o'clock in the morning; Louis did not come, according to custom, to take his master's orders. They arrived at

Tenay about three, stopped there a couple of hours to dine, and it was eight o'clock when they reached the bourg of Rossillon, where they waited half an hour to bait the horses.

"As they left Rossillon, the weather became bad, and the rain began to fall: Peytel told his domestic to get a covering for the articles in the open chariot; but Rey refused to do so, adding, in an ironical tone, that the weather was fine. For some days past, Peytel had remarked that his servant was gloomy, and scarcely spoke at all.

"After they had gone about 500 paces beyond the bridge of Andert, that crosses the river Furans, and ascended to the least steep part of the hill of Darde, Peytel cried out to his servant, who was seated in the car, to come down from it, and finish the ascent on foot.

"At this moment a violent wind was blowing from the south, and the rain was falling heavily: Peytel was seated back in the right corner of the carriage, and his wife, who was close to him, was asleep, with her head on his left shoulder. All of a sudden he heard the report of a fire-arm (he had seen the light of it at some paces' distance), and Madame Peytel cried out, 'My poor husband, take your pistols;' the horse was frightened, and began to trot. Peytel immediately drew the pistol, and fired, from the interior of the carriage, upon an individual whom he saw running by the side of the road.

"Not knowing, as yet, that his wife had been hit, he jumped out on one side of the carriage, while Madame Peytel descended from the other; and he fired a second pistol at his domestic, Louis Rey, whom he had just recognised. Redoubling his pace, he came up with Rey, and struck him, from behind, a blow with the hammer. Rey turned at this, and raised up his arm to strike his master with the pistol which he had just discharged at him; but Peytel, more quick than he, gave the domestic a blow with the hammer, which felled him to the ground (he fell his face forwards), and then Peytel, bestriding the body, despatched him, although the brigand asked for mercy.

"He now began to think of his wife; and ran back, calling out her name repeatedly, and seeking for her, in vain, on both sides of the road. Arrived at the bridge of Andert, he recognised his wife, stretched in a field, covered with water, which bordered the Furans. This horrible discovery had so much the more astonished him, because he had no idea, until now, that his wife had been wounded: he endeavoured to draw her from the water; and it was only after considerable exertions that he was enabled to do so, and to place her, with her face towards the ground, on the side of the road. Supposing that, here, she would be sheltered from any farther danger, and believing, as yet, that she was only wounded, he determined to ask for help at a lone house, situated on the road towards Rossillon; and at this instant he perceived, without at all being able to explain how, that his horse had followed him back to the spot, having turned back of its own accord, from the road to Belley.

"The house at which he knocked was inhabited by two men, of the name of Thannet, father and son, who opened the door to him, and whom he entreated to come to his aid, saying, that his wife had just been assassinated by his servant. The elder Thannet approached to, and examined the body, and told Peytel that it was quite dead; he and his son took up the corpse, and placed it in the bottom of the carriage, which they all mounted themselves, and pursued their route to Belley. In order to do so, they had to pass by Rey's body, on the road, which Peytel wished to crush under the wheels of his carriage. It was to rob him of 7,500 francs, said Peytel, that the attack had been made."

Our friend, the Procureur's Substitut, has dropped, here, the eloquent and pathetic style altogether, and only gives the unlucky prisoner's narrative in the baldest and most unimaginative style. How is a jury to listen to such a fellow? they ought to condemn him, if but for making such an uninteresting statement. Why not have helped poor Peytel with some of those rhetorical graces which have been so plentifully bestowed in the opening part of the act of accusation. He might have said :—

"Monsieur Peytel is an eminent notary at Belley; he is a man distinguished for his literary and scientific acquirements; he has lived long in the best society of the capital; he had been but a few months married to that young and unfortunate lady, whose loss has plunged her bereaved husband into despair — almost into madness. Some early differences had marked, it is true, the commencement of their union; but these,—which, as can be proved by evidence, were almost all the unhappy lady's fault,—had happily ceased, to give place to sentiments far more delightful and tender. Gentlemen, Madame Peytel bore in her bosom a sweet pledge of future concord between herself and her husband: in three brief months she was to become a mother.

"In the exercise of his honourable profession,—in which, to succeed, a man must not only have high talents, but undoubted probity,—and, gentlemen, Monsieur Peytel *did* succeed—*did* inspire respect and confidence, as you, his neighbours, well know;—in the exercise, I say, of his high calling, Monsieur Peytel, towards the end of October last, had occasion to make a journey in the neighbourhood, and visit some of his many clients.

"He travelled in his own carriage, his young wife beside him. Does this look like want of affection, gentlemen? or is it not a mark of love—of love and paternal care on his part towards the being with whom his lot in life was linked,—the mother of his coming child,—the young girl, who had everything to gain from the union with a man of his attainments of intellect, his kind temper, his great experience, and his high position? In this manner they travelled, side by side, lovingly together. Monsieur Peytel was not a lawyer merely, but a man of letters and varied learning; of the noble and sublime science of geology he was, especially, an ardent devotee."

(Suppose, here, a short panegyric upon geology. Allude to the creation of this mighty world, and then, naturally, to the Creator. Fancy the conversations which Peytel, a religious man,* might have with his young wife upon the subject.)

* He always went to mass; it is in the evidence.

"Monsieur Peytel had lately taken into his service a man named Louis Rey. Rey was a foundling, and had passed many years in a regiment—a school, gentlemen, where much besides bravery, alas! is taught; nay, where the spirit which familiarizes one with notions of battle and death, I fear, may familiarize one with ideas, too, of murder. Rey, a dashing reckless fellow, from the army, had lately entered Peytel's service; was treated by him with the most singular kindness; accompanied him (having charge of another vehicle) upon the journey before alluded to; and *knew that his master carried with him a considerable sum of money;* for a man like Rey an enormous sum, 7,500 francs. At midnight, on the 1st of November, as Madame Peytel and her husband were returning home, an attack was made upon their carriage. Remember, gentlemen, the hour at which the attack was made; remember the sum of money that was in the carriage; and remember that the Savoy frontier *is within a league of the spot* where the desperate deed was done."

Now, my dear Briefless, ought not Monsieur Procureur, in common justice to Peytel, after he had so eloquently proclaimed, not the facts, but the suspicions, which weighed against that worthy, to have given a similar florid account of the prisoner's case? Instead of this, you will remark, that it is the advocate's endeavour to make Peytel's statements as uninteresting in style as possible; and then he demolishes them in the following way:—

"Scarcely was Peytel's statement known, when the common sense of the public rose against it. Peytel had commenced his story upon the bridge of Andert, over the cold body of his wife. On the 2nd November he had developed it in detail, in the presence of the physicians, in the presence of the assembled neighbours—of the persons who, on the day previous only, were his friends. Finally, he had completed it in his interrogatories, his conversations, his writings, and letters to the magistrates ; and everywhere these words, repeated so often, were only received with a painful incredulity. The fact was that, besides the singular character which Peytel's appearance, attitude, and talk had worn ever since the event, there was in his narrative an inexplicable enigma ; its contradictions and impossibilities were such, that calm persons were revolted at it, and that even friendship itself refused to believe it."

Thus Mr. Attorney speaks, not for himself alone, but for the whole French public ; whose opinions, of course, he knows. Peytel's statement is discredited *everywhere ;* the statement which he had made over the cold body of his wife—the monster ! It is not enough simply to prove that the man committed the murder, but to make the jury violently angry against him, and cause them to shudder in the jury-box, as the exposes he horrid details of the crime.

" Justice," goes on Mr. Substitute (who answers for the feelings of everybody), " *disturbed by the pre-occupations of public opinion,* commenced, without delay, the most active researches. The bodies of the victims were submitted to the investigations of men of art ; the wounds and projectiles were examined ; the place where the event took place explored with care. The morality of the authors of this frightful scene became the object of rigorous examination ; the *exigeances* of the prisoner, the forms affected by him, his calculated silence, and his answers, coldly insulting, were feeble obstacles; and justice at length arrived, by its prudence, and by the discoveries it made, to the most cruel point of certainty."

You see that a man's demeanour is here made a crime against him; and that Mr. Substitute wishes to consider him guilty, because he has actually the audacity to hold his tongue. Now follows a touching description of the domestic, Louis Rey:—

"Louis Rey, a child of the Hospital at Lyons, was confided, at a very early age, to some honest country people, with whom he stayed until he entered the army. At their house, and during this long period of time, his conduct, his intelligence, and the sweetness of his manners, were such, that the family of his guardians became to him as an adopted family; and that his departure caused them the most sincere affliction. When Louis quitted the army, he returned to his benefactors, and was received as a son. They found him just as they had ever known him (I acknowledge that this pathos beats my humble defence of Rey entirely), except that he had learned to read and write; and the certificates of his commanders proved him to be a good and gallant soldier.

"The necessity of creating some resources for himself, obliged him to quit his friends, and to enter the service of Monsieur de Montrichard, a lieutenant of gendarmerie, from whom he received fresh testimonials of regard. Louis, it is true, might have a fondness for wine, and a passion for women; but he had been a soldier, and these faults were, according to the witnesses, amply compensated for by his activity, his intelligence, and the agreeable manner in which he performed his service. In the month of July, 1839, Rey quitted, voluntarily, the service of M. de Montrichard; and Peytel, about this period, meeting him at Lyons, did not hesitate to attach him to his service. Whatever may be the prisoner's present language, it is certain that, up to the day of Louis's death, he served Peytel with diligence and fidelity.

"More than once his master and mistress spoke well of him. *Everybody* who has worked, or been at the house of Madame Peytel, has spoken in praise of his character: and, indeed, it may be said, that these testimonials were general.

" On the very night of the 1st of November, and immediately after the catastrophe, we remark how Peytel begins to make insinuations against his servant; and how artfully, in order to render them more sure, he disseminates them through the different parts of his narrative. But, in the course of the proceeding, these charges have met with a most complete denial. Thus we find the disobedient servant, who, at Pont d' Ain, refused to carry the money-chest to his master's room, under the pretext that the gates of the inn were closed securely, occupied with tending the horses, after their long journey: meanwhile Peytel was standing by, and neither master nor servant exchanged a word; and the witnesses who beheld them both, have borne testimony to the zeal and care of the domestic.

" In like manner, we find that the servant, who was so remiss, in the morning, as to neglect to go to his master for orders, was ready for departure before seven o'clock, and had eagerly informed himself whether Monsieur and Madame Peytel were awake; learning, from the maid of the inn, that they had ordered nothing for their breakfast. This man, who refused to carry with him a covering for the car, was, on the contrary, ready to take off his own cloak, and with it shelter articles of small value; this man, who had been, for many days, so silent and gloomy, gave, on the contrary, many proofs of his gaiety—almost of his indiscretion, speaking, at all the inns, in terms of praise of his master and mistress. The waiter at the inn, at Dauphin, says he was a tall young fellow, mild and good-natured; we talked, for some time, about horses, and such things; he seemed to be perfectly natural, and not preoccupied at all. At Pont d'Ain, he talked of his being a foundling; of the place where he had been brought up, and where he had served; and, finally, at Rossillon, an hour before his death, he conversed familiarly with the master of the port, and spoke on indifferent subjects.

"All Peytel's insinuations against his servant had no other end than to show, in every point of Rey's conduct, the behaviour of a man who was premeditating attack. Of what, in fact, does he accuse him? Of wishing to rob him of 7,500 francs, and of having had recourse to assassination, in order to effect the robbery. But, for a premeditated crime, consider what singular improvidence the person showed who had determined on committing it; what folly and what weakness there is in the execution of it.

"How many insurmountable obstacles are there in the way of committing and profiting by crime! On leaving Belley, Louis Rey, according to Peytel's statement, knowing that his master would return with money, provided himself with a holster pistol, which Madame Peytel had once before perceived among his effects. In Peytel's cabinet there were some balls; four of these were found in Rey's trunk, on the 6th of November. And, in order to commit the crime, this domestic had brought away with him a pistol, and no ammunition! for Peytel has informed us that Rey, an hour before his departure from Macon, purchased six balls at a gunsmith's. To gain his point, the assassin must immolate his victims; for this, he has only one pistol, knowing, perfectly well, that Peytel, in all his travels, had two on his person; knowing that, at a late hour of the night, his shot might fail of effect; and that, in this case, he would be left to the mercy of his opponent.

"The execution of the crime is, according to Peytel's account, still more singular. Louis does not get off the carriage, until Peytel tells him to descend. He does not think of taking his master's life until he is sure that the latter has his eyes open. It is dark, and the pair are covered in one cloak; and Rey only fires at them at six paces' distance: he fires at hazard, without disquieting himself as to the choice of his victim; and the soldier, who was bold enough to undertake this double murder, has not force nor courage to consummate it. He flies, carrying in his hand a useless whip, with a heavy mantle on his shoulders, in spite of the detonation of two pistols at his ears, and the rapid steps of an angry master in pursuit, which ought to have set him upon some better means of escape. And we find this man, full of youth and vigour, lying with his face to the ground, in the midst of a public road, falling without a struggle, or resistance, under the blows of a hammer!

"And suppose the murderer had succeeded in his criminal projects, what fruit could he have drawn from them?—Leaving, on the road, the two bleeding bodies; obliged to lead two carriages at a time, for fear of discovery; not able to return himself, after all the pains he had taken to speak, at every place at which they had stopped, of the money which his master was carrying with him; too prudent to appear alone at Belley; arrested at the frontier, by the excise officers, who would present an impassable barrier to him till morning,—what could he do, or hope to do? The examination of the car has shown that Rey, at the moment of the crime, had neither linen, nor clothes, nor effects of any kind. There was found in his pockets, when the body was examined, no passport, nor certificate; one of his pockets contained a ball, of large calibre, which he had shown, in play, to a girl, at the inn at Macon, a little horn-handled knife, a snuff-box, a little packet of gunpowder, and a purse, containing only a halfpenny and some string. Here is all the baggage, with which, after the execution of his homicidal plan, Louis Rey intended to take refuge in a foreign country.* Beside these absurd contradictions, there is another remarkable fact, which must not be passed over; it is this:—the pistol, found by Rey, is of antique form, and the original owner of it has been found. He is a curiosity merchant, at Lyons; and, though he cannot affirm that Peytel was the person who bought this pistol of

* This sentence is taken from another part of the "Acte d'accusation."

him, he perfectly recognizes Peytel as having been a frequent customer at his shop!

"No, we may fearlessly affirm, that Louis Rey was not guilty of the crime which Peytel lays to his charge. If, to those who knew him, his mild and open disposition, his military career, modest and without a stain, the touching regrets of his employers, are sufficient proofs of his innocence,—the calm and candid observer, who considers how the crime was conceived, was executed, and what consequences would have resulted from it, will likewise acquit him, and free him of the odious imputation which Peytel endeavours to cast upon his memory.

"But justice has removed the veil, with which an impious hand endeavoured to cover itself. Already, on the night of the 1st of November, suspicion was awakened by the extraordinary agitation of Peytel; by those excessive attentions towards his wife, which came so late; by that excessive and noisy grief, and by those calculated bursts of sorrow, which are such as Nature does not exhibit. The criminal, whom the public conscience had fixed upon; the man whose frightful combinations have been laid bare, and whose falsehoods, step by step, have been exposed, during the proceedings previous to the trial; the murderer, at whose hands a heart-stricken family, and society at large, demands an account of the blood of a wife;—that murderer is Peytel!"

When, my dear Briefless, you are a judge (as I make no doubt you will be, when you have left off the club all night, cigar-smoking of mornings, and reading novels in bed), will you ever find it in your heart to order a fellow-sinner's head off, upon such evidence as this? Because a romantic Substitute du Procureur de Roi chooses to compose and recite a little drama, and draw tears from juries, let us hope that severe Rhadamanthine judges are not to be melted by such trumpery. One wants but the description of the characters to render the piece complete, as thus:—

Personages.		Costumes.
SEBASTIEN PEYTEL	Meurtrier	Habillement complet de notaire perfide: figure pâle, barbe noire, cheveux noirs.
LOUIS REY..................	Soldat rétiré, bon, brave, franc, jovial, aimant le vin, les femmes, la gaieté, ses maîtres surtout; vrai Français, enfin	Costume ordinaire; il porte sur ses épaules une couverture de cheval.
WOLFF	Lieutenant de gendarmerie.	
FELICITÉ D'ALCAZAR	Femme et victime de Peytel.	

Médecins, Villageois, Filles d'Auberge, Garçons d'Ecurie, &c. &c.

La scène se passe sur le pont d'Andert, entre Mâcon et Belley. Il est minuit. La pluie tombe: les tonnerres grondent. Le ciel est couvert de nuages, et sillonné d'éclairs.

All these personages are brought into play in the Procureur's drama; the villagers come in with their chorus; the old lieutenant of gendarmes, with his suspicions; Rey's frankness and gaiety, the romantic circumstances of his birth, his gallantry and fidelity, are all introduced, in order to form a contrast with Peytel, and to call down the jury's indignation against the latter. But are these proofs? or anything like proofs? And the suspicions, that are to serve instead of proofs, what are they?

"My servant, Louis Rey, was very sombre and reserved," says Peytel; "he refused to call me in the morning, to carry my money-chest to my room, to cover the open car when it rained." The Prosecutor disproves this, by stating, that Rey talked with the inn maids and servants, asked if his master was up, and stood in the inn-yard, grooming the horses, with his master by his side, neither speaking to the other. Might he not have talked to the maids, and yet been sombre when speaking to his master? Might he not have neglected to call his master, and yet have asked whether he was awake? Might he not have said that the inn gates were safe, out of hearing of the ostler witness? Mr. Substitute's answers to Peytel's statements are no answer at all. Every word Peytel said might be true, and yet Louis Rey might not have committed the murder; or every word might have been false, and yet Louis Rey might have committed the murder.

"Then," says Mr. Substitute, "how many obstacles are there to the commission of the crime? And these are—

"1. Rey provided himself with *one* holster pistol, to kill two people, knowing well that one of them had always a brace of pistols about him.

"2. He does not think of firing until his master's eyes are open: fires at six paces, not caring at whom he fires, and then runs away.

"3. He could not have intended to kill his master, because he had no passport in his pocket, and no clothes; and because he must have been detained at the frontier until morning; and because he would have had to drive two carriages, in order to avoid suspicion.

" 4. And, a most singular circumstance, the very pistol, which was found by his side, had been bought at the shop of a man at Lyons, who perfectly recognized Peytel as one of his customers, though he could not say he had sold that particular weapon to Peytel."

Does it follow, from this, that Louis Rey is not the murderer; much more, that Peytel is? Look at argument No. 1. Rey had no need to kill two people: he wanted the money, and not the blood. Suppose he had killed Peytel, would he not have mastered Madame Peytel easily?—a weak woman, in an excessively delicate situation, incapable of much energy, at the best of times.

2. "He does not fire till he knows his master's eyes are open." Why, on a stormy night, does a man driving a carriage go to sleep? Was Rey to wait until his master snored? "He fires at six paces, not caring whom he hits;" —and might not this happen too? The night is not so dark but that he can see his master, in *his usual place*, driving. He fires and hits—whom? Madame Peytel, who had left her place, *and was wrapped up with Peytel in his cloak*. She screams out, "Husband, take your pistols." Rey knows that his master has a brace, thinks that he has hit the wrong person, and, as Peytel fires on him, runs away. Peytel follows, hammer in hand; as he comes up with the fugitive, he deals him a blow on the back of the head, and Rey falls—his face to the ground. Is there anything unnatural in this story?—anything so monstrously unnatural, that is, that it might not be true?

3. These objections are absurd. Why need a man have change of linen? If he had taken none for the journey,

why should he want any for the escape? Why need he drive two carriages?—He might have driven both into the river, and Mrs. Peytel in one. Why is he to go to the douane, and thrust himself into the very jaws of danger? Are there not a thousand ways for a man to pass a frontier? Do smugglers, when they have to pass from one country to another, choose exactly those spots where a police is placed?

And, finally, the gunsmith of Lyons, who knows Peytel quite well, cannot say that he sold the pistol to him; that is, he did *not* sell the pistol to him; for you have only one man's word, in this case (Peytel's), to the contrary; and the testimony, as far as it goes, is in his favour. I say, my lud, and gentlemen of the jury, that these objections of my learned friend, who is engaged for the Crown, are absurd, frivolous, monstrous; that to *suspect* away the life of a man upon such suppositions as these, is wicked, illegal, and inhuman; and, what is more, that Louis Rey, if he wanted to commit the crime—if he wanted to possess himself of a large sum of money, chose the best time and spot for so doing; and, no doubt, would have succeeded, if Fate had not, in a wonderful manner, caused Madame Peytel *to take her husband's place*, and receive the ball intended for him in her own head.

But whether these suspicions are absurd or not, hit or miss, it is the advocate's duty, as it appears, to urge them. He wants to make as unfavourable an impression as possible with regard to Peytel's character; he, therefore, must, for contrast's sake, give all sorts of praise to his victim, and awaken every sympathy in the poor fellow's favour. Having done this, as far as lies in his power, having exaggerated every circumstance that can be unfavourable to Peytel, and given his own tale in the baldest manner possible—having declared that Peytel is the murderer of his wife and servant, the Crown now proceeds to back this assertion, by showing what interested motives he had, and by relating, after its own fashion, the circumstances of his marriage.

They may be told briefly here. Peytel was of a good family, of Macon, and entitled, at his mother's death, to a considerable property. He had been educated as a notary, and had lately purchased a business, in that line, in Belley, for which he had paid a large sum of money; part of the sum, 15,000 francs, for which he had given bills, was still due.

Near Belley, Peytel first met Felicité Alcazar, who was residing with her brother-in-law, Monsieur de Montrichard; and, knowing that the young lady's fortune was considerable, he made an offer of marriage to the brother-in-law, who thought the match advantageous, and communicated on the subject with Felicité's mother, Madame Alcazar, at Paris. After a time Peytel went to Paris, to press his suit, and was accepted. There seems to have been no affectation of love on his side; and some little repugnance on the part of the lady, who yielded, however, to the wishes of her parents, and was married. The parties began to quarrel on the very day of the marriage, and continued their disputes almost to the close of the unhappy connexion. Felicité was half blind, passionate, sarcastic, clumsy in her person and manners, and ill-educated; Peytel, a man of considerable intellect and pretensions, who had lived for some time at Paris, where he had mingled with good literary society. The lady was, in fact, as disagreeable a person as could well be, and the evidence describes some scenes which took place between her and her husband, showing how deeply she must have mortified and enraged him.

A charge very clearly made out against Peytel, is that of dishonesty; he procured from the notary of whom he bought his place an acquittance in full, whereas there were 15,000 francs owing, as we have seen. He also, in the contract of marriage, which was to have resembled, in all respects, that between Monsieur Broussais and another Demoiselle Alcazar, caused an alteration to be made in his favour, which gave him command over his wife's funded property, without furnishing the guarantees by which the other son-in-law was bound. And, almost immediately after his marriage, Peytel sold out of the funds a sum of 50,000 francs, that belonged to his wife, and used it for his own purposes.

About two months after his marriage, *Peytel pressed his wife to make her will.* He had made his, he said, leaving everything to her, in case of his death: after some parley, the poor thing consented.* This is a cruel

* "Peytel," says the act of accusation, " did not fail to see the danger which would menace him, if this will (which had escaped the magistrates in their search of Peytel's papers) was discovered. He, therefore, instructed his agent to take possession of it, which he did, and the fact was not mentioned for several months afterwards. Peytel and his agent were called upon to explain the circumstance, but refused, and their silence for a long time interrupted the 'instruction' (getting up of the evidence). All that could be obtained from them was an avowal, that such a will existed, constituting Peytel his wife's sole legatee; and a promise, on their parts, to produce it before the court gave its sentence." But why keep the will secret? The anxiety about it was surely absurd and unnecessary: the

suspicion against him ; and Mr. Substitute has no need to enlarge upon it. As for the previous fact, the dishonest statement about the 15,000 francs, there is nothing murderous in that—nothing which a man very eager to make a good marriage might not do. The same may be said of the suppression, in Peytel's marriage contract, of the clause to be found in Broussais', placing restrictions upon the use of the wife's money. Mademoiselle d'Alcazar's friends read the contract before they signed it, and might have refused it, had they so pleased.

After some disputes, which took place between Peytel and his wife (there were continual quarrels, and continual letters passing between them from room to room), the latter was induced to write him a couple of exaggerated letters, swearing "by the ashes of her father," that she would be an obedient wife to him, and entreating him to counsel and direct her. These letters were seen by members of the lady's family, who, in the quarrels between the couple, always took the husband's part. They were found in Peytel's cabinet, after he had been arrested for the murder, and after he had had full access to all his papers, of which he destroyed or left as many as he pleased. The accusation makes it a matter of suspicion against Peytel, that he should have left these letters of his wife's in a conspicuous situation.

" All these circumstances," says the accusation, "throw a frightful light upon Peytel's plans. The letters and whole of Madame Peytel's family knew that such a will was made. She had consulted her sister concerning it, who said—" If there is no other way of satisfying him, make the will ;" and the mother, when she heard of it, cried out—" Does he intend to poison her ? "

will of Madame Peytel are in the hands of her husband. Three months pass away, and this poor woman is brought to her home, in the middle of the night, with two balls in her head, stretched at the bottom of her carriage, by the side of a peasant!

"What other than Sebastian Peytel could have committed this murder?—whom could it profit?—who but himself had an odious chain to break, and an inheritance to receive? Why speak of the servant's projected robbery? The pistols found by the side of Louis's body, the balls bought by him at Macon, and those discovered at Belley, among his effects, were only the result of a perfidious combination. The pistol, indeed, which was found on the hill of Darde, on the night of the 1st of November, could only have belonged to Peytel, and must have been thrown by him, near the body of his domestic, with the paper which had before enveloped it. Who had seen this pistol in the hands of Louis? Among all the gendarmes, workwomen, domestics, employed by Peytel and his brother-in-law, is there one single witness who had seen this weapon in Louis's possession? It is true that Madame Peytel did, on one occasion, speak to M. de Montrichard of a pistol; which had nothing to do, however, with that found near Louis Rey."

Is this justice, or good reason? Just reverse the argument, and apply it to Rey. "Who but Rey could have committed this murder?—who but Rey had a large sum of money to seize upon?—a pistol is found by his side, balls and powder in his pocket, other balls in his trunks at home. The pistol found near his body could not, indeed, have belonged to Peytel: did any man ever see it in his possession? The very gunsmith who sold it, and who knew Peytel, would he not have known that he had sold him this pistol? At his own house, Peytel has a collection of weapons of all kinds; everybody has seen them—a man who makes such collections is anxious to display them. Did any one ever see this weapon?—Not one. And Madame Peytel did, in her lifetime, remark a pistol in the valet's possession. She was short-sighted, and could not particularize what kind of pistol it was; but she spoke of it to her husband and her brother-in-law." This is not satisfactory, if you please; but, at least, it is as satisfactory as the other set of suppositions. It is the very chain of argument which would have been brought against Louis Rey by this very same compiler of the act of accusation, had Rey survived, instead of Peytel, and had he, as most undoubtedly would have been the case, been tried for the murder.

This argument was shortly put by Peytel's counsel:— "*If Peytel had been killed by Rey in the struggle, would you not have found Rey guilty of the murder of his master and mistress?*" It is such a dreadful dilemma, that I wonder how judges and lawyers could have dared to persecute Peytel in the manner which they did.

After the act of accusation, which lays down all the suppositions against Peytel as facts, which will not admit the truth of one of the prisoner's allegations in his own defence, comes the trial. The judge is quite as impartial as the preparer of the indictment, as will be seen by the following specimens of his interrogatories:—

Judge. "The act of accusation finds in your statement

contradictions, improbabilities, impossibilities. Thus your domestic, who had determined to assassinate you, in order to rob you, and who *must have calculated upon the consequence of a failure,* had neither passport nor money upon him. This is very unlikely; because he could not have gone far with only a single halfpenny, which was all he had."

Prisoner. " My servant was known, and often passed the frontier without a passport."

Judge. " *Your domestic had to assassinate two persons,* and had no weapon but a single pistol. He had no dagger; and the only thing found on him was a knife."

Prisoner. "In the car there were several turner's implements, which he might have used."

Judge. " But he had not those arms upon him, because you pursued him immediately. He had, according to you, only this old pistol."

Prisoner. " I have nothing to say."

Judge. " Your domestic, instead of flying into woods, which skirt the road, ran straight forward on the road itself: *this, again, is very unlikely.*"

Prisoner. " This is a conjecture I could answer by a another conjecture ; I can only reason on the facts."

Judge. " How far did you pursue him ? "

Prisoner. " I don't know exactly."

Judge. " You said, ' two hundred paces.' "

No answer from the prisoner.

Judge. " Your domestic was young, active, robust, and tall. He was ahead of you. You were in a carriage, from which you had to descend : you had to take your pistols from a cushion, and *then* your hammer;—how are we to believe that you could have caught him, if he ran? It is *impossible.*"

Prisoner. " I can't explain it; I think that Rey had some defect in one leg. I, for my part, run tolerably fast."

Judge. " At what distance from him did you fire your first shot?"

Prisoner. " I can't tell."

Judge. " Perhaps he was not running when you fired."

Prisoner. " I saw him running."

Judge. " In what position was your wife?"

Prisoner. " She was leaning on my left arm, and the man was on the right side of the carriage."

Judge. " The shot must have been fired *à bout portant,* because it burned the eyebrows and lashes entirely. The assassin must have passed his pistol across your breast."

Prisoner. " The shot was not fired so close, I am convinced of it: professional gentlemen will prove it."

Judge. " *That is what you pretend, because you understand perfectly the consequences of admitting the fact.* Your wife was hit with two balls — one striking downwards, to the right, by the nose, the other going horizontally through the cheek, to the left."

Prisoner. " The contrary will be shown by the witnesses called for the purpose."

Judge. " *It is a very unlucky combination for you* that these balls, which went, you say, from the same pistol, should have taken two different directions."

Prisoner. " I can't dispute about the various combinations of fire-arms—professional persons will be heard."

Judge. " According to your statement, your wife said to you, ' My poor husband, take your pistols.' "

Prisoner. " She did."

Judge. " In a manner quite distinct ? "

" *Prisoner.* " Yes."

" *Judge.* " So distinct that you did not fancy she was hit ? "

Prisoner. " Yes ; that is the fact."

Judge. " *Here, again, is an impossibility;* and nothing is more precise than the declaration of the medical men. They affirm that your wife could not have spoken—their report is unanimous.

Prisoner. " I can only oppose to it quite contrary opinions from professional men, also : you must hear them."

Judge. " What did your wife do next ? "

* * * * *

Judge. " You deny the statements of the witnesses : " (they related to Peytel's demeanour and behaviour, which the judge wishes to show were very unusual ;—and what if they were ?) " Here, however, are some mute witnesses, whose testimony, you will not, perhaps, refuse. Near Louis Rey's body was found a horse-cloth, a pistol, and a whip. * * Your domestic must have had this cloth upon him when he went to assassinate you : it was wet and heavy. An assassin disencumbers himself of anything that is likely to impede him, especially when he is going to struggle with a man as young as himself."

Prisoner. " My servant had, I believe, this covering on his body; it might be useful to him to keep the priming of his pistol dry."

The president caused the cloth to be opened, and showed that there was no hook, or tie, by which it could be held together; and that Rey must have held it with one hand, and, in the other, his whip, and the pistol with which he intended to commit the crime; which was impossible.

Prisoner. " These are only conjectures."

And what conjectures, my God! upon which to take away the life of a man. Jeffreys, or Fouquier Tinville, could scarcely have dared to make such. Such prejudice, such bitter persecution, such priming of the jury, such monstrous assumptions and unreason—fancy them coming from an impartial judge! The man is worse than the public accuser.

"Rey," says the Judge, "could not have committed the murder, *because he had no money in his pocket, to fly, in case of failure.*" And what is the precise sum that his lordship thinks necessary for a gentleman to have, before he makes such an attempt? Are the men who murder for money, usually in possession of a certain independence before they begin? How much money was Rey, a servant, who loved wine and women, had been stopping at a score of inns on the road, and had, probably, an annual income of 400 francs,--how much money was Rey likely to have?

" *Your servant had to assassinate two persons.*" This I have mentioned before. Why had he to assassinate two persons,* when one was enough? If he had killed

* M. Balzac's theory of the case is, that Rey had intrigued with Madame Peytel; having known her previous to her marriage, when she was staying in the house of her brother-in-law, Monsieur de Montrichard; where Rey had been a servant.

Peytel, could he not have seized and gagged his wife immediately?

"*Your domestic ran straight forward, instead of taking to the woods, by the side of the road: this is very unlikely.*" How does his worship know? Can any judge, however enlightened, tell the exact road that a man will take, who has just missed a coup of murder, and is pursued by a man who is firing pistols at him? And has a judge a right to instruct a jury in this way, as to what they shall, or shall not, believe?

"You have to run after an active man, who has the start of you: to jump out of a carriage; to take your pistols; and, *then*, your hammer. *This is impossible.*" By heavens! does it not make a man's blood boil, to read such blundering, blood-seeking sophistry? This man, when it suits him, shows that Rey would be slow in his motions; and when it suits him, declares that Rey ought to be quick; declares, *ex cathedrâ*, what pace Rey should go, and what direction he should take; shows, in a breath, that he must have run faster than Peytel; and then, that he could not run fast, because the cloak clogged him; settles how he is to be dressed when he commits a murder, and what money he is to have in his pocket; gives these impossible suppositions to the jury, and tells them that the previous statements are impossible; and, finally, informs them of the precise manner in which Rey must have stood holding his horse-cloth in one hand, his whip and pistol in the other, when he made the supposed attempt at murder. Now, what is the size of a horse-cloth? Is it as big as a pocket-handkerchief? Is there no possibility that it might hang over one shoulder; that the whip should be held under that very arm? Did you never see a carter so carry it, his hands in his pocket all the while? Is it monstrous, abhorrent to nature, that a man should fire a pistol from under a cloak, on a rainy day?—that he should, after firing the shot, be frightened, and run; run straight before him, with the cloak on his shoulders, and the weapon in his hand? Peytel's story is possible, and very possible; it is almost probable. Allow that Rey had the cloth on, and you allow that he must have been clogged in his motions; that Peytel may have come up with him—felled him with a blow of the hammer: the doctors say that he would have so fallen by one blow—he would have fallen on his face, as he was found: the paper might have been thrust into his breast, and tumbled out as he fell. Circumstances far more impossible have occurred ere this; and men have been hanged for them, who were as innocent of the crime laid to their charge, as the judge on the bench, who convicted them.

In like manner, Peytel may not have committed the crime charged to him; and Mr. Judge, with his arguments, as to possibilities, and impossibilities,—Mr. Public Prosecutor, with his romantic narrative, and inflammatory harangues to the jury,—may have used all these powers to bring to death an innocent man. From the animus with which the case has been conducted, from beginning to end, it was easy to see the result. Here it is, in the words of the provincial paper :—

"*Bourg*, 28 *October*, 1839.

"The condemned Peytel has just undergone his punishment, which took place four days before the anniversary of his crime. The terrible drama of the bridge of Andert, which cost the life of two persons, has just terminated on the scaffold. Midday had just sounded on the clock of the Palais : the same clock tolled midnight, when, on the 30th of August, his sentence was pronounced.

"Since the rejection of his appeal in Cassation, on which his principal hopes were founded, Peytel spoke little of his petition to the King. The notion of transportation was that which he seemed to cherish most. However, he made several inquiries from the gaoler of the prison, when he saw him at meal-time, with regard to the place of execution, the usual hour, and other details on the subject. From that period, the words 'Champ de Foire' (the fair-field, where the execution was to be held,) were frequently used by him in conversation.

"Yesterday, the idea that the time had arrived seemed to be more strongly than ever impressed upon him, especially after the departure of the curé, who latterly has been with him every day. The documents connected with the trial had arrived in the morning. He was ignorant of this circumstance, but sought to discover from his guardians what they tried to hide from him; and to find out whether his petition was rejected, and when he was to die.

"Yesterday, also, he had written to demand the presence of his counsel, M. Margerand, in order that he might have some conversation with him, and regulate his affairs, before he ——; he did not write down the word, but left in its place a few points of the pen.

"In the evening, whilst he was at supper, he begged

earnestly to be allowed a little wax candle, to finish what he was writing; otherwise, he said, *Time might fail.* This was a new, indirect, manner of repeating his ordinary question. As light, up to that evening, had been refused him, it was thought best to deny him in this, as in former instances; otherwise his suspicions might have been confirmed. The keeper refused his demand.

"This morning, Monday, at nine o'clock, the Greffier of the Assize Court, in fulfilment of the painful duty which the law imposes upon him, came to the prison, in company with the curé of Bourg, and announced to the convict that his petition was rejected, and that he had only three hours to live. He received this fatal news with a great deal of calmness, and showed himself to be no more affected than he had been on the trial. 'I am ready; but I wish they had given me four-and-twenty hours' notice,'—were all the words he used.

"The Greffier now retired, leaving Peytel alone with the curé, who did not, thenceforth, quit him. Peytel breakfasted at ten o'clock.

"At eleven, a picquet of mounted gendarmerie and infantry took their station upon the place before the prison, where a great concourse of people had already assembled. An open car was at the door. Before he went out, Peytel asked the gaoler for a looking-glass; and having examined his face for a moment, said, 'At least, the inhabitants of Bourg will see that I have not grown thin.'

"As twelve o'clock sounded, the prison gates opened, an aide appeared, followed by Peytel, leaning on the arm of the curate. Peytel's face was pale, he had a long black beard, a blue cap on his head, and his great-coat flung over his shoulders, and buttoned at the neck.

"He looked about at the place and the crowd; he asked if the carriage would go at a trot; and on being told that that would be difficult, he said he would prefer walking, and asked what the road was. He immediately set out, walking at a firm and rapid pace. He was not bound at all.

"An immense crowd of people encumbered the two streets through which he had to pass to the place of execution. He cast his eyes alternately upon them and upon the guillotine, which was before him.

"Arrived at the foot of the scaffold, Peytel embraced the curé, and bade him adieu. He then embraced him again; perhaps, for his mother and sister. He then mounted the steps rapidly, and gave himself into the hands of the executioner, who removed his coat and cap. He asked how he was to place himself, and, on a sign being made, he flung himself briskly on the plank, and stretched his neck. In another moment he was no more.

"The crowd, which had been quite silent, retired, profoundly moved by the sight it had witnessed. As at all executions, there was a very great number of women present.

"Under the scaffold there had been, ever since the morning, a coffin. The family had asked for his remains, and had them immediately buried, privately: and, thus, the unfortunate man's head escaped the modellers in wax, several of whom had arrived to take an impression of it."

Down goes the axe; the poor wretch's head rolls gasping into the basket; the spectators go home, pondering; and Mr. Executioner and his aids have, in half an hour, removed all traces of the august sacrifice, and of the altar on which it had been performed. Say, Mr. Briefless, do you think that any single person, meditating murder, would be deterred therefrom by beholding this—nay, a thousand more executions? It is not for moral improvement, as I take it, nor for opportunity to make appropriate remarks upon the punishment of crime, that people make a holiday of a killing-day, and leave their homes and occupations, to flock and witness the cutting off of a head. Do we crowd to see Mr. Macready, in the new tragedy, or Mademoiselle Elssler in her last new ballet, and flesh-coloured stockinnet pantaloons, out of a pure love of abstract poetry and beauty; or from a strong notion that we shall be excited, in different ways, by the actor and the dancer? And so, as we go to have a meal of fictitious terror at the tragedy, of something more questionable in the ballet, we go for a glut of blood to the execution. The lust is in every man's nature, more or less. Did you ever witness a wrestling or boxing match? The first clatter of the kick on the shins, or the first drawing of blood, makes the stranger shudder a little; but soon the blood is his chief enjoyment, and he thirsts for it with a fierce delight. It is a fine grim pleasure that we have in seeing a man killed; and I make no doubt that the organs of destructiveness must begin to throb and swell as we witness the delightful, savage spectacle.

Three or four years back, when Fieschi and Lacenaire

were executed, I made attempts to see the execution of both, but was disappointed in both cases. In the first instance, the day for Fieschi's death was, purposely, kept secret; and he was, if I remember rightly, executed at some remote quarter of the town. But it would have done a philanthropist good, to witness the scene which we saw on the morning when his execution did *not* take place.

It was Carnival time, and the rumour had pretty generally been carried abroad that he was to die on that morning. A friend, who accompanied me, came many miles, through the mud and dark, in order to be in at the death. We set out before light, floundering through the muddy Champs Elysées, where, besides, were many other persons floundering, and all bent upon the same errand. We passed by the Concert of Musard, then held in the Rue St. Honoré; and round this, in the wet, a number of coaches were collected. The ball was just up, and a crowd of people, in hideous masquerade, drunk, tired, dirty, dressed in horrible old frippery, and daubed with filthy rouge, were trooping out of the place; tipsy women and men, shrieking, jabbering, gesticulating, as French will do; parties swaggering, staggering forwards, arm in arm, reeling to and fro across the street, and yelling songs in chorus; hundreds of these were bound for the show, and we thought ourselves lucky in finding a vehicle to the execution place, at the Barrière d'Enfer. As we crossed the river, and entered the Enfer Street, crowds of students, black workmen, and more drunken devils, from more carnival balls, were filling it ; and on the grand place there were thousands of these assembled, looking out for Fieschi and his cortège. We waited and waited; but, alas! no fun for us that morning ; no throat-cutting ; no august spectacle of satisfied justice ; and the eager spectators were obliged to return, disappointed of their expected breakfast of blood. It would have been a fine scene, that execution, could it but have taken place in the midst of the mad mountebanks, and tipsy strumpets, who had flocked so far to witness it, wishing to wind up the delights of their carnival by a bonne-bouche of a murder.

The other attempt was equally unfortunate. We arrived too late on the ground to be present at the execution of Lacenaire and his co-mate in murder, Avril. But as we came to the ground (a gloomy round space, within the barrier—three roads lead to it—and, outside, you see the wine-shops and restaurateurs of the barrier looking gay and inviting,)—as we came to the ground, we only found, in the midst of it, a little pool of ice, just partially tinged with red. Two or three idle street-boys were dancing and stamping about this pool ; and when I asked one of them whether the execution had taken place, he began dancing more madly than ever, and shrieked out with a loud fantastical theatrical voice, " *Venez tous Messieurs et Dames, voyez ici le sang du monstre Lacenaire, et de son compagnon le traître Avril,*" or words to that effect ; and, straightway, all the other gamins screamed out the words in chorus, and took hands and danced round the little puddle.

O august Justice, your meal was followed by a pretty appropriate grace! Was any man, who saw the show, deterred, or frightened, or moralized in any way? He had gratified his appetite for blood, and this was all. There is something singularly pleasing, both in the amusement of execution-seeing, and in the results. You are not only delightfully excited at the time, but most pleasingly relaxed afterwards; the mind, which has been wound up painfully until now, becomes quite complacent and easy. There is something agreeable in the misfortunes of others, as the philosopher has told us. Remark what a good breakfast you eat, after an execution; how pleasant it is to cut jokes after it, and upon it. This merry, pleasant mood is brought on by the blood tonic.

But, for God's sake, if we are to enjoy this, let us do so in moderation; and let us, at least, be sure of a man's guilt, before we murder him. To kill him, even with the full assurance that he is guilty, is hazardous enough. Who gave you the right to do so?—you, who cry out against suicides, as impious and contrary to Christian law? What use is there in killing him? You deter no one else from committing the crime by so doing: you give us, to be sure, half an hour's pleasant entertainment; but it is a great question whether we derive much moral profit from the sight. If you want to keep a murderer from farther inroads upon society, are there not plenty of hulks and prisons, God wot; treadmills, galleys, and houses of correction? Above all, as in the case of Sebastian Peytel and his family, there have been two deaths already, was a third death absolutely necessary? and, taking the fallibility of judges and lawyers into his heart, and remembering the thousand instances of unmerited punishment that have been suffered upon similar and stronger evidence before, can any man declare, positively, and upon his oath, that Peytel was guilty, and that this was not *the third murder in the family?*

FOUR IMITATIONS OF BERANGER.

LE ROI D'YVETOT.

Il était un roi d'Yvetot,
   Peu connu dans l'histoire ;
Se levant tard, se couchant tôt,
   Dormant fort bien sans gloire,
Et couronné par Jeanneton
D'un simple bonnet de coton,
        Dit-on.
   Oh! oh! oh! oh! ah! ah! ah! ah!
   Quel bon petit roi c'était là!
        La, la.

Il fesait ses quatre repas
   Dans son palais de chaume,
Et sur un âne, pas à pas,
   Parcourait son royaume.
Joyeux, simple et croyant le bien,
Pour toute garde il n'avait rien
        Qu'un chien.
   Oh! oh! oh! oh! ah! ah! ah! ah! &c.
        La, la.

Il n'avait de goût onéreux
    Qu'une soif un peu vive ;
Mais, en rendant son peuple heureux,
    Il faut bien qu'un roi vive.
Lui-même à table, et sans suppôt,
Sur chaque muid levait un pot
        D'impôt.
    Oh ! oh ! oh ! oh ! ah ! ah ! ah ! ah ! &c.
        La, la.

Aux filles de bonnes maisons
    Comme il avait su plaire,
Ses sujets avaient cent raisons
    De le nommer leur père :
D'ailleurs il ne levait de ban
Que pour tirer quatre fois l'an
        Au blanc.
    Oh ! oh ! oh ! oh ! ah ! ah ! ah ! ah ! &c.
        La, la.

Il n'agrandit point ses états,
    Fut un voisin commode,
Et, modèle des potentats,
    Prit le plaisir pour code.
Ce n'est que lorsqu'il expira,
Que le peuple qui l'enterra
        Pleura.
    Oh ! oh ! oh ! oh ! ah ! ah ! ah ! ah ! &c.
        La, la.

On conserve encor le portrait
 De ce digne et bon prince ;
C'est l'enseigne d'un cabaret
 Fameux dans la province.
Les jours de fête, bien souvent,
La foule s'écrie en buvant
 Devant :
 Oh ! oh ! oh ! oh ! ah ! ah ! ah ! ah !
 Quel bon petit roi c'était là !
 La, la.

THE KING OF YVETOT.

There was a king of Yvetot,
Of whom renown hath little said,
Who let all thoughts of glory go,
    And dawdled half his days a-bed;
And every night, as night came round,
By Jenny, with a nightcap crowned,
        Slept very sound.
    Sing, ho, ho, ho! and he, he, he!
    That's the kind of king for me.

And every day it came to pass,
    That four lusty meals made he;
And, step by step, upon an ass,
    Rode abroad, his realms to see;
And wherever he did stir,
What think you was his escort, sir?
        Why, an old cur.
    Sing, ho, ho, ho! &c.

THE KING OF YVETOT.

If e'er he went into excess,
    'Twas from a somewhat lively thirst ;
But he who would his subjects bless,
    Odd's fish!—must wet his whistle first ;
And so from every cask they got,
Our king did to himself allot,
          At least a pot,
    Sing, ho, ho ! &c.

To all the ladies of the land,
    A courteous king, and kind, was he ;
The reason why you'll understand,
    They named him Pater Patriæ.
Each year he called his fighting men,
And marched a league from home, and then
          Marched back again.
    Sing, ho, ho ! &c.

Neither by force nor false pretence,
    He sought to make his kingdom great,
And made (oh ! princes, learn from hence)—
    " Live and let live," his rule of state.
'Twas only when he came to die,
That his people, who stood by,
          Were known to cry.
    Sing, ho, ho ! &c.

The portrait of this best of kings
Is extant still, upon a sign
That on a village tavern swings,
   Famed in the country for good wine.
The people, in their Sunday trim,
Filling their glasses to the brim,
       Look up to him.
    Singing, ha, ha, ha! and he, he, he!
    That's the sort of king for me.

THE KING OF BRENTFORD.

ANOTHER VERSION.

THERE was a king in Brentford,—of whom no legends tell,
But who, without his glory,—could eat and sleep right well.
His Polly's cotton nightcap,—it was his crown of state,
He slept of evenings early,—and rose of mornings late.

All in a fine mud palace,—each day he took four meals,
And for a guard of honour,—a dog ran at his heels,
Sometimes, to view his kingdoms,—rode forth this monarch good,
And then a prancing jackass—he royally bestrode.

There were no costly habits—with which this king was curst,
Except (and where's the harm on't?)—a somewhat lively thirst;
But people must pay taxes,—and kings must have their sport,
So out of every gallon—His Grace he took a quart.

He pleased the ladies round him,—with manners soft and bland;
With reason good, they named him,—the father of his land.
Each year his mighty armies—marched forth in gallant show;
Their enemies were targets,—their bullets they were tow.

He vexed no quiet neighbour,—no useless conquest made,
But by the laws of pleasure,—his peaceful realm he swayed.
And in the years he reigned,—through all this country wide,
There was no cause for weeping,—save when the good man died.

The faithful men of Brentford,—do still their king deplore,
His portrait yet is swinging,—beside an alehouse door.
And topers, tender-hearted,—regard his honest phiz,
And envy times departed,—that knew a reign like his.

LE GRENIER.

Je viens revoir l'asile où ma jeunesse
De la misère a subi les leçons.
J'avais vingt ans, une folle maîtresse,
De francs amis et l'amour des chansons :
Bravant le monde et les sots et les sages,
Sans avenir, riche de mon printemps,
Leste et joyeux je montais six étages.
Dans un grenier qu'on est bien à vingt ans !

C'est un grenier, point ne veux qu'on l'ignore.
Là fut mon lit, bien chétif et bien dur ;
Là fut ma table ; et je retrouve encore
Trois pieds d'un vers charbonnés sur le mur.
Apparaissez, plaisirs de mon bel âge,
Que d'un coup d'aile a fustigés le temps.
Vingt fois pour vous j'ai mis ma montre en gage.
Dans un grenier qu'on est bien à vingt ans !

Lisette ici doit surtout apparaître,
Vive, jolie, avec un frais chapeau ;
Déjà sa main à l'étroite fenêtre
Suspend son schal, en guise de rideau.
Sa robe aussi va parer ma couchette ;
Respecte, Amour, ses plis longs et flottans.
J'ai su depuis qui payait sa toilette.
Dans un grenier, qu'on est bien à vingt ans !

A table un jour, jour de grande richesse,
De mes amis les voix brillaient en chœur,
Quand jusqu'ici monte un cri d'allégresse :
A Marengo, Bonaparte est vainqueur.
Le canon gronde ; un autre chant commence ;
Nous célébrons tant de faits éclatans.
Les rois jamais n'envahiront la France.
Dans un grenier qu'on est bien à vingt ans !

Quittons ce toit où ma raison s'enivre.
Oh ! qu'ils sont loin ces jours si regrettés !
J'échangerais ce qu'il me reste à vivre
Contre un des mois qu'ici Dieu m'a comptés.
Pour rêver gloire, amour, plaisir, folie,
Pour dépenser sa vie en peu d'instans,
D'un long espoir pour la voir embellie,
Dans uns grenier qu'on est bien à vingt ans !

THE GARRET.

With pensive eyes the little room I view,
    Where, in my youth, I weathered it so long ;
With a wild mistress, a stanch friend or two,
    And a light heart still breaking into song :
Making a mock of life, and all its cares,
    Rich in the glory of my rising sun,
Lightly I vaulted up four pair of stairs,
    In the brave days when I was twenty-one.

Yes ; 'tis a garret—let him know't who will—
    There was my bed—full hard it was and small.
My table there—and I decipher still
    Half a lame couplet charcoaled on the wall.
Ye joys, that Time hath swept with him away,
    Come to mine eyes, ye dreams of love and fun ;
For you I pawned my watch how many a day,
    In the brave days when I was twenty-one.

And see my little Jessy, first of all ;
    She comes with pouting lips and sparkling eyes :
Behold, how roguishly she pins her shawl
    Across the narrow casement, curtain-wise ;
Now by the bed her petticoat glides down,
    And when did woman look the worse in none ?
I have heard since who paid for many a gown,
    In the brave days when I was twenty-one.

One jolly evening, when my friends and I
    Made happy music with our songs and cheers,
A shout of triumph mounted up thus high,
    And distant cannon opened on our ears :
We rise,—we join in the triumphant strain,—
    Napoleon conquers—Austerlitz is won—
Tyrants shall never tread us down again,
    In the brave days when I was twenty-one.

Let us begone—the place is sad and strange—
    How far, far off, these happy times appear ;
All that I have to live I'd gladly change
    For one such month as I have wasted here—
To draw long dreams of beauty, love, and power,
    From founts of hope that never will outrun,
And drink all life's quintessence in an hour,
    Give me the days when I was twenty-one !

ROGER-BONTEMPS.

Aux gens atrabilaires
Pour exemple donné,
En un temps de misères
Roger-Bontemps est né.
Vivre obscur à sa guise,
Narguer les mécontens ;
Eh gai ! c'est la devise
Du gros Roger-Bontemps.

Du chapeau de son père
Coiffé dans les grands jours,
De roses ou de lierre
Le rajeunir toujours ;
Mettre un manteau de bure,
Vieil ami de vingt ans ;
Eh gai ! c'est la parure
Du gros Roger-Bontemps.

Posséder dans sa hutte
Une table, un vieux lit,
Des cartes, une flûte,
Un broc que Dieu remplit ;

Un portrait de maîtresse,
Un coffre et rien dedans ;
Eh gai ! c'est la richesse
Du gros Roger-Bontemps.

Aux enfans de la ville
Montrer de petits jeux ;
Etre fesseur habile
De contes graveleux ;
Ne parler que de danse
Et d'almanachs chantans :
Eh gai ! c'est la science
Du gros Roger-Bontemps.

Faute de vins d'élite,
Sabler ceux du canton :
Préférer Marguerite
Aux dames du grand ton :
De joie et de tendresse
Remplir tous ses instans ;
Eh gai ! c'est la sagesse
Du gros Roger-Bontemps.

Dire au ciel : Je me fie,
Mon père, à ta bonté ;
De ma philosophie
Pardonne le gaîté :
Que ma saison dernière
Soit encore un printemps ;
Eh gai ! c'est la prière
Du gros Roger-Bontemps.

Vous, pauvres pleins d'envie,
Vous, riches désireux,
Vous, dont le char dévie
Après un cours heureux ;
Vous, qui perdrez peut-être
Des titres éclatans,
Eh gai ! prenez pour maitre
Le gros Roger-Bontemps.

JOLLY JACK.

When fierce political debate
  Throughout the isle was storming,
And Rads attacked the throne and state,
  And Tories the reforming,
To calm the furious rage of each,
  And right the land demented,
Heaven sent us Jolly Jack, to teach
  The way to be contented.

Jack's bed was straw, 'twas warm and soft,
  His chair, a three-legged stool ;
His broken jug was emptied oft,
  Yet, somehow, always full.

His mistress' portrait decked the wall,
    His mirror had a crack;
Yet, gay and glad, though this was all
    His wealth, lived Jolly Jack.

To give advice to avarice,
    Teach pride its mean condition,
And preach good sense to dull pretence,
    Was honest Jack's high mission.
Our simple statesman found his rule
    Of moral in the flagon,
And held his philosophic school
    Beneath the George and Dragon.

When village Solons cursed the Lords,
    And called the malt-tax sinful,
Jack heeded not their angry words,
    But smiled, and drunk his skin full.
And when men wasted health and life,
    In search of rank and riches,
Jack marked, aloof, the paltry strife,
    And wore his threadbare breeches.

" I enter not the church," he said,
    " But I'll not seek to rob it;"
So worthy Jack Joe Miller read,
    While others studied Cobbett.
His talk it was of feast and fun;
    His guide the Almanack;
From youth to age thus gaily run
    The life of Jolly Jack.

And when Jack prayed, as oft he would,
   He humbly thanked his Maker;
"I am," said he, "O Father good!
   Nor Catholic, nor Quaker:
Give each his creed, let each proclaim
   His catalogue of curses;
I trust in Thee, and not in them,
   In Thee, and in Thy mercies!"

"Forgive me if, 'midst all Thy works,
   No hint I see of damning;
And think there's faith among the Turks,
   And hope for e'en the Bramin.
Harmless my mind is, and my mirth,
   And kindly is my laughter;
I cannot see the smiling earth,
   And think there's hell hereafter."

Jack died; he left no legacy,
   Save that his story teaches:—
Content to peevish poverty;
   Humility to riches.
Ye scornful great, ye envious small,
   Come, follow in his track;
We all were happier, if we all
   Would copy JOLLY JACK.

FRENCH DRAMAS AND MELODRAMAS.

THERE are three kinds of drama in France, which you may subdivide as much as you please.

There is the old classical drama, well nigh dead, and full time too. Old tragedies, in which half a dozen characters appear, and spout sonorous Alexandrines for half a dozen hours—the fair Rachel has been trying to revive this *genre*, and to untomb Racine; but be not alarmed, Racine will never come to life again, and cause audiences to weep as of yore. Madame Rachel can only galvanize the corpse, not revivify it. Ancient French tragedy, red-heeled, patched, and be-periwigged, lies in the grave; and it is only the ghost of it that we see, which the fair Jewess has raised. There are classical comedies in verse, too, wherein the knavish valets, rakish heroes, stolid old guardians, and smart, free-spoken serving-women, discourse in Alexandrines, as loud as the Horaces or the Cid. An Englishman will seldom reconcile himself to the *ronflement* of the verses, and the painful recurrence of the rhymes; for my part, I had rather go to Madame Saqui's, or see Deburau dancing on a rope; his lines are quite as natural and poetical.

Then there is the comedy of the day, of which Monsieur

Scribe is the father. Good heavens! with what a number of gay colonels, smart widows, and silly husbands has that gentleman peopled the play-books. How that unfortunate seventh commandment has been maltreated by him and his disciples. You will see four pieces, at the Gymnase, of a night; and so sure as you see them, four husbands shall be wickedly used. When is this joke to cease? Mon Dieu! Play-writers have handled it for about two thousand years, and the public, like a great baby, must have the tale repeated to it over and over again.

Finally, there is the Drama, that great monster which has sprung into life of late years; and which is said, but I don't believe a word of it, to have Shakspeare for a father. If Mr. Scribe's plays may be said to be so many ingenious examples how to break one commandment, the *drame* is a grand and general chaos of them all; nay, several crimes are added, not prohibited in the Decalogue, which was written before dramas were. Of the drama, Victor Hugo and Dumas are the well-known and respectable guardians. Every piece Victor Hugo has written, since *Hernani*, has contained a monster—a delightful monster, saved by one virtue. There is Triboulet, a foolish monster; Lucrèce Borgia, a maternal monster; Mary Tudor, a religious monster; Monsieur Quasimodo, a hump-backed monster; and others, that might be named, whose monstrosities we are induced to pardon—nay, admiringly to witness—because they are agreeably mingled with some exquisite display of affection. And, as the great Hugo has one monster to each play, the great Dumas has, ordinarily, half a dozen, to whom murder is nothing; common intrigue, and simple breakage of the before-mentioned commandment, nothing; but who live and move in a vast, delightful complication of crime, that cannot be easily conceived in England, much less described.

When I think over the number of crimes that I have seen Mademoiselle Georges, for instance, commit, I am filled with wonder at her greatness, and the greatness of the poets who have conceived these charming horrors for her. I have seen her make love to, and murder, her sons, in the *Tour de Nesle*. I have seen her poison a company of no less than nine gentlemen, at Ferrara, with an affectionate son in the number; I have seen her, as Madame de Brinvilliers, kill off numbers of respectable relations in the four first acts; and, at the last, be actually burned at the stake, to which she comes shuddering, ghastly, barefooted, and in a white sheet. Sweet excitement of tender sympathies! Such tragedies are not so good as a real, downright execution; but, in point of interest, the next thing to it: with what a number of moral emotions do they fill the breast; with what a hatred for vice, and yet a true pity and respect for that grain of virtue that is to be found in us all; our bloody, daughter-loving Brinvilliers; our warm-hearted, poisonous Lucretia Borgia; above all, what a smart appetite for a cool supper afterwards, at the Café Anglais, when the horrors of the play act as a piquant sauce to the supper!

Or, to speak more seriously, and to come, at last, to the point. After having seen most of the grand dramas which have been produced at Paris, for the last half-dozen years, and thinking over all that one has seen,—the fictitious murders, rapes, adulteries, and other crimes, by which one has been interested and excited,—a man may take leave to be heartily ashamed of the manner in which he has spent his time; and of the hideous kind of mental intoxication in which he has permitted himself to indulge.

Nor are simple society outrages the only sort of crime in which the spectator of Paris plays has permitted himself to indulge; he has recreated himself with a deal of blasphemy besides, and has passed many pleasant evenings in beholding religion defiled and ridiculed.

Allusion has been made, in a former paper, to a fashion that lately obtained in France, and which went by the name of Catholic reaction; and as, in this happy country, fashion is everything, we have had not merely Catholic pictures and quasi religious books, but a number of Catholic plays have been produced, very edifying to the frequenters of the theatres or the Boulevards, who have learned more about religion from these performances than they have acquired, no doubt, in the whole of their lives before. In the course of a very few years we have seen—*The Wandering Jew; Belshazzar's Feast; Nebuchadnezzar:* and the *Massacre of the Innocents; Joseph and his Brethren; The Passage of the Red Sea;* and *The Deluge.*

The great Dumas, like Madame Sand, before mentioned, has brought a vast quantity of religion before the footlights. There was his famous tragedy of *Caligula*, which, be it spoken to the shame of the Paris critics, was coldly received; nay, actually hissed, by them. And why? Because, says Dumas, it contained a great deal too much piety for the rogues. The public, he says, was much more religious, and understood him at once.

"As for the critics," says he, nobly, "let those who cried out against the immorality of Antony and Marguerite de Bourgogne, reproach me for *the chastity of Messalina.*" (This dear creature is the heroine of the play of *Caligula.*) "It matters little to me. These people have but seen the form of my work; they have walked round the tent, but have not seen the arch which it covered; they have examined the vases and candles of the altar, but have not opened the tabernacle!

"The public alone has, instinctively, comprehended that there was, beneath this outward sign, an inward and mysterious grace: it followed the action of the piece in all its serpentine windings; it listened for four hours, with pious attention (avec recueillement et religion), to the sound of this rolling river of thoughts, which may have appeared to it new and bold, perhaps, but chaste and grave; and it retired, with its head on its breast, like a man who had just perceived, in a dream, the solution of a problem which he has long and vainly sought in his waking hours."

You see that not only Saint Sand is an apostle, in her way; but Saint Dumas is another. We have people in England who write for bread, like Dumas and Sand, and are paid so much for their line; but they don't set up for prophets. Mrs. Trollope has never declared that her novels are inspired by Heaven; Mr. Buckstone has written a great number of farces, and never talked about the altar and the tabernacle. Even Sir Edward Bulwer (who, on a similar occasion, when the critics found fault with a play of his, answered them by a pretty decent declaration of his own merits,) never ventured to say that he had received a divine mission, and was uttering five-act revelations.

All things considered, the tragedy of "Caligula" is a decent tragedy; as decent as the decent characters of the hero and heroine can allow it to be; it may be almost said, provokingly decent: but this, it must be remembered, is the characteristic of the modern French school (nay, of the English school too); and if the writer take the character of a remarkable scoundrel, it is ten to one but he turns out an amiable fellow, in whom we have all the warmest sympathy. Caligula is killed at the end of the performance; Messalina is comparatively well-behaved; and the sacred part of the performance, the tabernacle-characters apart from the mere "vase" and "candlestick" personages, may be said to be depicted in the person of a Christian convert, Stella, who has had the good fortune to be converted by no less a person than Mary Magdalene, when she, Stella, was staying on a visit to her aunt, near Narbonne.

  Stella (*continuant*.)   Voilà
  Que je vois s'avancer, sans pilote et sans rames,
  Une barque portant deux hommes et deux femmes,
  Et, spectacle inoui qui me ravit encor,
  Tous quatre avaient au front une auréole d'or
  D'où partaient des rayons de si vive lumière
  Que je fus obligée à baisser la paupière ;
  Et, lorsque je rouvris les yeux avec effroi,
  Les voyageurs divins étaient auprès de moi.
  Un jour de chacun d'eux et dans toute sa gloire
  Je te raconterai la marveilleuse histoire,
  Et tu l'adoreras, j'espère ; en ce moment,
  Ma mère, il te suffit de savoir seulement
  Que tous quatre venaient du fond de la Syrie :
  Un édit les avait bannis de leur patrie,

Et, se faisant bourreaux, des hommes irrités,
Sans avirons, sans eau, sans pain et garrottés,
Sur une frêle barque échouée au rivage,
Les avaient à la mer poussés dans un orage.
Mais à peine l'esquif eut-il touché les flots
Qu'au cantique chanté par les saints matelots
L'ouragan replia ses ailes frémissantes,
Que la mer aplanit ses vagues mugissantes,
Et qu'un soleil plus pur, reparaissant aux cieux,
Enveloppa l'esquif d'un cercle radieux !...
  Junia.—Mais c'était un prodige.
  Stella.—   Un miracle, ma mère !
Leurs fers tombèrent seuls, l'eau cessa d'être amère,
Et deux fois chaque jour le bateau fut couvert
D'une manne pareille à celle du désert :
C'est ainsi que, poussés par une main céleste,
Je les vis aborder.
  Junia.— Oh ! dis vîte le reste !
  Stella.—A l'aube, trois d'entre eux quittèrent la maison :
Marthe prit le chemin qui mène à Tarascon,
Lazare et Maximin celui de Massilie,
Et celle qui resta . . . . *c'était la plus jolie*, (how truly French!)
Nous faisant appeler vers le milieu du jour,
Demanda si les monts ou les bois d'alentour
Cachaient quelque retraite inconnue et profonde,
Qui la pût séparer à tout jamais du monde. . . . .
Aquila se souvint qu'il avait pénétré
Dans un antre sauvage et de tous ignoré,
Grotte creusée aux flancs de ces Alpes sublimes,
Où l'aigle fait son aire au-dessus des abîmes.
Il offrit cet asile, et dès le lendemain
Tous deux, pour l'y guider, nous étions en chemin.
Le soir du second jour nous touchâmes sa base :
Là, tombant à genoux dans une sainte extase,
Elle pria long-temps, puis vers l'antre inconnu,
Dénouant sa chaussure, elle marcha pied nu.
Nos prières, nos cris restèrent sans réponses :
Au milieu des cailloux, des épines, des ronces,
Nous la vîmes monter, un bâton à la main,
Et ce n'est qu'arrivée au terme du chemin,
Qu'enfin elle tomba sans force et sans haleine . . . .
  Junia.—Comment la nommait-on, ma fille ?
  Stella.—   Madeleine.

Walking, says Stella, by the sea-shore, "A bark drew near, that had nor sail nor oar; two women and two men the vessel bore: each of that crew, 'twas wondrous to behold, wore round his head a ring of blazing gold; from which such radiance glittered all around, that I was fain to look towards the ground. And when once more I raised my frightened eyne, before me stood the travellers divine; their rank, the glorious lot that each befel, at better season, mother, will I tell. Of this anon: the time will come, when thou shalt learn to worship as I worship now. Suffice it, that from Syria's land they came; an edict from their country banished them. Fierce, angry men, had seized upon the four, and launched them in that vessel from the shore. They launched these victims on the waters rude; nor rudder gave to steer, nor bread for food. As the doomed vessel cleaves the stormy main, that pious crew uplifts a sacred strain; the angry waves are silent as it sings; the storm, awe-stricken, folds its quivering wings. A purer sun appears the heavens to light, and wraps the little bark in radiance bright.

"Junia.—Sure 'twas a prodigy.

"Stella.—A miracle. Spontaneous from their hands the fetters fell. The salt sea-wave grew fresh; and, twice a day, manna (like that which on the desert lay) covered the bark, and fed them on their way. Thus, hither led, at Heaven's divine behest, I saw them land—

"Junia.—My daughter, tell the rest.

"Stella.—Three of the four, our mansion left at dawn. One, Martha, took the road to Tarascon; Lazarus and Maximin to Massily; but one remained (the fairest of the three), who asked us, if, i' the woods or mountains near, there chanced to be some cavern lone and drear; where she might hide, for ever, from all men. It chanced, my cousin knew of such a den; deep hidden in a mountain's hoary breast, on which the eagle builds his airy nest. And thither offered he the saint to guide. Next day upon the journey forth we hied; and came, at the second eve, with weary pace, unto the lonely mountain's rugged base. Here the worn traveller, falling on her knee, did pray awhile in sacred ecstasy; and, drawing off her sandals from her feet, marched, naked, towards that desolate retreat. No answer made she to our cries or groans; but, walking, midst the prickles and rude stones, a staff in hand, we saw her upwards toil; nor ever did she pause, nor rest the while, save at the entry of that savage den. Here, powerless and panting, fell she then.

"JUNIA.—What was her name, my daughter?
"STELLA.   MAGDALEN."

Here the translator must pause—having no inclination to enter "the tabernacle," in company with such a spotless high-priest as Monsieur Dumas.

Something "tabernacular" may be found in Dumas's famous piece of "Don Juan de Marana." The poet has laid the scene of his play in a vast number of places: in heaven (where we have the Virgin Mary, and little angels, in blue, swinging censers before her!)—on earth, under the earth, and in a place still lower, but not mentionable to ears polite; and the plot, as it appears from a dialogue between a good and a bad angel, with which the play commences, turns upon a contest between these two worthies for the possession of the soul of a member of the family of Marana.

Don Juan de Marana not only resembles his namesake, celebrated by Mozart and Molière, in his peculiar successes among the ladies, but possesses further qualities which render his character eminently fitting for stage representation; he unites the virtues of Lovelace and Lacenaire; he blasphemes upon all occasions; he murders, at the slightest provocation, and without the most trifling remorse; he overcomes ladies of rigid virtue, ladies of easy virtue, and ladies of no virtue at all; and the poet, inspired by the contemplation of such a character, has depicted his hero's adventures and conversation with wonderful feeling and truth.

The first act of the play contains a half-dozen of murders and intrigues, which would have sufficed humbler genius than M. Dumas's, for the completion of, at least, half-a-dozen tragedies. In the second act our hero flogs his elder brother, and runs away with his sister-in-law; in the third, he fights a duel with a rival, and kills him: whereupon the mistress of his victim takes poison, and dies, in great agonies, on the stage. In the fourth act, Don Juan, having entered a church for the purpose of carrying off a nun, with whom he is in love, is seized by the statue of one of the ladies whom he has previously victimized, and made to behold the ghosts of all those unfortunate persons whose deaths he has caused.

This is a most edifying spectacle. The ghosts rise solemnly, each in a white sheet, preceded by a wax candle;

and, having declared their names and qualities, call, in chorus, for vengeance upon Don Juan, as thus:—

Don Sandoval *loquitur*.

"I am Don Sandoval d'Ojedo. I played against Don Juan my fortune, the tomb of my fathers, and the heart of my mistress;—I lost all: I played against him my life, and I lost it. Vengeance against the murderer! vengeance!"—(*The candle goes out.*)

The candle goes out, and an angel descends—a flaming sword in his hand—and asks: "Is there no voice in favour of Don Juan?" when, lo! Don Juan's father (like one of those ingenious toys called "Jack-in-the-box,") jumps up from his coffin, and demands grace for his son.

When Martha, the nun, returns, having prepared all things for her elopement, she finds Don Juan fainting upon the ground.—"I am no longer your husband," says he, upon coming to himself; "I am no longer Don Juan; I am brother Juan, the Trappist. Sister Martha, recollect that you must die!"

This was a most cruel blow upon Sister Martha, who is no less a person than an angel, an angel in disguise—the good spirit of the house of Marana, who has gone to the length of losing her wings, and forfeiting her place in heaven, in order to keep company with Don Juan on earth, and, if possible, to convert him. Already, in her angelic character, she had exhorted him to repentance, but in vain; for, while she stood at one elbow, pouring not merely hints, but long sermons, into his ear, at the other elbow stood a bad spirit, grinning and sneering at all her pious counsels, and obtaining by far the greater share of the Don's attention.

In spite, however, of the utter contempt with which Don Juan treats her,—in spite of his dissolute courses, which must shock her virtue,—and his impolite neglect, which must wound her vanity, the poor creature (who, from having been accustomed to better company, might have been presumed to have had better taste), the unfortunate angel, feels a certain inclination for the Don, and actually flies up to heaven to ask permission to remain with him on earth.

And when the curtain draws up, to the sound of harps, and discovers white-robed angels walking in the clouds, we find the angel of Marana upon her knees, uttering the following address :—

LE BON ANGE.

Vierge, à qui le calice à la liqueur amère
    Fut si souvent offert,
Mère, que l'on nomma la douloureuse mère,
    Tant vous avez souffert !

Vous, dont les yeux divins sur la terre des hommes
    Ont versé plus de pleurs
Que vos pieds n'ont depuis, dans le ciel où nous sommes,
    Fait éclore de fleurs,

Vase d'élection, étoile matinale,
    Miroir de pureté,
Vous qui priez pour nous, d'une voix virginale,
    La suprême bonté ;

A mon tour, aujourd'hui, bienheureuse Marie,
    Je tombe à vos genoux ;
Daignez donc m'écouter, car c'est vous que je prie,
    Vous qui priez pour nous.

Which may be thus interpreted :—

O Virgin blest ! by whom the bitter draught
    So often has been quaffed,
That, for thy sorrow, thou are named by us
    The Mother Dolorous !

Thou, from whose eyes have fallen more tears of woe,
    Upon the earth below,
Than 'neath thy footsteps, in this heaven of ours,
    Have risen flowers !

O beaming morning star ! O chosen vase !
    O mirror of all grace !
Who, with thy virgin voice, dost ever pray
    Man's sins away ;

Bend down thine ear, and list, O blessed saint !
    Unto my sad complaint ;
Mother ! to thee I kneel, on thee I call,
    Who hearest all.

She proceeds to request that she may be allowed to return to earth, and follow the fortunes of Don Juan ; and, as there is one difficulty, or, to use her own words,—

> Mais, comme vous savez qu'aux voûtes éternelles,
> Malgré moi, tend mon vol,
> *Soufflez sur mon étoile et détachez mes ailes,*
> *Pour m'enchaîner au sol ;*

her request is granted, her star is *blown out* (O poetic allusion !) and she descends to earth to love, and to go mad, and to die for Don Juan !

The reader will require no further explanation, in order to be satisfied as to the moral of this play ; but is it not a very bitter satire upon the country, which calls itself the politest nation in the world, that the incidents, the indecency, the coarse blasphemy, and the vulgar wit of this piece, should find admirers among the public, and procure reputation for the author? Could not the Government, which has re-established, in a manner, the theatrical censorship, and forbids or alters plays which touch on politics, exert the same guardianship over public morals ? The honest English reader, who has a faith in his clergyman, and is a regular attendant at Sunday worship, will not be a little surprised at the march of intellect among our neighbours across the Channel, and at the kind of consideration in which they hold their religion. Here is a man who seizes upon saints and angels, merely to put sentiments in their mouths which might suit a nymph of Drury Lane. He shows heaven, in order that he may carry debauch into it ; and avails himself of the most sacred and sublime parts of our creed as a vehicle for a scene-painter's skill, or an occasion for a handsome actress to wear a new dress.

M. Dumas's piece of "Kean" is not quite so sublime; it was brought out by the author as a satire upon the French critics, who, to their credit be it spoken, had generally attacked him, and was intended by him, and received by the public, as a faithful portraiture of English manners. As such, it merits special observation and praise. In the first act you find a Countess and an Ambassadress, whose conversation relates purely to the great actor. All the ladies in London are in love with him, especially the two present. As for the Ambassadress, she prefers him to her husband (a matter of course in all French plays), and to a more seducing person still—no less a person than the Prince of Wales! who presently waits on the ladies, and joins in their conversation concerning Kean. "This man," says His Royal Highness, "is the very pink of fashion. Brummell is nobody when compared to him; and I myself only an insignificant private gentleman. He has a reputation among ladies, for which I sigh in vain; and spends an income twice as great as mine." This admirable historic touch at once paints the actor and the Prince; the estimation in which the one was held, and the modest economy for which the other was so notorious.

Then we have Kean, at a place called the *Trou de Charbon*, the Coal Hole, where, to the edification of the public, he engages in a fisty combat with a notorious boxer. This scene was received by the audience with loud exclamations of delight, and commented on, by the journals, as a faultless picture of English manners. The Coal Hole being on the banks of the Thames, a nobleman—*Lord Melbourn!*—has chosen the tavern as a rendezvous for a gang of pirates, who are to have their ship in waiting, in order to carry off a young lady, with whom his lordship is enamoured. It need not be said that Kean arrives at the nick of time, saves the innocent *Meess Anna*, and exposes the infamy of the Peer. A violent tirade against noblemen ensues, and Lord Melbourn slinks away, disappointed, to meditate revenge. Kean's triumphs continue through all the acts; the Ambassadress falls madly in love with him; the Prince becomes furious at his ill success, and the Ambassador dreadfully jealous. They pursue Kean to his dressing-room, at the theatre, where, unluckily, the Ambassadress herself has taken refuge. Dreadful quarrels ensue; the tragedian grows suddenly mad upon the stage, and so cruelly insults the Prince of Wales, that His Royal Highness determines to send *him to Botany Bay*. His sentence, however, is commuted to banishment to New York; whither, of course, Miss Anna accompanies him, rewarding him, previously, with her hand, and twenty thousand a year!

This wonderful performance was gravely received and admired by the people of Paris; the piece was considered to be decidedly moral, because the popular candidate was made to triumph throughout, and to triumph in the most virtuous manner; for, according to the French code of morals, success among women is, at once, the proof and the reward of virtue.

The sacred personage introduced in Dumas's play, behind a cloud, figures bodily in the piece of the *Massacre of the Innocents*, represented at Paris last year. She appears under a different name, but the costume is exactly that of Carlo-Dolce's Madonna; and an ingenious fable is arranged, the interest of which hangs upon the grand Massacre of the Innocents, perpetrated in the fifth act. One of the chief characters is *Jean le Précurseur*, who threatens woe to Herod and his race, and is beheaded by the orders of that sovereign.

In the *Festin de Balthazar*, we are similarly introduced to Daniel, and the first scene is laid by the waters of Babylon, where a certain number of captive Jews are seated in melancholy postures; a Babylonian officer enters, exclaiming, "Chantez nous quelques Chansons de Jerusalem," and the request is refused in the language of the Psalm. Belshazzar's Feast is given in a grand tableau, after Martin's picture. That painter, in like manner, furnished scenes for the *Deluge*. Vast numbers of schoolboys and children are brought to see these pieces; the lower classes delight in them. The famous *Juif Errant*, at the theatre of the Porte St. Martin, was the first of the kind, and its prodigious success, no doubt, occasioned the number of imitations which the other theatres have produced.

The taste of such exhibitions, of course, every English person will question; but we must remember the manners of the people among whom they are popular; and, if I may be allowed to hazard such an opinion, there is, in every one of these Boulevard mysteries, a kind of rude moral. The Boulevard writers don't pretend to "tabernacles" and divine gifts, like Madame Sand and Dumas, before mentioned. If they take a story from the sacred books, they garble it without mercy, and take sad liberties with the text; but they do not deal in descriptions of the agreeably wicked, or ask pity and admiration for tender-hearted criminals and philanthropic murderers, as their betters do. Vice is vice on the Boulevard; and it is fine to hear the audience, as a tyrant king roars out cruel sentences of death, or a bereaved mother pleads for the life of her child, making their remarks on the circumstances of the scene. "Ah, le gredin!" growls an indignant countryman: "Quel monstre!" says a grisette, in a fury. You see very fat old men crying like babies; and, like babies, sucking enormous sticks of barley-sugar. Actors and audience enter warmly into the illusion of the piece, and so especially are the former affected, that, at Franconi's, where the battles of the Empire are represented, there is as regular gradation in the ranks of the mimic army, as in the real imperial legions. After a man has served, with credit, for a certain number of years in the line, he is promoted to be an officer—an acting officer. If he conducts himself well, he may rise to be a Colonel, or a General of Division; if ill, he is degraded to the ranks again; or, worse degradation of all, drafted into a regiment of Cossacks, or Austrians. Cossacks is the lowest depth, however; nay, it is said that the men who perform these Cossack parts receive higher wages than the mimic grenadiers and old guard. They will not consent to be beaten every night, even in play; to be pursued in hundreds, by a handful of French; to fight against their beloved Emperor. Surely there is fine hearty virtue in this, and pleasant child-like simplicity.

The Gallery at l'Odéon—Matinée—Sketched from Nature.

So that while the drama of Victor Hugo, Dumas, and the enlightened classes, is profoundly immoral and absurd, the *drama* of the common people is absurd, if you will, but good and right-hearted. I have made notes of one or two of these pieces, which all have good feeling and kindness in them, and which turn, as the reader will see, upon one or two favourite points of popular morality. A drama that obtained a vast success at the Porte Saint Martin, was "La Duchesse de la Vauballière." The Duchess is the daughter of a poor farmer, who was carried off in the first place, and then married by M. le Duc de la Vauballière, a terrible *roué*, the farmer's landlord, and the intimate friend of Philippe d'Orléans, the Regent of France.

Now, the Duke, in running away with the lady, intended to dispense altogether with ceremony, and make of Julie anything but his wife; but Georges, her father, and one Morisseau, a notary, discovered him in his dastardly act, and pursued him to the very feet of the Regent, who compelled the pair to marry and make it up.

Julie complies, but though she becomes a Duchess, her heart remains faithful to her old flame, Adrian, the doctor; and she declares that, beyond the ceremony, no sort of intimacy shall take place between her husband and herself.

Then the Duke begins to treat her in the most ungentlemanlike manner; he abuses her in every possible way; he introduces improper characters into her house; and, finally, becomes so disgusted with her, that he determines to make away with her altogether.

For this purpose, he sends forth into the highways and

seizes a doctor, bidding him, on pain of death, to write a poisonous prescription for Madame la Duchesse. She swallows the potion; and, oh! horror! the doctor turns out to be Dr. Adrian, whose woe may be imagined, upon finding that he has been thus committing murder on his true love!

Let not the reader, however, be alarmed as to the fate of the heroine; no heroine of a tragedy ever yet died in the third act; and, accordingly, the Duchess gets up perfectly well again in the fourth, through the instrumentality of Morisseau, the good lawyer.

And now it is that vice begins to be really punished. The Duke, who, after killing his wife, thinks it necessary to retreat, and take refuge in Spain, is tracked to the borders of that country by the virtuous notary, and there receives such a lesson as he will never forget to his dying day.

Morisseau, in the first instance, produces a deed (signed by His Holiness the Pope), which annuls the marriage of the Duke de la Vauballière; then another deed, by which it is proved that he was not the eldest son of old La Vauballière, the former duke; then another deed, by which he shows that old La Vauballière (who seems to have been a disreputable old fellow) was a bigamist, and that, in consequence, the present man, styling himself Duke, is illegitimate; and, finally, Morisseau brings forward another document, which proves that the *reg'lar* Duke is no other than Adrian, the doctor!

Thus it is that love, law, and physic, combined, triumph over the horrid machinations of this star-and-gartered libertine.

"Hermann l'Ivrogne" is another piece of the same order; and, though not very refined, yet possesses considerable merit. As in the case of the celebrated Captain Smith, of Halifax, who "took to drinking ratafia, and thought of poor Miss Bailey,"—a woman and the bottle have been the cause of Hermann's ruin. Deserted by his mistress, who has been seduced from him by a base Italian Count, Hermann, a German artist, gives himself entirely up to liquor and revenge: but when he finds that force, and not infidelity, have been the cause of his mistress's ruin, the reader can fancy the indignant ferocity with which he pursues the *infâme ravisseur*. A scene, which is really full of spirit, and excellently well acted, here ensues! Hermann proposes to the Count, on the eve of their duel, that the survivor should bind himself to espouse the unhappy Marie; but the Count declares himself to be already married, and the student, finding a duel impossible (for his object was to restore, at all events, the honour of Marie), now only thinks of his revenge, and murders the Count. Presently, two parties of men enter Hermann's apartment; one is a company of students, who bring him the news that he has obtained the prize of painting; the other, the policemen, who carry him to prison, to suffer the penalty of murder.

I could mention many more plays in which the popular morality is similarly expressed. The seducer, or rascal of the piece, is always an aristocrat,—a wicked Count, or licentious Marquis,—who is brought to condign punishment just before the fall of the curtain. And too good reason have the French people had to lay such crimes to the charge of the aristocracy, who are expiating now, on the stage, the wrongs which they did a hundred years since. The aristocracy is dead now; but the theatre lives upon traditions: and don't let us be too scornful at such simple legends that are handed down by the people, from race to race. Vulgar prejudice against the great it may be; but prejudice against the great is only a rude expression of sympathy with the poor; long, therefore, may fat épiciers blubber over mimic woes, and honest proletaires shake their fists, shouting—" Gredin, scélérat, monstre de Marquis!" and such republican cries.

Remark, too, another development of this same popular feeling of dislike against men in power. What a number of plays and legends have we (the writer has submitted to the public, in the preceding pages, a couple of specimens; one of French, and the other of Polish, origin), in which that great and powerful aristocrat, the Devil, is made to be miserably tricked, humiliated, and disappointed. A play of this class, which, in the midst of all its absurdities and claptraps, had much of good in it, was called "Le Maudit des Mers." Le Maudit is a Dutch captain, who, in the midst of a storm, while his crew were on their knees at prayers, blasphemed, and drank punch; but what was his astonishment at beholding an archangel with a sword, all covered with flaming resin, who told him that, as he, in this hour of danger, was too daring, or too wicked, to utter a prayer, he never should cease roaming the seas until he could find some being who would pray to Heaven for him!

Once, only, in a hundred years, was the skipper allowed

to land for this purpose; and this piece runs through four centuries, in as many acts, describing the agonies and unavailing attempts of the miserable Dutchman. Willing to go any lengths, in order to obtain his prayer, he, in the second act, betrays a Virgin of the Sun to a follower of Pizarro; and, in the third, assassinates the heroic William of Nassau; but ever before the dropping of the curtain, the angel and sword make their appearance :—" Treachery," says the spirit, " cannot lessen thy punishment;—crime will not obtain thy release!"—*A la mer! à la mer!* and the poor devil returns to the ocean, to be lonely, and tempest-tossed, and sea-sick, for a hundred years more.

But his woes are destined to end with the fourth act. Having landed in America, where the peasants on the sea-shore, all dressed in Italian costumes, are celebrating, in a quadrille, the victories of Washington, he is there lucky enough to find a young girl to pray for him. Then the curse is removed, the punishment is over, and a celestial vessel, with angels on the decks, and " sweet little cherubs," fluttering about the shrouds and the poop, appear to receive him.

This piece was acted at Franconi's, where, for once, an angel-ship was introduced in place of the usual horsemanship.

One must not forget to mention here, how the English nation is satirized by our neighbours, who have some droll traditions regarding us. In one of the little Christmas pieces, produced at the Palais Royal (satires upon the follies of the past twelve months, on which all the small theatres exhaust their wit), the celebrated flight of Messrs. Green and Monck Mason was parodied, and created a good deal of laughter at the expense of John Bull. Two English noblemen, Milor Cricri and ˉMilor Hanneton, appear as descending from a balloon, and one of them communicates to the public the philosophic observations which were made in the course of his aërial tour.

"On leaving Vauxhall," says his lordship, "we drank a bottle of Madeira, as a health to the friends from whom we parted, and crunched a few biscuits to support nature during the hours before lunch. In two hours we arrived at Canterbury, enveloped in clouds; lunch, bottled porter; at Dover, carried several miles in a tide of air, bitter cold, cherry brandy; crossed over the Channel safely, and thought, with pity, of the poor people who were sickening in the steam-boats below; more bottled porter; over Calais; dinner, roast beef of Old England; near Dunkirk,—night falling, lunar rainbow, brandy-and-water; night confoundedly thick; supper, nightcap of rum-punch, and so to bed. The sun broke beautifully through the morning mist, as we boiled the kettle, and took our breakfast over Cologne. In a few more hours we concluded this memorable voyage, and landed safely at Weilburg, in good time for dinner."

The joke here is smart enough; but our honest neighbours make many better, when they are quite unconscious of the fun. Let us leave plays, for a moment, for poetry, and take an instance of French criticism, concerning England, from the works of a famous French exquisite and man of letters. The hero of the poem addresses his mistress—

> Londres, tu le sais trop, en fait de capitale,
> Est ce que fit le ciel de plus froid et plus pâle,
> C'est la ville du gaz, des marins, du brouillard ;
> On s'y couche à minuit, et l'on s'y lève tard ;
> Ses routs tant vantés ne sont qu'une boxade,
> Sur ses grands quais jamais échelle ou sérénade,
> Mais de volumineux bourgeois pris de porter
> Qui passent sans lever le front à Westminster ;
> Et n'était sa forêt de mâts perçant la brume,
> Sa tour dont à minuit le vieil œil s'allume,
> Et tes deux yeux, Zerline, illuminés bien plus,
> Je dirais que, ma foi, des romans que j'ai lus,
> Il n'en est pas un seul, plus lourd, plus léthargique
> Que cette nation qu'on nomme Britannique !

The writer of the above lines (which let any man who can translate) is Monsieur Roger de Beauvoir, a gentleman who actually lived many months in England, as an attaché to the embassy of M. de Polignac. He places the heroine of his tale in a *petit réduit près le Strand*, "with a green and fresh jalousie, and a large blind, let down all day; you fancied you were entering a bath of Asia, as soon as you had passed the perfumed threshold of this charming retreat!" He next places her—

> Dans un square écarté, morne et couverte de givre,
> Où se cache un hôtel, aux vieux lions de cuivre ;

and the hero of the tale, a young French poet, who is in London, is truly unhappy in that village.

> Arthur dessèche et meurt. Dans la ville de Sterne,
> Rien qu'en voyant le peuple il a le mal de mer ;

> Il n'aime ni le Parc, gai comme une citerne,
> Ni le tir au pigeon, ni le *soda-water*.*
>
> *Liston* ne le fait plus sourciller ! Il rumine
> Sur les trottoirs du Strand, droit comme un échiquier,
> Contre le peuple anglais, les nègres, la vermine,
> Et les mille *cokneys* du peuple boutiquier,
>
> Contre tous les bas-bleus, contre les pâtissières,
> Les paricurs d'Epsom, le gin, le parlement,
> La *quaterly*, le roi, la pluie et les libraires,
> Dont il ne touche plus, hélas ! un sou d'argent !
>
> Et chaque gentleman lui dit : L'heureux poète !

"L'heureux poète," indeed ! I question if a poet in this wide world is so happy as M. de Beauvoir, or has made such wonderful discoveries. "The bath of Asia, with green jalousies," in which the lady dwells; "the old hotel, with copper lions, in a lonely square;"—were ever such things heard of, or imagined, but by a Frenchman? The sailors, the negroes, the vermin, whom he meets in the street,—how great and happy are all these discoveries! Liston no longer makes the happy poet frown; and "gin," "cockneys," and the "quaterly" have not the least effect upon him! And this gentleman has lived many months amongst us; admires *Williams Shakspear*, the "grave et vieux prophète," as he calls him, and never, for an instant, doubts that his description contains anything absurd !

I don't know whether the great Dumas has passed any time in England; but his plays shew a similar intimate knowledge of our habits. Thus in *Kean*, the stage-manager

---

* The italics are the author's own.

is made to come forward and address the pit, with a speech beginning, "*My Lords and Gentlemen;*" and a company of English women are introduced (at the memorable Coal Hole), and they all wear *pinafores;* as if the British female were in the invariable habit of wearing this outer garment, or slobbering her gown without it. There was another celebrated piece, enacted some years since, upon the subject of Queen Caroline, where our late adored sovereign, George, was made to play a most despicable part; and where Signor Bergami fought a duel with Lord Londonderry. In the last act of this play, the House of Lords was represented, and Sir Brougham made an eloquent speech in the Queen's favour. Presently the shouts of the mob were heard without; from shouting they proceed to pelting; and pasteboard-brickbats and cabbages came flying among the representatives of our hereditary legislature. At this unpleasant juncture, *Sir Hardinge*, the Secretary-at-War, rises and calls in the military; the act ends in a general row, and the ignominious fall of Lord Liverpool, laid low by a brickbat from the mob!

The description of these scenes is, of course, quite incapable of conveying any notion of their general effect. You must have the solemnity of the actors, as they Mcess and Milor one another, and the perfect gravity and good faith with which the audience listen to them. Our stage Frenchman is the old Marquis, with sword, and pig-tail, and spangled court coat. The Englishman of the French theatre has, invariably, a red wig, and almost always leather gaiters, and a long white upper Benjamin : he remains as he was represented in the old caricatures after the peace, when Vernet designed him somewhat after the following fashion—

And to conclude this catalogue of blunders: in the famous piece of the *Naufrage de la Méduse*, the first act is laid on board an English ship-of-war, all the officers of which appeared in light blue or green coats (the lamp-light prevented our distinguishing the colour accurately), in little blue coats, and TOP-BOOTS!

* * * * *

Let us not attempt to deaden the force of this tremendous blow by any more remarks. The force of blundering can go no farther. Would a Chinese playwright or painter have stranger notions about the barbarians than our neighbours, who are separated from us but by two hours of salt water?

MEDITATIONS AT VERSAILLES.

THE palace of Versailles has been turned into a bricabrac shop of late years, and its time-honoured walls have been covered with many thousand yards of the worst pictures that eye ever looked on. I don't know how many leagues of battles and sieges the unhappy visitor is now obliged to march through, amidst a crowd of chattering Paris cockneys, who are never tired of looking at the glories of the Grenadier Français, to the chronicling of whose deeds this old palace of the old kings is now altogether devoted. A whizzing, screaming steam-engine rushes hither from Paris, bringing shoals of *badauds* in its wake. The old *coucous* are all gone, and their place knows them no longer. Smooth asphaltum terraces, tawdry lamps, and great hideous Egyptian obelisks, have frightened them away from the pleasant station they used to occupy under the trees of the Champs Elysées; and though the old coucous were just the most uncomfortable vehicles that human ingenuity ever constructed, one can't help looking back to the days of their existence with a tender regret, for there was pleasure, then, in the little trip of three leagues; and who ever had pleasure in a railroad journey? Does any reader of this venture to say that, on such a voyage, he ever dared to be pleasant? Do the most hardened stokers joke with one another? I don't believe it. Look into every single car of the train, and you will see that every single face is solemn. They take their seats gravely, and are silent, for the most part, during the journey; they dare not look out of window, for fear of being blinded by the smoke that comes whizzing by, or of losing their heads in one of the windows of the down train; they ride for miles in utter damp and darkness; through awful pipes of brick, that have been run pitilessly through the bowels of gentle mother earth, the cast-iron Frankenstein of an engine gallops on, puffing and screaming. Does any man pretend to say that he *enjoys* the journey?—he might as well say that he enjoyed having his hair cut; he bears it, but that is all: he will not allow the world to laugh at him, for any exhibition of slavish fear; and pretends, therefore, to be at his ease; but he *is* afraid, nay, ought to be, under the circumstances. I am sure Hannibal or Napoleon would, were they locked suddenly into a car; there kept close prisoners for a certain number of hours, and whirled along at this dizzy pace. You can't stop, if you would;—you may die, but you can't stop; the engine may explode upon the road, and up you go along with it; or, may be a bolter, and take a fancy to go down a hill, or into a river: all this you must bear, for the privilege of travelling twenty miles an hour.

This little journey, then, from Paris to Versailles, that used to be so merry of old, has lost its pleasures since the disappearance of the cuckoos; and I would as lief have for companions the statues that lately took a coach from the bridge opposite the Chamber of Deputies, and stepped out in the Court of Versailles, as the most part of the people who now travel on the railroad. The stone figures are not a whit more cold and silent than these persons, who used to be, in the old cuckoos, so talkative and merry. The prattling grisette, and her swain from the Ecole de Droit; the huge Alsacian carabinier, grim smiling under his sandy moustaches, and glittering brass helmet; the jolly nurse, in red calico, who had been to Paris, to show mamma her darling Lolo, or Guguste;—what merry companions used one to find squeezed into the crazy old vehicles that formerly performed the journey! But the age of horseflesh is gone—that of engineers, economists, and calculators has succeeded; and the pleasure of coucoudom is extinguished for ever. Why not mourn over it, as Mr. Burke did over his cheap defence of nations, and unbought grace of life; that age of chivalry, which he lamented, àpropos of a trip to Versailles, some half a a century back?

Without stopping to discuss (as might be done, in rather a neat and successful manner) whether the age of chivalry was cheap or dear, and whether, in the time of the unbought grace of life, there was not more bribery, robbery, villany, tyranny, and corruption, than exists even in our own happy days,—let us make a few moral and historical remarks upon the town of Versailles, where, between railroad and coucou, we are surely arrived by this time.

The town is, certainly, the most moral of towns. You

pass from the railroad station through a long, lonely suburb, with dusty rows of stunted trees on either side, and some few miserable beggars, idle boys, and ragged old women under them. Behind the trees are gaunt, mouldy houses, palaces once, where (in the days of the unbought grace of life) the cheap defence of nations gambled, ogled, swindled, intrigued; whence high-born duchesses used to issue, in old times, to act as chambermaids to lovely Du Barri, and mighty princes rolled away, in gilt caroches, hot for the honour of lighting his Majesty to bed, or of presenting his stockings when he rose, or of holding his napkin when he dined. Tailors, chandlers, tinmen, wretched hucksters, and greengrocers, are now established in the mansions of the old peers; small children are yelling at the doors, with mouths besmeared with bread and treacle; damp rags are hanging out of every one of the windows, steaming in the sun; oyster-shells, cabbage-stalks, broken crockery, old papers, lie basking in the same cheerful light. A solitary water-cart goes jingling down the wide pavement, and spirts a feeble refreshment over the dusty, thirsty stones.

After pacing for some time through such dismal streets, we *deboucher* on the *grand place:* and before us lies the palace dedicated to all the glories of France. In the midst of the great, lonely plain, this famous residence of King Louis looks low and mean.—Honoured pile! Time was, when tall musketeers and gilded body-guards allowed none to pass the gate. Fifty years ago, ten thousand drunken women from Paris broke through the charm; and now a tattered commissioner will conduct you through it for a penny, and lead you up to the sacred entrance of the palace.

We will not examine all the glories of France, as here they are portrayed in pictures and marble : catalogues are written about these miles of canvas, representing all the revolutionary battles, from Valmy to Waterloo,—all the triumphs of Louis XIV.—all the mistresses of his successor —and all the great men who have flourished since the French empire began. Military heroes are most of these —fierce constables in shining steel, marshals in voluminous wigs, and brave grenadiers in bearskin caps ; some dozens of whom gained crowns, principalities, dukedoms ; some hundreds, plunder and epaulets ; some millions, death in African sands, or in icy Russian plains, under the guidance, and for the good, of that arch-hero, Napoleon. By far the greater part of "all the glories" of France (as of most other countries) is made up of these military men ; and a fine satire it is, on the cowardice of mankind, that they pay such an extraordinary homage to the virtue called courage, filling their history books with tales about it, and nothing but it.

Let them disguise the place, however, as they will, and plaster the walls with bad pictures as they please, it will be hard to think of any family but one, as one traverses this vast gloomy edifice. It has not been humbled to the ground, as a certain palace of Babel was of yore ; but it is a monument of fallen pride, not less awful, and would afford matter for a whole library of sermons. The cheap defence of nations expended a thousand millions in the erection of this magnificent dwelling-place. Armies were employed, in the intervals of their warlike labours, to level hills, or pile them up; to turn rivers, and to build aqueducts, and transplant woods, and construct smooth terraces, and long canals. A vast garden grew up in a wilderness, and a stupendous palace in the garden, and a stately city round the palace: the city was peopled with parasites, who daily came to do worship before the creator of these wonders—the Great King. "Dieu seul est grand," said courtly Massillon; but next to him, as the prelate thought, was certainly Louis, his vicegerent here upon earth—God's lieutenant-governor of the world,—before whom courtiers used to fall on their knees, and shade their eyes, as if the light of his countenance, like the sun, which shone supreme in heaven, the type of him, was too dazzling to bear.

Did ever the sun shine upon such a king before, in such a palace?—or, rather, did such a king ever shine upon the sun? When Majesty came out of his chamber, in the midst of his superhuman splendours, viz. in his cinnamon-coloured coat, embroidered with diamonds; his pyramid of a wig;* his red-heeled shoes, that lifted him four inches from the ground, "that he scarcely seemed to touch;" when he came out, blazing upon the dukes and duchesses that waited his rising,—what could the latter do, but cover their eyes, and wink, and tremble? And did he not himself believe, as he stood there, on his high heels, under his ambrosial periwig, that there was something in him more than man—something above Fate?

* It is fine to think that, in the days of his youth, his Majesty Louis XIV. used to *powder his wig with gold-dust.*

This, doubtless, was he fain to believe; and if, on very fine days, from his terrace, before his gloomy palace of Saint Germains, he could catch a glimpse, in the distance, of a certain white spire of St. Denis, where his race lay buried, he would say to his courtiers, with a sublime condescension, "Gentlemen, you must remember that I, too, am mortal." Surely the lords in waiting could hardly think him serious, and vowed that his Majesty always loved a joke. However, mortal or not, the sight of that sharp spire wounded his Majesty's eyes; and is said, by the legend, to have caused the building of the palace of Babel-Versailles.

In the year 1681, then, the great king, with bag and baggage,—with guards, cooks, chamberlains, mistresses, jesuits, gentlemen, lackeys, Fenelons, Molières, Lauzuns, Bossuets, Villars, Villeroys, Louvois, Colberts,—transported himself to his new palace; the old one being left for James of England, and Jaquette his wife, when their time should come. And when the time did come, and James sought his brother's kingdom, it is on record, that Louis hastened to receive and console him, and promised to restore, incontinently, those islands from which the *canaille* had turned him. Between brothers such a gift was a trifle; and the courtiers said to one another, reverently,* "The Lord said unto my Lord, Sit thou on my right hand, until I make thine enemies my footstool." There was no blasphemy in the speech; on the contrary, it was gravely said,

* I think it is in the amusing *Memoirs of Madame de Créqui* (a forgery, but a work remarkable for its learning and accuracy) that the above anecdote is related.

by a faithful believing man, who thought it no shame to the latter, to compare his Majesty with God Almighty. Indeed, the books of the time will give one a strong idea how general was this Louis-worship. I have just been looking at one, which was written by an honest jesuit and protégé of Père la Chaise, who dedicates a book of medals to the august Infants of France, which does, indeed, go almost as far in print. He calls our famous monarch "Louis le Grand:—1, l'invincible; 2, le sage; 3, le conquérant; 4, la merveille de son siècle; 5, la terreur de ses ennemis; 6, l'amour de ses peuples; 7, l'arbitre de la paix et de la guerre; 8, l'admiration de l'univers; 9, et digne d'en être le maître; 10, le modèle d'un héros achevé; 11, digne de l'immortalité, et de la vénération de tous les siècles!"

A pretty jesuit declaration, truly, and a good honest judgment upon the great king! In thirty years more— 1. The invincible had been beaten a vast number of times. 2. The sage was the puppet of an artful old woman, who was the puppet of more artful priests. 3. The conqueror had quite forgotten his early knack of conquering. 5. The terror of his enemies (for 4, the marvel of his age, we pretermit, it being a loose term, that may apply to any person or thing) was now terrified by his enemies in turn. 6. The love of his people was as heartily detested by them, as scarcely any other monarch, not even his great grandson, has been, before or since. 7. The arbiter of peace and war was fain to send superb ambassadors to kick their heels in Dutch shopkeepers' antechambers. 8, is again a general term. 9. The man fit to be master of the universe, was scarcely master of his own kingdom. 10. The finished hero was all but finished, in a very common-place and vulgar way: and 11. The man worthy of immortality was just at the point of death, without a friend to soothe or deplore him; only withered old Maintenon, to utter prayers at his bedside, and croaking jesuits to prepare him,* with Heaven knows what wretched tricks and mummeries, for his appearance in that Great Republic that lies on the other side of the grave. In the course of his fourscore splendid miserable years, he never had but one friend, and he ruined and left her. Poor La Vallière, what a sad tale is yours! "Look at this Galerie des Glaces," cries Monsieur Vatout, staggering with surprise at the appearance of the room, two hundred and forty-two feet long, and forty high; "here it was that Louis displayed all the grandeur of royalty; and such was the splendour of his court, and the luxury of the times, that this immense room could hardly contain the crowd of courtiers that pressed around the monarch." Wonderful! wonderful! Eight thousand four hundred and sixty square feet of courtiers! Give a square yard to each, and you have a matter of three thousand of them. Think of three thousand courtiers per day, and all the chopping and changing of them for near forty years; some of them dying, some getting their wishes, and retiring to their provinces to enjoy their plunder: some disgraced, and going home to pine away out of the light of the sun;† new ones perpetually arriving,

* They made a jesuit of him on his death-bed.
† Saint Simon's account of Lauzun, in disgrace, is admirably facetious and pathetic; Lauzun's regrets are as monstrous as those of Raleigh, when deprived of the sight of his adorable Queen and Mistress, Elizabeth.

—pushing, squeezing, for their place, in the crowded Galerie des Glaces. A quarter of a million of noble countenances, at the very least, must those glasses have reflected. Rouge, diamonds, ribands, patches, upon the faces of smiling ladies: towering periwigs, sleek-shaven crowns, tufted moustaches, scars, and grizzled whiskers, worn by ministers, priests, dandies, and grim old commanders.—So many faces, O ye gods! and every one of them lies! So many tongues, vowing devotion and respectful love to the great king in his six-inch wig; and only poor La Vallière's, amongst them all, which had a word of truth for the dull ears of Louis of Bourbon.

"*Quand j'aurai de la peine aux Carmélites,*" says unhappy Louise, about to retire from these magnificent courtiers, and their grand Galerie des Glaces, "*je me souviendrai de ce que ces gens là m'ont fait souffrir!*"— A troop of Bossuets, inveighing against the vanities of courts, could not preach such an affecting sermon. What years of anguish and wrong has the poor thing suffered, before these sad words came from her gentle lips! How these courtiers have bowed and flattered, kissed the ground on which she trod, fought to have the honour of riding by her carriage, written sonnets, and called her goddess; who, in the days of her prosperity, was kind and beneficent, gentle and compassionate to all; then (on a certain day, when it is whispered that his Majesty hath cast the eyes of his gracious affection upon another) behold three thousand courtiers are at the feet of the new divinity.—" O divine Athenais! what blockheads have we been to worship any but you.—*That* a goddess?—a pretty goddess, forsooth;

—a witch, rather, who, for a while, kept our gracious monarch blind! Look at her; the woman limps as she walks; and, by sacred Venus, her mouth stretches almost to her diamond ear-rings!"* The same tale may be told of many more deserted mistresses; and fair Athenais de Montespan was to hear it of herself one day. Meantime, while La Vallière's heart is breaking, the model of a finished hero is yawning, as, on such paltry occasions, a finished hero should. *Let* her heart break: a plague upon her tears and repentance; what right has she to repent? Away with her to her convent. She goes, and the finished hero never sheds a tear. What a noble pitch of stoicism to have reached! Our Louis was so great, that the little woes of mean people were beyond him: his friends died, his mistresses left him; his children, one by one, were cut off before his eyes, and great Louis is not moved, in the slightest degree! As how, indeed, should a god be moved?

I have often liked to think about this strange character in the world, who moved in it, bearing about a full belief in his own infallibility; teaching his generals the art of war, his ministers the science of government, his wits taste, his courtiers dress; ordering deserts to become gardens, turning villages into palaces, at a breath; and, indeed, the august figure of the man, as he towers upon his throne, cannot fail to inspire one with respect and awe :— how grand those flowing locks appear; how awful that sceptre;

---

* A pair of diamond ear-rings, given by the King to La Vallière, caused much scandal; and some lampoons are extant, which impugn the taste of Louis XIV. for loving a lady with such an enormous mouth.

how magnificent those flowing robes! In Louis, surely, if in any one, the majesty of kinghood is represented.

But a king is not every inch a king, for all the poet may say; and it is curious to see how much precise majesty there is in that majestic figure of Ludovicus Rex. In the plate opposite, we have endeavoured to make the exact calculation. The idea of kingly dignity is equally strong in the two outer figures; and you see, at once, that majesty is made out of the wig, the high-heeled shoes, and cloak, all fleurs-de-lis bespangled. As for the little, lean, shrivelled, paunchy old man, of five feet two, in a jacket and breeches, there is no majesty in *him*, at any rate; and yet he has just stept out of that very suit of clothes. Put the wig and shoes on him, and he is six feet high;—the other fripperies, and he stands before you majestic, imperial, and heroic! Thus do barbers and cobblers make the gods that we worship: for do we not all worship him? Yes; though we all know him to be stupid, heartless, short, of doubtful personal courage, worship and admire him we must; and have set up, in our hearts, a grand image of him, endowed with wit, magnanimity, valour, and enormous heroical stature.

And what magnanimous acts are attributed to him! or, rather, how differently do we view the actions of heroes and common men, and find that the same thing shall be a wonderful virtue in the former, which, in the latter, is only an ordinary act of duty. Look at yonder window of the king's chamber;—one morning a royal cane was seen whirling out of it, and plumped among the courtiers and guard of honour below. King Louis had absolutely, and

with his own hand, flung his own cane out of the window, "because," said he, "I won't demean myself by striking a gentleman!" O miracle of magnanimity! Lauzun was not caned, because he besought Majesty to keep his promise,—only imprisoned for ten years in Pignerol, along with banished Fouquet;—and a pretty story is Fouquet's, too.

Out of the window the king's august head was one day thrust, when old Condé was painfully toiling up the steps of the court below. "Don't hurry yourself, my cousin," cries Magnanimity; "one who has to carry so many laurels cannot walk fast." At which all the courtiers, lackeys, mistresses, chamberlains, jesuits, and scullions, clasp their hands, and burst into tears. Men are affected by the tale to this very day. For a century and three-quarters, have not all the books that speak of Versailles, or Louis Quatorze, told the story?—"Don't hurry yourself, my cousin!" O admirable king and christian! what a pitch of condescension is here, that the greatest king of all the world should go for to say anything so kind, and really tell a tottering old gentleman, worn out with gout, age, and wounds, not to walk too fast!"

What a proper fund of slavishness is there in the composition of mankind, that histories like these should be found to interest and awe them. Till the world's end, most likely, this story will have its place in the history books, and unborn generations will read it, and tenderly be moved by it. I am sure that Magnanimity went to bed that night, pleased and happy, intimately convinced that he had done an action of sublime virtue, and had easy slumbers and sweet dreams,—especially if he had taken a light supper, and not too vehemently attacked his *en cas de nuit.*

That famous adventure, in which the *en cas de nuit* was brought into use, for the sake of one Poquelin, *alias* Molière;—how often has it been described and admired? This Poquelin, though king's valet de chambre, was, by profession, a vagrant; and, as such, looked coldly on by the great lords of the palace, who refused to eat with him. Majesty, hearing of this, ordered his *en cas de nuit* to be placed on the table, and positively cut off a wing, with his own knife and fork, for Poquelin's use. O thrice happy Jean Baptiste! The king has actually sate down with him, cheek by jowl, had the liver-wing of a fowl, and given Molière the gizzard; put his imperial legs under the same mahogany, *sub iisdem trabibus.* A man, after such an honour, can look for little else in this world: he has tasted the utmost conceivable earthly happiness, and has nothing to do now but to fold his arms, and look up to heaven, and sing "Nunc dimittis," and die.

Do not let us abuse poor old Louis, on account of this monstrous pride; but only lay it to the charge of the fools who believed and worshipped it. If, honest man, he believed himself to be almost a god, it was only because thousands of people had told him so—people, only half liars, too, who did, in the depths of their slavish respect, admire the man almost as much as they said they did. If, when he appeared in his five-hundred-million coat, as he is said to have done, before the Siamese ambassadors, the courtiers began to shade their eyes, and long for parasols, as if this

Bourbonic sun was too hot for them ; indeed, it is no wonder that he should believe that there was something dazzling about his person : he had half a million of eager testimonies to this idea. Who was to tell him the truth ? —Only in the last years of his life did trembling courtiers dare whisper to him, after much circumlocution, that a certain battle had been fought at a place called Blenheim, and that Eugene and Marlborough had stopped his long career of triumphs.

"*On n'est plus heureux à notre âge,*" says the old man, to one of his old generals, welcoming Tallard, after his defeat; and he rewards him with honours, as if he had come from a victory. There is, if you will, something magnanimous in this welcome to his conquered general, this stout protest against Fate. Disaster succeeds disaster ; armies after armies march out to meet fiery Eugene and that dogged fatal Englishman, and disappear in the smoke of the enemies' cannon. Even at Versailles you may almost hear it roaring at last; but when courtiers, who have forgotten their god, now talk of quitting this grand temple of his, old Louis plucks up heart, and will never hear of surrender. All the gold and silver at Versailles he melts, to find bread for his armies; all the jewels on his five-hundred-million coat he pawns resolutely; and, bidding Villars go and make the last struggle but one, promises, if his general is defeated, to place himself at the head of his nobles, and die King of France. Indeed, after a man, for sixty years, has been performing the part of a hero, some of the real heroic stuff must have entered into his composition, whether he would or not. When the great Elliston was enacting the part of King George the Fourth, in the play of "The Coronation," at Drury Lane, the galleries applauded very loudly his suavity and majestic demeanour, at which Elliston, inflamed by the popular loyalty (and by some fermented liqueur in which, it is said, he was in the habit of indulging), burst into tears, and, spreading out his arms, exclaimed : "Bless ye, bless ye, my people!" Don't let us laugh at his Ellistonian majesty, nor at the people who clapped hands, and yelled "bravo," in praise of him. The tipsy old manager did really feel that he was a hero at that moment; and the people, wild with delight and attachment for a magnificent coat and breeches, surely were uttering the true sentiments of loyalty, which consists in reverencing these and other articles of costume. In this fifth act, then, of his long royal drama, old Louis performed his part excellently; and, when the curtain drops upon him, he lies, dressed majestically, in a becoming kingly attitude, as a king should.

The king, his successor, has not left, at Versailles, half so much occasion for moralizing; perhaps the neighbouring Parc aux Cerfs would afford better illustrations of his reign. The life of his great grandsire, the grand Lama of France, seems to have frightened Louis, the well-beloved, who understood that loneliness is one of the necessary conditions of divinity ; and, being of a jovial, companionable turn, aspired not beyond manhood. Only in the matter of ladies did he surpass his predecessor, as Solomon did David. War he eschewed, as his grandfather bade him ; and his simple taste found little in this world to enjoy beyond the mulling of chocolate, and the frying of pancakes. Look, here is the room called Laboratoire du Roi, where, with his own hands, he made his mistress' breakfast :—here is the little door through which, from her apartments in the upper story, the chaste Du Barri came stealing down to the arms of the weary, feeble, gloomy, old man. But of women he was tired long since, and even pancake-frying had palled upon him. What had he to do, after forty years of reign; —after having exhausted everything? Every pleasure that Dubois could invent for his hot youth, or cunning Lebel could minister to his old age, was flat and stale; used up to the very dregs: every shilling in the national purse had been squeezed out, by Pompadour and Du Barri and such brilliant ministers of state. He had found out the vanity of pleasure, as his ancestor had discovered the vanity of glory: indeed it was high time that he should die. And die he did; and round his tomb, as round that of his grandfather before him, the starving people sang a dreadful chorus of curses, which were the only epitaphs, for good or for evil, that were raised to his memory.

As for the courtiers—the knights and nobles, the unbought grace of life—they, of course, forgot him in one minute after his death, as the way is. When the king dies, the officer appointed opens his chamber window, and calling out into the court below, *Le Roi est mort*, breaks his cane, takes another and waves it, exclaiming, *Vive le Roi!* Straightway all the loyal nobles begin yelling *Vive le Roi!* and the officer goes round solemnly, and sets yonder great clock in the Cour de Marbre to the hour of the king's death. This old Louis had solemnly ordained; but the Versailles clock was only set twice; there was no shouting of *Vive le Roi* when the successor of Louis XV. mounted to heaven to join his sainted family.

Strange stories of the deaths of kings have always been very recreating and profitable to us : what a fine one is that of the death of Louis XV., as Madame Campan tells it. One night the gracious monarch came back ill from Trianon ; the disease turned out to be the small-pox ; so violent that ten people of those who had to enter his chamber caught the infection and died. The whole court flies from him ; only poor old fat Mesdames the King's daughters persist in remaining at his bedside, and praying for his soul's welfare.

On the 10th May, 1774, the whole court had assembled at the château, the Œil de Bœuf was full. The Dauphin had determined to depart as soon as the king had breathed his last. And it was agreed by the people of the stables, with those who watched in the king's room, that a lighted candle should be placed in a window, and should be extinguished as soon as he had ceased to live. The candle was put out; at that signal, guards, pages, and squires mounted on horseback, and everything was made ready for departure. The Dauphin was with the Dauphiness, waiting together for the news of the king's demise. *An immense noise, as if of thunder, was heard in the next room;* it was the crowd of courtiers, who were deserting the dead king's apartment, in order to pay their court to the new power of Louis XVI. Madame de Noailles entered, and was the first to salute the queen by her title of Queen of France, and begged their Majesties to quit their apartments, to receive the princes and great lords of the court desirous to pay their homage to the new sovereigns. Leaning on her husband's arm, a handkerchief to her eyes, in the most touching attitude, Marie Antoinette received these first visits. On quitting the chamber where the dead king lay, the Duc de Villequier bade M. Andervillé, first surgeon of the king, to open and embalm the body:—it would have been certain death to the surgeon. "I am ready, sir," said he, "but, whilst I am operating, you must hold the head of the corpse; your charge demands it." The Duke went away without a word, and the body was neither opened nor embalmed. A few humble domestics and poor workmen watched by the remains, and performed the last offices to their master. The surgeons ordered spirits of wine to be poured into the coffin.

They huddled the king's body into a post-chaise; and, in this deplorable equipage, with an escort of about forty men, that Louis, the well-beloved, was carried, in the dead of night, from Versailles to Saint Denis, and then thrown into the tomb of the kings of France!

If any man is curious, and can get permission, he may mount to the roofs of the palace, and see where Louis XVI. used royally to amuse himself, by gazing upon the doings of all the townspeople below with a telescope. Behold that balcony, where, one morning, he, his queen, and the little Dauphin stood, with Cromwell Grandison Lafayette by their side, who kissed her Majesty's hand, and protected her; and then, lovingly surrounded by his people, the king got into a coach, and came to Paris: nor did his Majesty ride much in coaches after that.

There is a portrait of the king, in the upper galleries,

clothed in red and gold, riding a fat horse, brandishing a sword, on which the word "Justice" is inscribed, and looking remarkably stupid and uncomfortable. You see that the horse will throw him at the very first fling; and as for the sword, it never was made for such hands as his, which were good at holding a corkscrew or a carving knife, but not clever at the management of weapons of war. Let those pity him who will: call him saint and martyr if you please; but a martyr to what principle was he? Did he frankly support either party in his kingdom, or cheat and tamper with both? He might have escaped; but he must have his supper, and so his family was butchered, and his kingdom lost, and he had his bottle of Burgundy in comfort at Varennes. A single charge upon the fatal tenth of August, and the monarchy might have been his once more; but he is so tender-hearted, that he lets his friends be murdered before his eyes almost: or, at least, when he has turned his back upon his duty and his kingdom, and has skulked for safety into the reporter's box, at the National Assembly. There were hundreds of brave men who died that day, and were martyrs, if you will; poor neglected tenth-rate courtiers, for the most part, who had forgotten old slights and disappointments, and left their places of safety, to come and die, if need were, sharing in the supreme hour of the monarchy. Monarchy was a great deal too humane to fight along with these, and so left them to the pikes of Santerre, and the mercy of the men of the Sections. But we are wandering a good ten miles from Versailles, and from the deeds which Louis XVI. performed there.

He is said to have been such a smart journeyman blacksmith, that he might, if Fate had not perversely placed a crown on his head, have earned a couple of louis every week by the making of locks and keys. Those who will, may see the workshop, where he employed many useful hours; Madame Elizabeth was at prayers; meanwhile, the queen was making pleasant parties with her ladies; Monsieur, the Count d'Artois, was learning to dance on the tight-rope; and Monsieur de Provence was cultivating *l'eloquence du billet*, and studying his favourite Horace. It is said that each member of the august family succeeded remarkably well in his or her pursuits; big Monsieur's little notes are still cited. At a minuet or sillabub, poor Antoinette was unrivalled; and Charles, on the tight-rope, was so graceful and so *gentil*, that Madame Saqui might envy him. The time only was out of joint. O cursed spite, that ever such harmless creatures as these were bidden to right it!

A walk to the little Trianon is both pleasing and moral; no doubt the reader has seen the pretty fantastical gardens which environ it; the groves and temples; the streams and caverns (whither, as the guide tells you, during the heat of summer, it was the custom of Marie Antoinette to retire, with her favourite, Madame de Lamballe): the lake, and Swiss village, are pretty little toys, moreover; and the cicerone of the place does not fail to point out the different cottages which surround the piece of water, and tell the names of the royal masqueraders who inhabited each. In the long cottage, close upon the lake, dwelt the Seigneur du Village, no less a personage than Louis XV.; Louis

XVI., the Dauphin, was the Bailli; near his cottage is that of Monseigneur the Count d'Artois, who was the miller; opposite, lived the Prince de Condé, who enacted the part of gamekeeper (or, indeed, any other rôle, for it does not signify much); near him was the Prince de Rohan, who was the aumônier; and yonder is the pretty little dairy, which was under the charge of the fair Marie Antoinette herself.

I forget whether Monsieur the fat Count of Provence took any share of this royal masquerading; but look at the names of the other six actors of the comedy, and it will be hard to find any person for whom Fate had such dreadful visitations in store. Fancy the party, in the days of their prosperity, here gathered at Trianon, and seated under the tall poplars, by the lake, discoursing familiarly together: suppose, of a sudden, some conjuring Cagliostro of the time is introduced among them, and foretells to them the woes that are about to come. "You, Monsieur l'Aumônier, the descendant of a long line of princes, the passionate admirer of that fair queen who sits by your side, shall be the cause of her ruin and your own,* and shall die in disgrace and exile. You, son of the Condés, shall live long enough to see your royal race overthrown, and shall die by the hands of a hangman.† You, oldest son of Saint Louis, shall perish by the executioner's axe; that beautiful head, O Antoinette, the same ruthless blade shall sever." "They shall kill me first," says Lamballe, at the queen's side. "Yes, truly," replies the soothsayer, "for Fate prescribes

* In the diamond-necklace affair.
† He was found hanging in his own bed-room.

ruin for your mistress, and all who love her."* "And," cries Monsieur d'Artois, " do I not love my sister, too ? I pray you not to omit me in your prophecies."

To whom Monsieur Cagliostro says, scornfully, "You may look forward to fifty years of life, after most of these are laid in the grave. You shall be a king, but not die one; and shall leave the crown only; not the worthless head that shall wear it. Thrice shall you go into exile : you shall fly from the people, first, who would have no more of you and your race ; and you shall return home over half a million of human corpses, that have been made for the sake of you, and of a tyrant as great as the greatest of your family. Again driven away, your bitterest enemy shall bring you back. But the strong limbs of France are not to be chained by such a paltry yoke as you can put on her : you shall be a tyrant, but in will only ; and shall have a sceptre, but to see it robbed from your hand."

"And, pray, Sir Conjuror, who shall be the robber ? " asked Monsieur the Count d'Artois.

* * * * *

This I cannot say, for here my dream ended. The fact is, I had fallen asleep, on one of the stone-benches in the Avenue de Paris ; and, at this instant, was awakened by a whirling of carriages, and a great clattering of national

---

* Among the many lovers that rumour gave to the queen, poor Ferseu is the most remarkable. He seems to have entertained for her a high and perfectly pure devotion. He was the chief agent in the luckless escape to Varennes; was lurking in Paris during the time of her captivity; and was concerned in the many fruitless plots that were made for her rescue. Ferseu lived to be an old man, but died a dreadful and violent death. He was dragged from his carriage by the mob, in Stockholm, and murdered by them.

guards, lancers, and outriders, in red. HIS MAJESTY, LOUIS PHILIPPE, was going to pay a visit to the palace, which contains several pictures of his own glorious actions, and which has been dedicated, by him, to all the glories of France.

THE END.

www.ingramcontent.com/pod-product-compliance
Lightning Source LLC
Chambersburg PA
CBHW051858300426
44117CB00006B/451